Culture
Reexamined

Culture Reexamined

Broadening Our
Understanding
of Social and
Evolutionary
Influences

Edited by
Adam B. Cohen

American Psychological Association • Washington, DC

Published by
American Psychological Association
750 First Street, NE
Washington, DC 20002
www.apa.org

To order
APA Order Department
P.O. Box 92984
Washington, DC 20090-2984
Tel: (800) 374-2721; Direct: (202) 336-5510
Fax: (202) 336-5502; TDD/TTY: (202) 336-6123
Online: www.apa.org/pubs/books
E-mail: order@apa.org

In the U.K., Europe, Africa, and the Middle East, copies may be ordered from
American Psychological Association
3 Henrietta Street
Covent Garden, London
WC2E 8LU England

Typeset in Goudy by Circle Graphics, Inc., Columbia, MD

Printer: United Book Press, Baltimore, MD
Cover Designer: Naylor Design, Washington, DC

The opinions and statements published are the responsibility of the authors, and such opinions and statements do not necessarily represent the policies of the American Psychological Association.

Library of Congress Cataloging-in-Publication Data

Cohen, Adam B.
  Culture reexamined : broadening our understanding of social and evolutionary influences / Adam B. Cohen.
      pages cm
  Includes bibliographical references and index.
  ISBN 978-1-4338-1587-4 — ISBN 1-4338-1587-7 1. Social psychology. 2. Culture and psychology. I. Title.
  HM1033.C615 2014
  302—dc23

                                    2013021737

British Library Cataloguing-in-Publication Data

A CIP record is available from the British Library.

Printed in the United States of America
First Edition

http://dx.doi.org/10.1037/14274-000

CONTENTS

CONTRIBUTORS

W. Keith Campbell, PhD, Department of Psychology, University of Georgia, Athens

Chi-yue Chiu, PhD, Division of Strategy, Management and Organisation, Nanyang Business School, Nanyang Technological University, Singapore, and Institute of Sociology, Chinese Academy of Social Sciences, Beijing, China

Adam B. Cohen, PhD, Department of Psychology, Arizona State University, Tempe

Brittany Gentile, PhD, Department of Psychology, University of Georgia, Athens

P. J. Henry, PhD, Department of Psychology, New York University—Abu Dhabi, Abu Dhabi, United Arab Emirates

Vanessa E. Hettinger, MA, Department of Psychology, University of South Florida, Tampa

Shinobu Kitayama, PhD, Robert B. Zajonc Collegiate Professor of Psychology, Institute for Social Research, University of Michigan, Ann Arbor

Letty Y.-Y. Kwan, PhD, Institute on Asian Consumer Insight, Nanyang Technological University, Singapore

Shyhnan Liou, PhD, Institute of Creative Industries Design, National Cheng Kung University, Tainan City, Taiwan

Ariel Malka, PhD, Department of Psychology, Yeshiva University, New York, NY

Hazel Rose Markus, PhD, Department of Psychology, Stanford University, Stanford, CA

Kenneth Michniewicz, MA, Department of Psychology, University of South Florida, Tampa

Benoît Monin, PhD, Department of Organizational Behavior and Psychology, Stanford Graduate School of Business, Stanford, CA

Angela G. Pirlott, PhD, Department of Psychology, University of Wisconsin—Eau Claire

Benjamin Grant Purzycki, PhD, Centre for Human Evolution, Cognition, and Culture, University of British Columbia, Vancouver, British Columbia, Canada

David P. Schmitt, PhD, Caterpillar Inc., Professor of Psychology, Department of Psychology, Bradley University, Peoria, IL

A. Timur Sevincer, PhD, Department of Psychology, University of Hamburg, Hamburg, Germany

Azim F. Shariff, PhD, Department of Psychology, University of Oregon, Eugene

Richard Sosis, PhD, Department of Anthropology, University of Connecticut, Storrs

Lauren M. Szczurek, MA, Department of Psychology, Stanford University, Stanford, CA

Jean M. Twenge, PhD, Department of Psychology, San Diego State University, San Diego, CA

Joseph A. Vandello, PhD, Department of Psychology, University of South Florida, Tampa

Michael E. W. Varnum, PhD, Department of Psychology, Arizona State University, Tempe

FOREWORD

In the last 3 decades, cultural psychology has come of age, and this remarkable volume celebrates that fact. The transition from a culture-blind psychology to a culture-contingent psychology has been a rocky one and is far from complete. Yet hundreds of experiments, simulations, surveys, and analyses of cultural products and practices now provide increasingly robust support for Geertz's (1973) assertion that "there is no such thing as a human nature independent of culture" (p. 49) as well as for Bruner's (1990) claim that "it is impossible to construct a human psychology on the basis of the individual alone" (p. 12).

People, the essays collected here explain, require the public and shared meanings and practices of their various communities and activities to become people. Moreover, there is an ongoing mutual constitution between people and their many cultures. People are culturally shaped shapers. This is their human nature.

When my colleague Shinobu Kitayama and I began our work on culture, we theorized that individuals were sociocultural beings (Markus & Kitayama, 1991). Together with many of our colleagues, we imagined a cultural approach in psychology as the logical extension of a social psychological approach. Cultures were social situations writ larger. As social psychologists, we came by this idea honestly. For the founders of our field, behavior was both a social product and an ongoing social process. For example, in 1948, Kurt Lewin wrote

> The social climate in which a child lives is for the child as important as the air it breathes. The group to which the child belongs is the ground on which he stands. His relation to the group and his status in it are the most important factors for his feeling of security or insecurity. No wonder that the group the person is part of, and the culture in which he lives, determine to a very high degree his behavior and character. (p. 82)

The ways in which people are dynamic sociocultural constructions were also central to the theorizing of Solomon Asch (1952). In his view, biological beings become human only through social transactions with other people and their products, that is, with their cultures—their ideas, interactions, and institutions. As he described it

> The paramount fact is that men come into the world not alone with the objects of nature but also with other men, and through this encounter they are transformed into human beings. The environment of others and the products of their labor become a powerful, comprehensive region of forces within which each moves and has being. (p. 6)

As Shinobu and I compared two of the *regions of forces* that each of us knew best—Japan and the United States—it seemed to us that there were clear differences in North American and Japanese patterns of modes of being. Building on the work of Shweder and Bourne (1984), who asked whether the concept of the person varies cross-culturally, and also that of Harry Triandis (1989), who mapped out the behavioral syndromes of individualism and collectivism, we proposed two different patterns of attuning to sociocultural contexts, which gave rise to two different schemas of self or agency. When an independent schema of self organizes behavior, the primary referent is the individual's own thoughts, feelings, and actions. Alternatively, when an interdependent schema of self organizes behavior, the immediate referent is the thoughts, feelings, and actions of the other with whom the person is in relationship.

The view was that if the schema for the self was different, all processes that implicate the self—cognition, emotion, motivation, morality, relationships, intergroup processes, health, and well-being—might well take different forms. We felt that the extent of this cultural dependence was a matter of empirical question. Initially, and still now in some circles, there was considerable resistance to these and other ideas emphasizing variability in psychological functioning. Some thought that describing agency in such terms was too homogenizing and bordered on stereotyping. It was too simple. No doubt, but compared with the taken-for-granted view that there was only one style of agency, the claim that there might be another way to be a self was a 100% increase in the assumed complexity of human nature.

Some independent selves argued against the idea of cultural conditioning, worried that it was cultural determinism. Still others thought that since the goal of science was to pursue the universal laws of human nature, uncovering diversity in psychological functioning was a spoiler. Critics worried that an emphasis on diversity could even work to undermine the entire endeavor of psychological science. Of course, a cultural psychology was not posed against universals, just universalistic fallacies. For example, one new universal that has emerged from cultural psychology is that *what* you think and feel influences *how* you think and feel—process and content are intertwined.

The rapidly expanding field of cultural psychology has succeeded in providing an empirical foundation for the theoretical insights of Lewin, Asch, and Geertz (Fiske, Kitayama, Markus, & Nisbett, 1998; Heine, 2011; Kitayama & Cohen, 2007; Shweder, 1991). Humans are culture bearing, culture making, and culture sharing animals. Culture, then, is not something to be stripped away in the service of finding the really real or uncovering the basic elements of human behavior. The psychological is cultural. The cultural is psychological.

Although psychology has yet to fully absorb the consequences of this fact, many psychologists are now aware that much of what we have assumed to be universal and characteristic of humans in general is, in fact, characteristic of North Americans who live lives structured by particular sets of cultural meanings and practices. Psychology as we know it is not yet a comprehensive psychology; it is an indigenous psychology of America or perhaps, more specifically, a psychology of secular, middle-class Anglo America, a psychology of WEIRD people in the label of Henrich, Heine, and Norenzayan (2010). As fish who have now become aware of the water, we can now ask, as the authors in this volume do, how have our Western cultures fostered our particular ways of being? And what are cultures? How do they work? What gives rises to them? Why do we have them?

This volume, then, will go a long distance in completing the cultural turn in psychology. The emphasis here is on how cultures make psyches but also on how psyches make culture. The word is out. Culture is not just something that East Asians have. Here we find culture in many forms. These cultures derive from the many social distinctions that organize and animate our lives—professions, social classes, gender, the frontier, politics, religion, generation, food. Each of us interacts with multiple cultures in a lifetime and in a single day. We are shaped by these cultures, and we shape them.

Because of culture, people don't have to wait around for natural selection or genetic mutation to produce the biology to live in a different terrain or cope with a change in climate. Together we can invent new shelters and climate-appropriate clothing. Or we can save ourselves the trouble of innovating new technologies by copying our fellow humans (Markus &

Conner, 2013). People's capacity to be shaped by the meanings that are pervasive in their environments, to make meaning, to share these meanings, and to build worlds according to these meanings is their great evolutionary advantage.

This insightful and provocative collection offers the careful reader many gifts. It is an illuminating example of its own message: Cultures evolve. The knowledge culture of psychology is evolving and finally giving full expression to some of the field's most powerful foundational ideas. The book also illuminates why psychologists should focus their attention on the systematic collective antecedents and consequences of individual actions. Finally, *Culture Reexamined* invites us to think about ourselves and other people in a new way. No one has just one culture. We all have many different cultures—of nation, region, race, gender, class, religion, profession, and so forth. We can embrace these cultures and use them as resources; we can resist them; and since they are products of human agency, we can also change them.

Hazel Rose Markus

REFERENCES

Asch, S. (1952). *Social psychology*. Englewood Cliffs, NJ: Prentice Hall.

Bruner, J. (1990). *Acts of meaning*. Cambridge, MA: Harvard University Press.

Fiske, A., Kitayama, S., Markus, H. R., & Nisbett, R. E. (1998). The cultural matrix of social psychology. In D. Gilbert, S. Fiske, & G. Lindzey (Eds.), *The handbook of social psychology* (4th ed., pp. 915–981). San Francisco, CA: McGraw-Hill.

Geertz, C. (1973). *The interpretations of cultures*. New York, NY: Basic Books.

Heine, S. J. (2011). Evolutionary explanations need to account for cultural variability (Commentary). *Behavioral and Brain Sciences, 34*, 26–27. doi:10.1017/S0140525X10002669

Henrich, J., Heine, S. J., & Norenzayan, A. (2010). The weirdest people in the world? *Behavioral and Brain Sciences, 33*(2–3), 61–83. doi:10.1017/S0140525X0999152X

Kitayama, S., & Cohen, D. (2007). *Handbook of cultural psychology*. New York, NY: Guilford Press.

Lewin, K. (1948). *Resolving social conflicts: Selected papers on group dynamics* (G. W. Lewin, Ed.). New York, NY: Harper & Row.

Markus, H., & Kitayama, S. (1991). Culture and the self: Implications for cognition, emotion, and motivation. *Psychological Review, 98*, 224–253. doi:10.1037/0033-295X.98.2.224

Markus, H. R., & Conner, A. (2013). *Clash!: 8 cultural conflicts that make us who we are*. New York, NY: Hudson Street Press.

Shweder, R. A. (1991). *Thinking through cultures: Expeditions in cultural psychology.* Cambridge, MA: Harvard University Press.

Shweder, R. A., & Bourne, L. (1984). Does the concept of the person vary cross-culturally? In R. A. Shweder & R. A. LeVine (Eds.), *Culture theory: Essays on mind, self, and emotion* (pp. 158–199). New York, NY: Cambridge University Press.

Triandis, H. C. (1989). The self and social behavior in differing cultural contexts. *Psychological Review, 93,* 506–520. doi:10.1037/0033-295X.96.3.506

Culture
Reexamined

INTRODUCTION

ADAM B. COHEN

Before the advent of cultural psychology, I am given to believe, social psychological laws were framed in the same universal ways as physical laws. Just as an apple would unfailingly fall on Sir Isaac Newton's head, so too would it have fallen on Confucius' head, although separated by multiple forms of distance—geographical miles, temporal centuries, and cultural divides. Psychological laws seemed like this too. A wealthy, Protestant, English subject or a poor, Confucian, Chinese individual would equally feel cognitive dissonance if they acted inconsistently with their self-views (Festinger, 1957); they would equally attribute people's behaviors to their autonomous selves (Jones & Harris, 1967); and they would equally be motivated to put themselves ahead of their close others and cultivate their own personal self-esteem (Heine, Lehman, Markus, & Kitayama, 1999). All of these tendencies were apparently part of universal laws of human nature.

But whereas apples the world over are equally subject to the laws of gravity, people are not like this. People are inextricably made up by, and

http://dx.doi.org/10.1037/14274-010
Culture Reexamined: Broadening Our Understanding of Social and Evolutionary Influences,
A. B. Cohen (Editor)

themselves constitute, culture (Fiske, Kitayama, Markus, & Nisbett, 1998; Shweder, 1991). When I studied cultural psychology in graduate school, primarily with Drs. Paul Rozin and Steven Heine, I was enthralled to learn that all of these social psychological phenomena were actually inextricably bound up in culture. People in East or Southeast Asia, for example, are not prone to dissonance effects; they are much more sensitive to how context affects people's behaviors; and they are motivated to put others before themselves and to improve themselves rather than to feel good about themselves. These cultural differences are understood to reflect cultural-level variation in individualism versus collectivism, creating and being constituted by selves that are independent or interdependent (Markus & Kitayama, 1991; Triandis, 1995).

The more I learned about these culturally contextualized psychological laws, though, the more puzzled I became. Like an East Asian, I often felt that my behavior was relatively subject to situational demands, and I felt that I had been raised from a young age to feel as much part of a group as an individual and to be bound as much by duty and obligation as by my own personal choices. How could this be, when I am a European American who was born in Philadelphia, not a Japanese person born in Kyoto?

I began to theorize that perhaps it was my Jewish religion, not my nationality, that had created these collectivistic tendencies in me. Jewish culture (perhaps like Eastern cultures) is in many ways more collectivistic than the prototypical Western culture (Cohen, Hall, Koenig, & Meador, 2005; Cohen & Hill, 2007). Thus, I began to wonder whether religion could be as important a kind of culture as the country in which one was born. Perhaps it was a different apple than the one that struck Sir Isaac that led me to be interested in how culture shapes psychology and vice versa—not a falling apple, but the fruit of the tree of the knowledge of good and evil from which Adam and Eve ate in the Garden of Eden in Genesis (if indeed it was an apple; the Hebrew text does not specify the species of fruit).

In my dissertation, I investigated religion as a cultural influence on morality—specifically, how members of different religions reckon their knowledge of good and evil. For Jews, thinking lustful thoughts, as long as they are not acted on, is not a sin, but such thoughts are adulterous according to Protestants (Cohen, 2003; Cohen & Rankin, 2004; Cohen & Rozin, 2001). In all, I showed that Jews and Christians would make social psychological judgments in accordance with the doctrines of their religious cultures. This type of result had significance in several ways for understanding culture. For one thing, it suggested that the array of cultural influences is wider than had been the focus of study in psychology—including religion. Furthermore, it meant that ancient religious tenets and texts exerted an influence on people's thoughts, speaking to why cultures develop as they do, an understudied question in cultural psychology.

These kinds of issues were the impetus for this edited volume, which is intended to broaden the psychology of culture in two ways. First, the chapters discuss an impressive array of cultural influences—not just country of origin but also professional and disciplinary cultures, historical changes in cultures, social class, frontier settlement and geographical regions, political cultures, religion, and gender. Although this is surely not an exhaustive list of the kinds of culture that psychology should be interested in, understanding how these distinct and intersecting forms of culture affect and are made up by thoughts, feelings, and behaviors is an exciting and fruitful new direction for psychology.

The second major advance provided by these chapters is that they broaden our thinking about the processes by which cultures come about and are maintained. Psychological theories about the origins or processes of cultural development are relatively impoverished. These chapters offer a wide set of theories and explanations, ranging from biological evolution to the division of labor and other aspects of social class.

WHAT'S IN THE BOOK

This book represents an attempt to capture two of the most exciting directions in theory and research on culture in psychology, one of which is to broaden the kinds of cultures that psychologists think about and study.

In Chapter 1, Chi-yue Chiu, Letty Y.-Y. Kwan, and Shyhnan Liou consider professional and disciplinary cultures. By studying these kinds of cultures, Chiu et al. remind us how cultures have intersubjective sharedness and continuity, and they alert us to some cultural differences that do not garner attention when we think about other kinds of cultures. For example, disciplinary cultures vary in precision of vocabulary. (My favorite fact learned in editing this book was that "in an introductory lecture of their respective discipline, humanists make an average of almost five filled pauses (e.g., *ums*, *ers*) per minute and social scientists make an average of four filled pauses per minute, compared with 1.5 filled pauses per minute for natural scientists" (Chapter 1, p. 15). Such insights can have broad-ranging benefits, ranging from helping to improve interdisciplinary collaboration to helping to understand why different kinds of groups are relatively disadvantaged in different kinds of fields.

In Chapter 2, Brittany Gentile, W. Keith Campbell, and Jean M. Twenge explore generational cultures. Theoretically, they develop the generational change model to emphasize how cultures can change over time; even that psychological hallmark of U.S. culture, individualism, has not always been as pervasive as it is now (Twenge, Konrath, Foster, Campbell, & Bushman, 2008). Moreover, Gentile et al. provide guidance on the strengths and weaknesses of a variety of individual- and cultural-level methods that can be used to study such temporal changes in cultures.

In Chapter 3, P. J. Henry considers culture and social class. Studying social class as a culture reminds us to deconfound our variables of interest in studying culture (e.g., ethnicity and even caste vs. social class). Moreover, by theorizing distinct social classes as cultures in their own right, we might avoid perpetuating some hegemonic styles of thinking, such as assuming that upper-class people only influence lower-class people, rather than a more dynamic process of mutual influence. Henry also shows that variables that go with social class, such as stigmatization, agency, and individual choice, can enrich our understanding of well-studied cultural phenomena such as individual-ism–collectivism and culture of honor; enrich dominant perspectives in the study of culture, such as mutual constitution; and tell us something about the processes by which cultures form, including multiple kinds of adaptive processes. Finally, social class reminds us to think of culture at multiple levels of analysis.

In Chapter 4, Joseph A. Vandello, Vanessa E. Hettinger, and Kenneth Michniewicz consider regional culture. How can it be that, all within one country, the United States, Easterners are more intrusive and rude than Midwesterners, Southerners are particularly hospitable, and New England-ers are obdurately pragmatic? Vandello et al. review regional cultural dif-ferences in domains such as individualism–collectivism, well-being, honor and retribution, and personality; theorize about how ecology might promote such cultural variation; make methodological and conceptual recommenda-tions about how best to study regional cultures; and share some ideas about whether regional cultures will disappear or persist in the United States.

In Chapter 5, Shinobu Kitayama, Michael E. W. Varnum, and A. Timur Sevincer delve into how settling wild frontiers requires and promotes indi-vidualism. They proffer the intriguing hypothesis that new ideas are more likely to come from the sort of people who embrace an ethos of individual-ism enough to voluntarily settle a new frontier and from the individualism-promoting demands that such settlement requires (including not only psychological demands but perhaps even genes and germs). Provocatively, they consider evidence from the perspective of not just the United States as a whole but also of the U.S. frontier, Japan's Hokkaido region, and finally cosmopolitan cities, productively viewed as modern frontiers because they are centers of innovation in science, technology, art, fashion, and business.

In Chapter 6, Ariel Malka theorizes about political culture and democ-racy. Of importance given the general goals of the book, his views question how expansive definitions of culture can and remain useful. Malka considers political cultural orientations to consensus and cleavage and the cultural dif-ferences between political conservatives and liberals. He provides compelling theory on and evidence of why the same sort of person favors a suite of attitudes that are independent in principle—gun rights, abortion restrictions, and small government—or even principles that at some level of abstraction seem incompatible, such as being antiabortion but pro–death penalty. Malka explains why these relations are stronger among people who are politically engaged—because the political messages that people hear tell them which political identities and which issues go together, including messages from polarized cultural elites.

In Chapter 7 on food and culture, Benoît Monin and Lauren M. Szczurek discuss what cultural psychologists can learn from food. Building on my mentor Paul Rozin's germinal work on food and culture, this chapter is a great argument for the deep cultural significance of food, and it speaks to broad issues such as societal relations, the confluence of multiple cultural influences, and how institutions shape culture.

The second exciting direction in the study of culture that I wanted to capture in this book was the synthesis of theory about evolution and theory about culture. This synthesis is a very new way of thinking about culture, and so this focus on evolution was not intended to overshadow the first, major goal of the book (broadening the kinds of culture studied in psychology). This goal is, however, an important one because most people intuitively falsely dichotomize evolution and culture. When faced with a behavior, people often ask, "Is this a behavior that varies between places (and is therefore cultural), or is this a behavior that is the same everywhere (and is therefore evolutionary)?" I have previously asserted that psychologists interested in culture should consider both culturally universal and culturally variable aspects of human behavior (Cohen, 2010) and can be much more sophisticated in their thinking about evolution and culture, including asking how evolution might shape cultural development. Chapters 8 and 9 focus most on these issues, though of course other chapters also raise relevant points.

In Chapter 8, Angela G. Pirlott and David P. Schmitt discuss gendered sexual cultures from the perspective that gender norms and roles can be evoked facultatively as a result of environmental features, such as sex ratios. At the same time that variation in a host of gender- and sex-related variables may be transmitted and shared (and hence be cultural in the intuitive sense), they might also be caused by and interact with evolved sexual strategies.

Finally, in Chapter 9, Azim F. Shariff, Benjamin Grant Purzycki, and Richard Sosis consider religions as cultural solutions to social living, and they also provide a rich and nuanced discussion of evolution and culture. Shariff et al. propose that religion offers solutions to social and ecological problems, such as by coordinating group living via mechanisms such as supernatural monitoring, providing mechanisms for resource management, encouraging costly signaling, containing rituals that encourage cohesion, having ways of dealing with defectors, and regulating marriage and sexuality. A particular bonus in this chapter is their rich discussion of cultural and evolutionary functionalism.

WHO THIS BOOK IS FOR

I, and all of this book's authors, are psychologists. However, we are psychologists of many different cultural backgrounds, from many different places, who study many different cultural things—from food to politics to religion. I believe that psychologists, if they study human beings of any kind and in any context, would be well advised to take culture into account because—as the chapters in this book explain—culture affects nearly every domain of life.

These chapters will help psychologists and other social scientists think more deeply about several aspects of culture. I have previously argued that broadening the cultures that psychologists study can help us improve our theorizing regarding what cultures are, whether practices and ideas are culturally specific or culturally universal (cf. Norenzayan & Heine, 2005), how research on culture is done, and what is interesting about culture (Cohen, 2009). I claimed, therefore, that broadening psychologists' view of culture would be important in applied, basic research, and clinical contexts in psychology.

Of course, it is not just psychologists who study culture, and any professional in any field might find it helpful to think about the different kinds of cultures discussed in this book. A businessperson might find it sensible and intuitive to remind her- or himself to be culturally sensitive when interacting with a colleague from another country, but that same businessperson might need to be reminded about cultural sensitivity when encountering someone with a different religion or political outlook or from a different region of her or his own country.

Studying culture can help us understand each other better and prevent conflict resulting from clashing worldviews (Markus & Conner, 2013). If you want to understand why East Asians and Westerners might have trouble seeing eye to eye and what to do about that, psychology has decades of top-notch studies. This book might help you better understand your neighbors' puzzling food habits (Chapter 7), why parents just don't understand (Chapter 2), why the U.S. South (Chapter 4) and the Wild West (Chapter 5) seem like different countries, and why engineering professors and psychology professors speak totally different languages (Chapter 1). It also provides some new perspectives on old debates about cultural clashes between Democrats and Republicans (Chapter 6), between men and women (Chapter 8), between members of different religions (Chapter 9), and between rich and poor people (Chapter 3).

Finally, the cultures presented in this book are just fascinating. People in any walk of life might enjoy reading about their own and others' multiple cultural viewpoints, and the chapters here have been written to be accessible to people without a strong background in the social sciences.

Taken together, the contributions to this book will surely help inspire generations of psychologists interested in culture. The chapters will encourage psychologists to think about a wider set of kinds of culture than they traditionally have (professional and disciplinary, historical cultures, regions within the country, frontiers, political landscapes, sex and gender, and religion, among others) and to think more broadly about the processes that give shape to a wide set of cultural influences (settlement, political pressures, and evolution, among others). Thus, I offer my sincerest thanks to all the authors for their thought-provoking contributions to this volume.

REFERENCES

Cohen, A. B. (2003). Religion, likelihood of action, and the morality of mentality. *The International Journal for the Psychology of Religion, 13*, 273–285. doi:10.1207/S15327582IJPR1304_4

Cohen, A. B. (2009). Many forms of culture. *American Psychologist, 64*, 194–204. doi:10.1037/a0015308

Cohen, A. B. (2010). Just how many different forms of culture are there? *American Psychologist, 65*, 59–61. doi:10.1037/a0017793

Cohen, A. B., Hall, D. E., Koenig, H. G., & Meador, K. G. (2005). Social versus individual motivation: Implications for normative definitions of religious orientation. *Personality and Social Psychology Review, 9*, 48–61. doi:10.1207/s15327957pspr0901_4

Cohen, A. B., & Hill, P. C. (2007). Religion as culture: Religious individualism and collectivism among American Catholics, Jews, and Protestants. *Journal of Personality, 75*, 709–742. doi:10.1111/j.1467-6494.2007.00454.x

Cohen, A. B., & Rankin, A. (2004). Religion and the morality of positive mentality. *Basic and Applied Social Psychology, 26*, 45–57. doi:10.1207/s15324834basp2601_5

Cohen, A. B., & Rozin, P. (2001). Religion and the morality of mentality. *Journal of Personality and Social Psychology, 81*, 697–710. doi:10.1037/0022-3514.81.4.697

Festinger, L. (1957). *A theory of cognitive dissonance*. Stanford, CA: Stanford University Press.

Fiske, A. P., Kitayama, S., Markus, H. R., & Nisbett, R. E. (1998). The cultural matrix of social psychology. In D. T. Gilbert, S. Fiske, & G. Lindzey (Eds.), *Handbook of social psychology* (4th ed., Vol. 2, pp. 915–981). Boston, MA: McGraw-Hill.

Heine, S. J., Lehman, D. R., Markus, H. R., & Kitayama, S. (1999). Is there a universal need for positive self-regard? *Psychological Review, 106*, 766–794. doi:10.1037/0033-295X.106.4.766

Jones, E. E., & Harris, V. A. (1967). The attribution of attitudes. *Journal of Experimental Social Psychology, 3,* 1–24. doi:10.1016/0022-1031(67)90034-0

Markus, H. R., & Conner, A. (2013). *Clash! 8 cultural conflicts that make us who we are.* New York, NY: Hudson Street Press.

Markus, H. R., & Kitayama, S. (1991). Culture and the self: Implications for cognition, emotion, and motivation. *Psychological Review, 98,* 224–253. doi:10.1037/0033-295X.98.2.224

Norenzayan, A., & Heine, S. J. (2005). Psychological universals: What are they and how can we know? *Psychological Bulletin, 131,* 763–784. doi:10.1037/0033-2909.131.5.763

Shweder, R. A. (1991). *Thinking through cultures: Expeditions in cultural psychology.* Cambridge, MA: Harvard University Press.

Triandis, H. C. (1995). *Individualism and collectivism.* Boulder, CO: Westview Press.

Twenge, J. M., Konrath, S., Foster, J. D., Campbell, W. K., & Bushman, B. (2008). Egos inflating over time: A cross-temporal meta-analysis of the narcissistic personality inventory. *Journal of Personality, 76,* 875–902. doi:10.1111/j.1467-6494.2008.00507.x

1

PROFESSIONAL AND DISCIPLINARY CULTURES

CHI-YUE CHIU, LETTY Y.-Y. KWAN, AND SHYHNAN LIOU

Cultural and cross-cultural research has uncovered many cultural similarities and differences across nations and ethnic groups and discovered many psychological effects of national or ethnic cultures (Chiu & Hong, 2006; Lehman, Chiu, & Schaller, 2004). By comparison, the effects of intellectual traditions in established disciplines and professions on human behaviors have not received much research attention (see Sanchez-Burks & Lee, 2007). In this chapter, we argue that each established academic discipline or profession has a distinctive culture. Moreover, the knowledge tradition in an academic profession affects its practitioners' behaviors in important ways. Furthermore, taking a cultural perspective on academic disciplines and professions has significant intellectual benefits. For example, it invites critical reflections on the uneven representation of different national groups in

We acknowledge the support of a research grant awarded to Chi-yue Chiu by the Ministry of Education, Singapore, for the preparation of this chapter.

http://dx.doi.org/10.1037/14274-001
Culture Reexamined: Broadening Our Understanding of Social and Evolutionary Influences,
A. B. Cohen (Editor)

academic disciplines and professions. Including professional and disciplinary cultures in cultural psychological inquiry can also promote nuanced research into cultural processes.

CULTURE AS A KNOWLEDGE TRADITION

Our argument that established disciplines and professions have cultures is based on the definition of *culture* as a knowledge tradition in the anthropology of knowledge (Barth, 2002). According to Barth (2002), "Knowledge provides people with materials for reflection and premises for action" and "actions become knowledge to others after the fact" (p. 1). For a tradition of knowledge to achieve the status of a culture, it has, aside from containing a corpus of assumptions and assertions about aspects of the world that are partially instantiated and communicated in one or several media, to be "distributed, communicated, employed, and transmitted within a series of instituted social relations" (Barth, 2002, p. 2). This idea resonates with the argument that two defining characteristics of a cultural knowledge tradition are its sharedness and continuity (Chiu, Leung, & Hong, 2010). Unlike a family tradition or an individual's eccentric beliefs and values, culture is widely (albeit not perfectly) shared in a human community. Unlike a fad that enjoys temporary popularity, culture has a history.

Sharedness of Cultural Ideas and Practices

Cultural ideas and practices are represented and shared at multiple levels (Chiu & Hong, 2006). At the supraindividual level, culture exists in the form of tangible, public representations that are embodied in the culture's instituted social relations and are accessible to all members of the culture (Morling & Lamoreaux, 2008). As are national cultures, disciplinary and professional cultures are embodied in various instituted practices. In disciplinary and professional cultures, institutionalization often occurs through the professional codes, textbooks, training programs, and in-class social interactions in academia. As Barth (2002) put it, "Mathematical knowledge has its computations, gross anatomy its atlases, microbiology its technical apparatus and chemical models, and so on. These representations shape both thought and action and thus the practices of scholars in different disciplines" (p. 9). Indeed, knowledge in an academic discipline is often represented via its characteristic framing images and metaphors (e.g., the metaphor of war games in immunology), which shape construction of research projects, communication of knowledge, and production of new knowledge in the field (Barth, 2002).

At the individual level, culture exists in the form of internalized individual-level characteristics, such as values and preferences. In the context of disciplinary and professional cultures, reliable individual differences exist between practitioners in the marketing and research and development (R&D) professions (Griffin & Hauser, 1992). Whereas marketing professionals focus on the market, prefer a short time horizon of incremental projects, and can accept a high degree of ambiguity and bureaucracy, R&D professionals focus on scientific development, have a high need for specificity, prefer a long time horizon of advanced projects, and have relatively little tolerance for ambiguity and bureaucracy. Naturally, these rules do not apply to every individual professional or even to every marketing or R&D department, but they do indicate trends that researchers have been able to identify.

Finally, culture is also represented in the form of intersubjective perceptions of culture—beliefs and values that members of a culture perceive to be widespread in their culture (Chiu, Gelfand, Yamagishi, Shteynberg, & Wan, 2010). Consistent with the idea that established disciplines have cultures, a recent study (Chiu & Kwan, 2011) showed that among both business school and engineering students, consensus exists that business students value a market orientation (including values such as organizational recognition, sales and profit, and market share) more than they do a research orientation (which consists of values such as knowledge, research for research's sake, creative environment, and freedom to solve problems). In contrast, both engineering students and business school students agree that engineering students value a research orientation more than they do a market orientation. In short, cultural ideas and practices are shared at different levels.

Socialization of Practitioners Into Disciplinary and Professional Cultures

Cultures are, moreover, transmitted in a series of instituted social relations. Core values in disciplinary and professional cultures are reproduced through institutionalization of the attendant cultural practices of these values. These values are transmitted to new generations of practitioners through disciplinary socialization. Acculturation of practitioners into a discipline or profession ensures the continuity of the disciplinary or professional culture.

Research has shown that as individuals acculturate into their professional cultures, the framing "idea network" and hidden metaphorical associations also permeate their general worldviews. Hence, individuals pursuing different academic disciplines have different sociopolitical attitudes. For example, students in commerce and business studies—disciplines traditionally associated with economic rationalism—tend to have relatively weaker proenvironment attitudes (Hodgkinson & Innes, 2001). Some of these disciplinary differences can be attributed to self-selection—individuals prefer to major in disciplines whose core values are congruent with personal values (Hastie, 2007). Nonetheless, longitudinal research findings have shown that institutional socialization can reinforce students' initial sociopolitical preferences (see Chatard & Selimbegovic, 2007). For example, social science students show a significant decrease in social dominance orientation over their course of study, largely as a result of the development of a stronger belief in environmental (vs. genetic) determinism during their study (Dambrun, Kamiejski, Haddadi, & Duarte, 2009). In a 3-year longitudinal study of commerce and social science students, Guimond and Palmer (1996) also found that over time, commerce students held increasingly stronger procapitalist values and antiunion values. They also displayed a stronger tendency to discount systemic factors as explanations for poverty and unemployment. In contrast, social science students were less likely over time to victimize people who were poor or unemployed. Furthermore, increased exposure to social science professors and courses appears to mediate the changes in social science students' sociopolitical attitudes. Another longitudinal study (Guimond, 1999) further showed that this acculturation effect results from informational influence (influence of the academic major pursued by the students) rather than conformity to peer influence.

In short, clear evidence has shown that established disciplines and professions have cultures that are shared at different levels of representation and are systematically transmitted to newer generations of practitioners.

Behavioral Consequences of Disciplinary and Professional Cultures

Each disciplinary or professional culture has its own language, mode of analysis, mores, and standards of validation. The shared representations of a discipline or profession shape the thoughts, actions, and practices of scholars in the discipline or profession. For example, the differences in the structure of knowledge across academic disciplines create a characteristic communicative style among its practitioners when they talk about knowledge in their discipline. Compared with ideas and concepts in the humanities and social sciences, those in the hard sciences are more exact and specific. For example, the ways to define or refer to a natural science concept (e.g., the law of relativity) tend to be invariant among natural scientists. By comparison, the ways to refer to social science concepts among social scientists are more variable (e.g., the relative deprivation hypothesis). As a consequence, natural sciences require a smaller academic vocabulary than social sciences and the humanities. For example, the average number of different words out of the first 400 words of a natural science publication is around 160, compared with 200 words for a humanities publication. The average number of different words of the first 400 words in an introductory natural science lecture is around 160 words, compared with 195 words for an introductory humanities lecture (Schachter, Rauscher, Christenfeld, & Crone, 1994). Because humanists and social scientists (vs. natural scientists) use more varied vocabularies to communicate ideas in their discipline, they pause more frequently when they talk about ideas in their field. In an introductory lecture for their respective discipline, humanists make an average of almost five filled pauses (e.g., *ums*, *ers*) per minute and social scientists make an average of four filled pauses per minute, compared with 1.5 filled pauses per minute for natural scientists (Schachter, Christenfeld, Ravina, & Bilous, 1991).

Individuals from markedly different disciplines or professions also process information differently. Findings from a recently completed study (Chiu & Kwan, 2011) help to illustrate this point. In this study, business and engineering students were supposedly invited by a worldwide commercial carrier to redesign its check-in service to reduce cost, improve efficiency, and satisfy customers' needs. Next, participants learned that they would receive two types of information that might be useful to them: (a) feedback from a consumer survey (market information) and (b) feedback from engineers and industrial designers (research information). The participants went through six pages of information, with two pieces of market information and two pieces of research information on each page. The locations of the four information items on each page were randomly determined. To control for the effect of information content, the same piece of information was framed as market information (e.g., "Customers should be able to easily check where their bags are, especially when the bags do not arrive as expected") for half of the participants and as research information (e.g., "Reusable GPS tracker prevents loss of bags and allows customers to track their own bag") for the remaining half. Participants' eye movements during the task were monitored. The dependent variables were the average length of time (across the six trials) until the participants attended to the first piece of market or research information, the total number of times the participants focused on each type of information, and the total number of times the participants looked at each type of information.

Recall that the general consensus is that business students value a market orientation more than they do a research orientation. Consistent with this pattern, Chiu and Kwan (2011) found that it took business students less time to attend to the first piece of market information than to the first piece of research information. They also focused on market information more often and spent more time reading the market information. Recall also that the general consensus is that engineering students value a research orientation more than they do a market orientation. Again, consistent with this pattern, it took engineering students a shorter length of time to attend to the first piece of research information than to the first piece of market information. They also focused on research information more often and spent more time processing research information. These results show that adhering to a disciplinary culture can be compared with a double-edged sword: On the one hand, it provides a foundational schema to structure attention; on the other hand, it also creates intellectual blind spots for practitioners in each discipline.

In summary, established disciplines and professions have knowledge traditions that meet the criteria of sharedness and continuity of a culture. These knowledge traditions also possess the functional characteristics of national cultures in guiding attention (and other cognitive processes) and communication (and other social interactions). Thus, the knowledge traditions in mature disciplines and professions can be treated as cultures.

VALUE OF STUDYING DISCIPLINARY AND PROFESSIONAL CULTURES: SOME EXAMPLES

Granted that mature disciplines and professions have cultures, two questions emerge. First, what are the advantages of taking a cultural perspective on academic disciplines and professions? Second, how may studying disciplinary and professional cultures improve understanding of cultural processes?

Advantages of Taking a Cultural Perspective on Academic Disciplines

Workways refer to the characteristic ideas of a culture about what is true, good, and efficient within the domain of work. In a recent review of the cultural psychology of workways, Sanchez-Burks and Lee (2007) concluded that studying culture in work contexts offers a unique perspective that is relevant for theory and research in cultural psychology. We agree with this conclusion. Indeed, taking a cultural perspective on academic disciplines has many benefits. For example, it confers new insights into why interdisciplinary collaborations do not always lead to increased creativity and productivity, which is a key problem in research on the psychology of team performance. It also invites critical reflections on the uneven representation of different national or ethnic groups in academia.

Understanding Interdisciplinary Collaboration

A key question in the psychology of team performance is how disciplinary or functional diversity in a work team affects team performance and creativity. The presence of disciplinary or functional diversity is expected to benefit the interdisciplinary work team and its members in several ways (Han, Peng, Chiu, & Leung, 2010). First, disciplinary diversity enlarges the team's pool of intellectual resources, allowing team members to access complementary ideas, knowledge, and skills that can be creatively integrated and synthesized to generate novel, creative solutions to current problems (Jehn, Northcraft, & Neale, 1999). Second, the multiple perspectives that employees with diverse disciplinary backgrounds bring to the work team invite the team to clarify, organize, and integrate new approaches to accomplishing its organizational goals (Thomas & Ely, 1996). Third, functional diversity within a work group may foster a more robust critical evaluation of an idea before it is accepted. Critical evaluation of initial ideas may in turn reduce risk aversion, increase problem-solving efficiency, and improve decision-making quality in the group (Lattimer, 1998). Finally, work units characterized by high levels of disciplinary diversity are likely to have access to broader networks of contacts, which would enable the work units to acquire otherwise inaccessible but useful information. With this information, work units can calibrate their decisions, increase their work commitment, and enhance their responsiveness to environmental turbulence (Donnellon, 1993; Tushman, 1977). Indeed, some empirical evidence has shown that diversity in team composition contributes to work team creativity (e.g., Woodman, Sawyer, & Griffin, 1993).

Nonetheless, despite the potential benefits of interdisciplinary collaborations, many collaborations result in conflicts rather than in increased creativity or productivity. Consider as an example the interface of R&D and marketing. The literature on managing technological innovation highlights the importance of managing organizational complexities, especially the complexities that exist at the boundary between R&D and marketing (Maltz, Souder, & Kumar, 2001). Nonetheless, engineers and scientists in R&D often fail to appreciate marketing's contributions to innovation, believing that customers do not know what they want, that marketing does not have the needed technological expertise to provide substantial input into product changes, and that marketing's time horizon is too short. Alternatively, marketing professionals often complain that engineers and scientists in R&D lack perspective, do not appreciate prior customer investments, and do not understand the concept of diverse market segments and that marketing's role is too narrowly defined as refining technically driven ideas rather than finding ways to technologically embody customer needs (Workman, 1997).

Treating entrenched knowledge traditions in R&D and marketing as cultures, we argue that the conflicts between R&D and marketing may arise in part from cultural clashes. Practitioners of R&D and marketing have been socialized to regard the dominant values and preferred cognitive and communication styles of their own discipline as normal and to pathologize those of the other discipline.

Indeed, the pattern of reactions to members from other disciplines on a multidisciplinary team resembles the pattern of reactions to foreign cultures in multicultural contexts (Chiu, Gries, Torelli, & Cheng, 2011). Research on multicultural psychology has shown that ideas and practices from foreign cultures may sometimes be regarded as cognitive resources that can be appropriated to improve one's performance (Leung & Chiu, 2010; Leung, Maddux, Galinsky, & Chiu, 2008). However, sometimes ideas and practices imported from other cultures may be seen as heretical and a threat to the purity, integrity, and vitality of one's own culture (Chiu & Cheng, 2007). If similar cultural processes mediate reactions to members of other disciplines on a multidisciplinary team and reactions to foreign national cultures in a multicultural environment, one would expect the cognitive and motivational factors that promote appreciative reactions or reduce exclusionary reactions to a foreign culture to have the same positive effects on the quality and outcomes of interdisciplinary collaborations. In multicultural psychology, awareness of cultural differences and being open-minded are two critical factors that enhance appreciative reactions to foreign cultures (Leung & Chiu, 2008, 2010). Individuals who are blind to cultural differences will not be able to appreciate the values of other cultures. Individuals who are aware of cultural differences are motivated to learn from other cultures only if they are open-minded. Likewise, our recent studies (Kwan & Chiu, 2011) showed that members of a multidisciplinary team do not appreciate the knowledge of members from other disciplines if they are unaware of the differences between disciplines. When they are aware of these differences, they appreciate another discipline only when they are motivated to learn from other disciplines. In short, taking a cultural perspective on disciplinary and professional traditions connects research on interdisciplinary collaboration to multicultural psychology and confers new insights into the psychological processes that mediate team performance and creativity in multidisciplinary teams.

Reflecting Critically on the Uneven Representation of Different National or Ethnic Groups in Academic Disciplines

Treating academic disciplines as culture increases the awareness of the compatibility of the core values of the discipline and those of national cultures. To take psychology as an example, as a science psychology emphasizes objectivity and impartiality in generating, validating, and disseminating knowledge. Nonetheless, some writers have recently highlighted the relevance of cultural factors at different stages of knowledge creation. For example, Chiu and Kwan (2011) posited that knowledge creation involves one or more iterations of these three stages: (a) authoring new ideas; (b) selecting, editing, and marketing new ideas; and (c) accepting the new ideas in the market. Of more importance, different evaluation criteria are used at different stages of knowledge creation. At the authoring stage, the primary criterion for evaluation is the novelty of the idea. Ideas that are novel, non-conventional, and counterintuitive in relation to current knowledge are preferred at this stage. At the selection, editing, and marketing stage, the primary objectives are to select an idea on the basis of its potential success in the marketplace of ideas, to modify and edit the selected idea to enhance its marketability, and to enhance acceptance of the idea by the target audiences. At this stage, knowledge creators will consider the assumed attitudes, values, and beliefs of the gatekeepers (e.g., reviewers, journal editors) and the end users (readers; Fast, Heath, & Wu, 2009). At the acceptance stage, the gatekeepers deliberating on the market-entry rights of an idea will consider the collective utility of the idea (including its practical and heuristic value) and the preferences of the pertinent authorities (e.g., opinions of the reviewers). The actual preferences of the end users (readers) determine the extent of acceptance of the idea in the market. In summary, although science values ideas that are novel vis-à-vis existing knowledge, the acceptance of an idea in the marketplace of ideas also depends on the assumed and actual consensus regarding the preferences of the gatekeepers and consumers of the idea. Such assumed and actual consensus is an integral part of the disciplinary culture.

Available bibliographic tools allow researchers to identify the knowledge workers who have been most successful in having their ideas accepted in their discipline. Analysis of the background of these workers reveals an uneven representation of different national groups in the discipline. Take *Psychological Science,* a premium psychology journal, as an example. Between May 2000 and December 2010, 2,363 articles or reviews were published in *Psychological Science.* Among these 2,363 articles or reviews, 339 (14.4%) were contributions from the 44 most prolific researchers who had published seven or more *Psychological Science* articles during this period (see Table 1.1). An analysis of the background of these researchers reveals that only two were of Asian descent, and all received their doctoral degree from a North American or European institution. Furthermore, 2,319 (98.1%) of these articles had at least one North American or European author, and only 140 (5.9%) had at least one author from outside North America or Europe. The dominance of North America and Europe in the production of psychological knowledge is particularly clear when considering the fact that more than 1 million psychologists were active around the globe, and only around 577,000 were from the United States and Europe (Stevens & Gielen, 2007).

One might expect a more even representation of successful knowledge producers across countries in social and personality psychology, a subdiscipline in psychology that emphasizes contextual influence on behaviors. Between

TABLE 1.1
Number of Psychological Science Articles or Reviews Published by the 44 Most Prolific Contributors to *Psychological Science* (2000–2010)

Contributor	No. of published articles	Awarding institution of PhD
Plomin, Robert	12	University of Texas at Austin
Cacioppo, John T.	11	Ohio State University
Davidson, Richard R.	11	Harvard University
Enns, James T.	11	Princeton University
Galinsky, Adam D.	11	Princeton University
Schwarz, Norbert	10	Universität Mannheim
Ariely, Dan	9	University of North Carolina at Chapel Hill
Blake, Randolph	9	Vanderbilt University
Bloom, Paul	9	Massachusetts Institute of Technology
Bushman, Brad J.	9	University of Missouri
Driver, Jon	9	University of Oxford
Kingstone, Alan	9	University of Manchester
Rayner, Keith	9	Cornell University
Reyna, Valerie F.	9	Rockefeller University
Rhodes, Gillian	9	Stanford University
Ambady, Nalin	8	Harvard University
Banaji, Mahzarin R.	8	Ohio State University
Diener, Ed	8	University of Washington
Gilbert, Daniel T.	8	Princeton University
Goldin-Meadow, Susan	8	University of Pennsylvania
Humphreys, Glyn W.	8	University of Bristol
McCrae, C. Neil	8	University of Aberdeen
Scholl, Brian J.	8	Rutgers, The State University of New Jersey
Schooler, Jonathan W.	8	University of Washington
Wilson, Tim D.	8	University of Michigan
Bentin, Shlomo	7	Hebrew University of Jerusalem
Dweck, Carol S.	7	Yale University
Epley, Nicholas	7	Cornell University
Harmon-Jones, Eddie	7	University of Arizona
Hasher, Lynn	7	University of California, Berkeley
Inzlicht, Michael	7	Brown University
Kramer, A. F.	7	University of Illinois
Lubinski, David	7	University of Minnesota
Luck, Steven J.	7	University of California, San Diego
Pratt, Jay	7	Washington University
Proffitt, Dennis R.	7	Pennsylvania State University
Robinson, Michael D.	7	University of California, Davis
Rosenthal, Robert	7	University of California, Los Angeles
Rozin, Paul	7	Harvard University
Schacter, Daniel L.	7	University of Toronto
Schyns, Philippe G.	7	Brown University
Seligman, Martin E. P.	7	University of Pennsylvania
Viken, Richard J.	7	University of Iowa
Wynn, Karen	7	McGill University

Note. Some of the 330 articles were published by two or more authors on the list and thus were counted more than once. Data from http://wokinfo.com/

1991 and 2010, a total of 3,269 articles were published in the *Journal of Personality and Social Psychology* (JPSP), a flagship journal in social and personality psychology. Of these 3,269 articles, 723 (22.1%) were contributions from the 45 most prolific researchers who had published 13 or more *JPSP* articles during this period. Again, the dominance of North America and Europe in the production of social and personality psychology knowledge can be discerned from an analysis of these researchers' backgrounds. As shown in Table 1.2, among these 45 researchers, only two were of Asian descent, and all received their doctoral degrees from a North American or European institution. In addition, 3,220 (98.5%) of the 3,269 published articles had at least one author from North America or Europe, and only 118 (3.6%) had at least one author not from North America or Europe. The dominance of Western-authored articles in *JPSP* may reflect a cultural bias in social and personality psychology identified by Edward Sampson (1977). According to Sampson, social and personality psychology emphasizes "a cultural and historical thesis of self-contained individualism; syntheses of opposing or desirable characteristics are located within the person rather than within an interdependent collectivity" (p. 767). Sampson issued a warning to social psychologists, arguing that "in an era in which collective problem solving is necessary, the perpetuation of self-contained, individualistic conceptions can stifle psychology's effort to contribute to resolving contemporary social issues" (p. 767).

The dominance of Western countries in other top science publications is also evident, but to lesser extent than in psychology. For example, of the 19,073 articles published in *Science* between 1991 and 2010, 92.7% had at least one author from North America or Europe, and 13.9% had at least one author not from North America or Europe.

One may argue that psychologists from Western backgrounds do not limit their research attention to behavioral patterns in Western cultures and may even refrain from generalizing their findings across cultures. Nonetheless, a recent review (Henrich, Heine, & Norenzayan, 2010) suggested otherwise. The authors of this review concluded that "behavioral scientists routinely publish broad claims about human psychology and behavior in the world's top journals based on samples drawn entirely from Western, Educated, Industrialized, Rich and Democratic (WEIRD) societies" (Henrich et al., 2010, p. 83) These results invite critical reflections on the possible cultural biases in psychological knowledge.

How Studying Disciplinary and Professional Cultures Enriches Cultural Psychology

Studying disciplinary and professional cultures also produces new insights into cultural processes. We illustrate this argument with two examples.

TABLE 1.2
Number of *JPSP* Articles Published by the 45 Most Prolific Contributors to *JPSP* (1991–2010)

Contributor	No. of published *JPSP* articles	No. of citing articles	No. of citing articles per *JPSP* article	Publication year of first *JPSP* article	Awarding institution of PhD
Baumeister, R. F.	34	2,193	64.50	1978	Princeton University
Mikulincer, M.	30	1,319	43.97	1986	Bar-Ilan University
Petty, R. E.	30	1,455	48.50	1976	Ohio State University
Diener, E.	27	2,355	87.22	1975	University of Washington
Greenberg, J.	24	919	38.29	1976	University of Kansas
Higgins, E. T.	23	1,130	49.13	1976	Columbia University
John, O. P.	23	2,363	102.74	1986	University of Oregon
Stapel, D. A.[a]	23	592	25.74	1996	University of Amsterdam
Elliot, A. J.	22	2,361	107.32	1991	University of Wisconsin
Holmes, J. G.	22	921	41.86	1970	University of North Carolina
Sedikides, C.	22	923	41.95	1989	Ohio State University
Simpson, J. A.	22	1,346	61.18	1983	University Minnesota
Pyszczynski, T.	21	756	36.00	1978	University of Kansas
Judd, C. M.	20	1,631	81.55	1980	Columbia University
Robins, R. W.	20	1,001	50.05	1994	University of California, Berkeley
Trope, Y.	20	793	39.65	1975	University of Michigan
Dunning, D.	19	1,125	59.21	1989	Stanford University
Gilovich, T.	19	663	34.89	1981	Stanford University
Spears, R.	19	973	51.21	1985	University of Exeter
Keltner, D.	18	1,302	72.33	1993	Stanford University
Kruglanski, A. W.	18	902	50.11	1973	University of California, Los Angeles

Arndt, J.	17	450	26.47	1997	University of Arizona
Solomon, S.	17	692	40.71	1977	University of Kansas
Wegner, D. M.	17	919	54.06	1975	Michigan State University
Finkel, E. J.	16	402	25.13	2001	North Carolina
Liberman, N.	16	625	39.06	1998	Tel Aviv University
Shaver, P. R.	16	896	56.00	1972	University of Michigan
Swann, W. B.	16	801	50.06	1976	University of Minnesota
Cacioppo, J.T.	15	1,329	88.60	1977	Ohio State University
McCrae, R. R.	15	1,542	102.80	1980	Boston University
Zanna, M.	15	891	59.40	1966	Yale University
De Dreu, C. K. W.	14	356	25.43	2000	University of Groningen
Galinsky, A. D.	14	563	40.21	2000	Princeton University
Gilbert, D. T.	14	1,337	95.50	1983	Princeton University
Harmon-Jones, E.	14	917	65.50	1995	University of Arizona
Murray, S. L.	14	696	49.71	1993	University of Waterloo
Neuberg, S. L.	14	824	58.86	1987	Carnegie Mellon University
Rusbult, C. E.	14	837	59.79	1979	University of North Carolina
Banaji, M. R.	13	1,525	117.31	1989	Ohio State University
Bargh, J. A.	13	2,585	198.85	1982	University of Michigan
Blascovich, J.	13	747	57.46	1975	University of Nevada
Chiu, C.Y.	13	488	37.54	1997	Columbia University
Hamilton, D. L.	13	421	32.38	1969	University of Illinois
Kenrick, D. T.	13	489	37.62	1976	Arizona State University
Taylor, S. E.	13	1,223	94.08	1971	Yale University

Note. Some of the 723 articles were published by two or more authors on the list and thus were counted more than once. *JPSP* = *Journal of Personality and Social Psychology*. Data from http://wokinfo.com/ and http://thomsonreuters.com/

[a]*JPSP* has retracted several articles published by Stapel because the published data were found to have questionable credibility.

Tracking Evolution of Subcultures

First, a major challenge in cultural psychological research is to examine the emergence of new cultures or subcultures (Cheng & Chiu, 2010). The availability of bibliographic tools allows researchers to quantify how ideas flow between different disciplines and subdisciplines, which in turn enables cultural researchers to track the emergence of subdisciplinary cultures. For example, Yang and Chiu (2009) analyzed 40 years (1979–2009) of journal citation data collected from 17 American Psychological Association (APA) journals. The analysis of the dynamic flow of knowledge between subfields of psychology revealed that although the subfields engage in a clear division of labor, they also engage in dynamic transactions of knowledge. Their results further showed that an emergent subfield would first obtain its intellectual nutrients from the established subdisciplines. Once it found its own niche, it turned into a spin-off and started to assume the role of knowledge supplier. For example, in the decade 1980–1989 APA began publishing *Behavioral Neuroscience, Health Psychology*, and the *Journal of Experimental Psychology: Learning, Memory, and Cognition*. During this period, these three new journals were not frequently cited by other APA journals. Instead, they functioned largely as consumers of knowledge from journals in the cognate subdisciplines. This result suggests that new journals, being relatively less established, are receptive to ideas and influences from the related subfields. In the next decade (1990–1999), these three journals were more frequently cited, probably because they were more established than before. In this decade, *Behavioral Neuroscience* exported knowledge to the *Journal of Experimental Psychology: Animal Behavior Processes*; the *Journal of Experimental Psychology: Learning, Memory, and Cognition* exported knowledge to the *Journal of Experimental Psychology: General*; and *Health Psychology* exported knowledge to the *Journal of Counseling Psychology* and *Psychological Assessment*. Of interest is that APA also introduced three new journals (*Neuropsychology, Psychological Assessment*, and *Psychological Methods*) in this decade, and these journals also took on the role of knowledge consumers, importing knowledge from journals in the cognate subdisciplines. These results suggest that a new intellectual tradition may emerge when a new constellation of ideas that is different from existing intellectual traditions can be identified. Next, the emergent knowledge tradition may seek intellectual input from related traditions, find a distinctive niche, and start to exert its influences on the cognate subdisciplines when it becomes more established. Similar processes may underline the emergence of other forms of subculture (e.g., religious domination and consumer subcultures; Cheng & Chiu, 2010). Nonetheless, investigation into the emergence of academic disciplines and subdisciplines is relatively easy because of ready availability of longitudinal, quantitative data on the directions and patterns of knowledge transactions between different academic disciplines and subdisciplines.

Modeling Cultural Transmission Process

The ready availability of bibliographic data also allows cultural researchers to test important theories of cultural transmission. For example, cultural learning can occur through direct interaction with the environment and hence can take place independent of any social influence. However, because asocial learning typically incurs additional effort and time investment, as well as risks ensuing from trial-and-error learning in an uncertain environment, individuals often prefer social learning or acquisition of information from other individuals (Whiten & Ham, 1992). According to the culture–gene coevolution theory (Kendal, Giraldeau, & Laland, 2009), natural selection has favored the evolution of social learning mechanisms that enable selective imitation and emulation for the purpose of acquiring relevant information in a changing environment. These evolved mechanisms of conformist cultural transmission also facilitate collective adherence to and sanctioning of the shared behavioral standards of the cultural community (Chudek & Henrich, 2011).

Within each human community and across different life domains, marked individual differences occur in the amount and quality of information one possesses. It is of critical importance for the fitness enhancement of both the individual and the culture that people learn from individuals who possess high-quality information. Hence, a key challenge in conformist cultural transmission research is to determine how individuals decide from whom to learn (Chudek, Heller, Birch, & Henrich, 2012). Culture–gene coevolution theorists have specified three strategies individuals may adopt to determine from whom to learn. One such strategy is to learn from those who possess better skills or a higher level of competence. However, direct perception of competence can be inaccurate. The challenge to form a veridical perception of competence is particularly serious for naïve learners. For example, junior social psychologists may not have sufficient experience and knowledge to determine which social psychologists possess better research skills. Thus, people, particularly naïve learners, often resort to heuristics for deciding from whom to learn.

One such decision heuristic is the success heuristic, one that biases learners to select models by accumulated record or symbols of success, such as greater wealth in a capitalist society. One indicator of success in an academic discipline is the number of publications in the discipline's premium journals. By this standard, the academics listed in Tables 1.1 and 1.2 can be considered successful practitioners in psychology and social and personality psychology, respectively.

Another decision heuristic is the prestige heuristic, one that biases learners to prefer learning from models who have received preferential attention or deference from other learners (Henrich & Gil-White, 2001). Note that the term *prestige* in culture–gene coevolution theory does not refer to the amount of admiration and respect received from others. Instead, it refers to the amount of attention or deference other learners willingly confer on certain models. The prestige heuristic can lead to more accurate and rapid learning because it capitalizes on others' knowledge about who is worthy of attention (Chudek et al., 2012). In academia, a good indicator of the prestige of a practitioner is how frequently others have cited the practitioner's published works. Column 3 of Table 1.2 shows the number of articles that have cited the JPSP articles published by the 45 most prolific contributors to JPSP (excluding self-citations). Column 4 of the same table shows the average number of articles citing each JPSP article (excluding self-citations). These citation data could be used as indices of the prestige of these social and personality psychologists in their discipline.

Learners may also select models for behavioral emulation on the basis of other information, such as the model's seniority (age or years of experiences in the field) or the quality of training the model has received. Again, using social and personality psychology as an example, an indicator of seniority could be the year in which a researcher published his or her first article in JPSP (Column 5 of Table 1.2), and the quality of training the model has received can be measured by the institution at which the researcher received his or her doctoral training (Column 6 of Table 1.2) and its ranking.

Evolutionary researchers have developed many ingenious experimental paradigms to test the influence of various heuristics on social learning. For example, in a series of studies, Chudek et al. (2012) manipulated the amount of attention bystanders gave to two adult models and observed how this manipulation affected young children's tendency to imitate the preferences of these models. They found that young children were likely to imitate the preferences of the model who had received some attention from others than to imitate the preferences of the one who had not.

An advantage of studying disciplinary cultures is that as we have illustrated here and in Table 1.2, quantitative data on different pertinent heuristic information are readily available. An interesting observation based on the (partial) data in Table 1.2 is that indicators of researcher success, prestige, and seniority are not highly correlated. For example, although the number of citing articles and the number of citing articles per published article are highly correlated ($r = .81$), indices of prestige do not correlate highly with the number of published articles (number of citing articles, $r = .43$; number of citing articles per published article $r = -.13$). Year of publication of the first JPSP article (a proxy for seniority) does not correlate with the number of published articles ($r = -.13$), the number of citing articles ($r = -.17$), or the number of citing articles per published article ($r = -.13$). Given the relative independence of the different types of heuristic information, it is possible to model their additive and multiplicative effects on learners' social learning preferences. In addition, outcome variables (the tendency that a certain model's domain-specific competence will be imitated) can also be easily quantified. For example, researchers can count how frequently the published articles of certain practitioners in the discipline are adopted as readings in graduate courses. The availability of such quantitative data allows researchers to test the differential effects of different heuristics on learners' social learning preferences in different academic disciplines.

CONCLUSION

National and ethnic cultures have received the most research attention in cross-cultural and cultural psychology. In this chapter, we argued that as do nations and ethnic groups, a mature discipline or profession also has its cultural traditions. Many practitioners in the discipline or profession have internalized the core symbolic elements of its tradition. These core elements are embodied in various instituted practices and represented in the shared, intersubjective representations of its practitioners. Furthermore, the core ideas and practices of a disciplinary or professional culture are transmitted across generations of practitioners and have a pronounced influence on its practitioners' values, communicative behaviors, and preferred information processing styles.

Including disciplinary and professional cultures as a form of culture in cultural psychology research has several benefits. First, we can apply principles of multicultural psychology to understand the cognitive and motivational factors that determine team creativity and productivity in interdisciplinary collaborations. Second, taking a cultural perspective on disciplinary inquiry invites critical reflections on the possible cultural biases in psychological research. Finally, treating intellectual traditions in a discipline or profession as cultures provides a new context for studying cultural processes. These benefits attest to the utility of broadening the scope of cultural and cross-cultural psychology to other forms of culture, including disciplinary and professional cultures (Sanchez-Burks & Lee, 2007).

REFERENCES

Barth, F. (2002). An anthropology of knowledge. *Current Anthropology, 43*, 1–18. doi:10.1086/324131

Chatard, A., & Selimbegovic, L. (2007). The impact of higher education on egalitarian attitudes and values: Contextual and cultural determinants. *Social and Personality Psychology Compass, 1*, 541–556. doi:10.1111/j.1751-9004.2007.00024.x

Cheng, S. Y.-Y., & Chiu, C.-y. (2010). A communication perspective to the emergence of a brand culture. In E. Morsella (Ed.), *Expressing oneself/expressing one's self: Communication, cognition, language, and identity* (pp. 125–142). Hillsdale, NJ: Erlbaum.

Chiu, C.-y., & Cheng, S. Y.-Y. (2007). Toward a social psychology of culture and globalization: Some social cognitive consequences of activating two cultures simultaneously. *Social and Personality Psychology Compass, 1,* 84–100. doi:10.1111/j.1751-9004.2007.00017.x

Chiu, C.-y., Gelfand, M., Yamagishi, T., Shteynberg, G., & Wan, C. (2010). Intersubjective culture: The role of intersubjective perceptions in cross-cultural research. *Perspectives on Psychological Science, 5,* 482–493. doi:10.1177/1745691610375562

Chiu, C.-y., Gries, P., Torelli, C. J., & Cheng, S. Y.-Y. (2011). Toward a social psychology of globalization. *Journal of Social Issues, 67,* 663–676. doi:10.1111/j.1540-4560.2011.01721.x

Chiu, C.-y., & Hong, Y. (2006). *Social psychology of culture.* New York, NY: Psychology Press.

Chiu, C.-y., & Kwan, L. Y.-y. (2011, September). *Intersubjective perspective to culture.* Invited keynote address presented at the 7th Chinese Psychologist Conference, Taipei, Taiwan.

Chiu, C.-y., Leung, K.-y., & Hong, Y.-y. (2010). Cultural processes: An overview. In A. K.-y. Leung, C.-y. Chiu, & Y.-y. Hong (Eds.), *Cultural processes: A social psychological perspective* (pp. 3–22). New York, NY: Cambridge University Press. doi:10.1017/CBO9780511779374.003

Chudek, M., Heller, S., Birch, S., & Henrich, J. (2012). Prestige-based cultural learning: Bystander's differential attention to potential models influences children's learning. *Evolution and Human Behavior, 33,* 46–56. doi:10.1016/j.evolhumbehav.2011.05.005

Chudek, M., & Henrich, J. (2011). Culture-gene coevolution, norm psychology and the emergence of human prosociality. *Trends in Cognitive Sciences, 15,* 218–226. doi:10.1016/j.tics.2011.03.003

Dambrun, M., Kamiejski, R., Haddadi, N., & Duarte, S. (2009). Why does social dominance orientation decrease with university exposure to the social sciences? The impact of institutional socialization and the mediating role of "geneticism." *European Journal of Social Psychology, 39,* 88–100. doi:10.1002/ejsp.498

Donnellon, A. (1993). Cross-functional teams in product development: Accommodating the structure to the process. *Journal of Product Innovation Management, 10,* 377–392. doi:10.1016/0737-6782(93)90096-9

Fast, N. J., Heath, C., & Wu, G. (2009). Common ground and cultural prominence: How conversation strengthens culture. *Psychological Science, 20,* 904–911. doi:10.1111/j.1467-9280.2009.02387.x

Griffin, A., & Hauser, J. R. (1992). Patterns of communication among marketing, engineering, and manufacturing: A comparison between two new product teams. *Management Science, 38,* 360–373. doi:10.1287/mnsc.38.3.360

Guimond, S. (1999). Attitude change during college: Normative or informational social influence. *Social Psychology of Education*, *2*, 237–261. doi:10.1023/A:1009662807702

Guimond, S., & Palmer, D. L. (1996). The political socialization of commerce and social science students: Epistemic authority and attitude change. *Journal of Applied Social Psychology*, *26*, 1985–2013. doi:10.1111/j.1559-1816.1996.tb01784.x

Han, J., Peng, S., Chiu, C.-y., & Leung, A. K.-y. (2010). Workforce diversity and creativity: A multilevel analysis. In A. K.-y. Leung, C.-y. Chiu, & Y.-y. Hong (Eds.), *Cultural processes: A social psychological perspective* (pp. 286–312). New York, NY: Cambridge University Press. doi:10.1017/CBO9780511779374.021

Hastie, B. (2007). Cold hearts and bleeding hearts: Disciplinary differences in university students' sociopolitical orientations. *Journal of Social Psychology*, *147*, 211–241. doi:10.3200/SOCP.147.3.211-241

Henrich, J., & Gil-White, F. (2001). The evolution of prestige: Freely conferred deference as a mechanism for enhancing the benefits of cultural transmission. *Evolution and Human Behavior*, *22*, 165–196. doi:10.1016/S1090-5138(00)00071-4

Henrich, J., Heine, S. J., & Norenzayan, A. (2010). The weirdest people in the world? *Behavioral and Brain Sciences*, *33*, 61–83. doi:10.1017/S0140525X0999152X

Hodgkinson, S. P., & Innes, J. M. (2001). The attitudinal influence of career orientation in first-year university students: Environmental attitudes as a function of degree choice. *Journal of Environmental Education*, *32*, 37–40. doi:10.1080/00958960109599144

Jehn, K. A., Northcraft, G. B., & Neale, M. A. (1999). Why some differences make a difference: A field study of diversity, conflict, and performance in workgroups. *Administrative Science Quarterly*, *44*, 741–763. doi:10.2307/2667054

Kendal, J., Giraldeau, L.-A., & Laland, K. (2009). The evolution of social learning rules: Payoff-biased and frequency-dependent biased transmission. *Journal of Theoretical Biology*, *260*, 210–219. doi:10.1016/j.jtbi.2009.05.029

Kwan, L. Y.-Y., & Chiu, C.-y. (2011, August). *Professional climate moderates the effect of perceived distance between professional cultures on quality of collaboration in functionally diverse innovation teams*. Paper presented at the Academy of Management Meeting, San Antonio, TX.

Lattimer, R. L. (1998). The case for diversity in global business, and the impact of diversity on team performance. *Competitiveness Review*, *8*, 3–17. doi:10.1108/eb046364

Lehman, D. R., Chiu, C.-y., & Schaller, M. (2004). Psychology and culture. *Annual Review of Psychology*, *55*, 689–714. doi:10.1146/annurev.psych.55.090902.141927

Leung, A. K.-y., & Chiu, C.-y. (2008). Interactive effects of multicultural experiences and openness to experience on creativity. *Creativity Research Journal*, *20*, 376–382. doi:10.1080/10400410802391371

Leung, A. K.-y., & Chiu, C.-y. (2010). Multicultural experiences, idea receptiveness, and creativity. *Journal of Cross-Cultural Psychology, 41*, 723–741. doi:10.1177/0022022110361707

Leung, A. K.-y., Maddux, W. W., Galinsky, A. D., & Chiu, C.-y. (2008). Multicultural experience enhances creativity: The when and how? *American Psychologist, 63*, 169–181. doi:10.1037/0003-066X.63.3.169

Maltz, E., Souder, W., & Kumar, A. (2001). Influencing R&D/marketing integration and the use of market information by R&D managers: Intended and unintended effects of managerial actions. *Journal of Business Research, 52*, 69–82. doi:10.1016/S0148-2963(99)00096-X

Morling, B., & Lamoreaux, M. (2008). Measuring culture outside the head: A meta-analysis of cultural products. *Personality and Social Psychology Review, 12*, 199–221. doi:10.1177/1088868308318260

Sampson, E. E. (1977). Psychology and the American ideal. *Journal of Personality and Social Psychology, 35*, 767–782. doi:10.1037/0022-3514.35.11.767

Sanchez-Burks, J., & Lee, F. (2007). Cultural psychology of workways. In S. Kitayama & D. Cohen (Eds.), *Handbook of cultural psychology* (pp. 346–369). New York, NY: Guilford Press.

Schachter, S., Christenfeld, N., Ravina, B., & Bilous, F. (1991). Speech disfluency and the structure of knowledge. *Journal of Personality and Social Psychology, 60*, 362–367. doi:10.1037/0022-3514.60.3.362

Schachter, S., Rauscher, F., Christenfeld, N., & Crone, K. (1994). The vocabularies of academia. *Psychological Science, 5*, 37–41. doi:10.1111/j.1467-9280.1994.tb00611.x

Stevens, M. J., & Gielen, U. P. (Eds.). (2007). *Toward a global psychology: Theory, research, intervention, and pedagogy.* Mahwah, NJ: Erlbaum.

Thomas, D. A., & Ely, R. J. (1996). Making differences matter: A new paradigm for managing diversity. *Harvard Business Review, 74*, 79–90.

Tushman, M. L. (1977). Special boundary roles in the innovation process. *Administrative Science Quarterly, 22*, 587–605. doi:10.2307/2392402

Whiten, A., & Ham, R. (1992). On the nature and evolution of imitation in the animal kingdom: Reappraisal of a century of research. *Advances in the Study of Behavior, 21*, 239–283. doi:10.1016/S0065-3454(08)60146-1

Woodman, R. W., Sawyer, J. E., & Griffin, R. W. (1993). Toward a theory of organizational creativity. *Academy of Management Review, 18*, 293–321.

Workman, J. (1997). Engineering's interactions with marketing groups in an engineering-driven organization. In R. Katz (Ed.), *The human side of managing technological innovation: A collection of readings* (pp. 535–549). New York, NY: Oxford University Press.

Yang, Y.-J., & Chiu, C.-y. (2009). Mapping the structure and dynamics of psychological knowledge: Forty years of APA journal citations (1970–2009). *Review of General Psychology, 13*, 349–356. doi:10.1037/a0017195

2

GENERATIONAL CULTURES

BRITTANY GENTILE, W. KEITH CAMPBELL, AND JEAN M. TWENGE

In discussions about culture, one very important variable is often left out: time. Culture is not static. Rather, it is inherently dynamic and evolves as the individuals living in it adopt and change elements over time (Boyd & Richerson, 1985). Generational or birth cohort differences can thus be thought of as a function of cultural change. Consider the case of a time traveler in the United States who goes back to the 1950s. Such a person would find himself or herself very out of place. Our time traveler would stand out in physical ways (e.g., hairstyle, more informal dress, a less formal manner of speaking) but might also be different in personality and behavior. This time traveler might appear less concerned with following social rules, more self-focused, more comfortable discussing personal issues, and more individualistic. Although in the same physical location, he or she might appear to be from a different culture because, for all intents and purposes, he or she is. In the intervening time period, the culture has changed enough that it can

http://dx.doi.org/10.1037/14274-002
Culture Reexamined: Broadening Our Understanding of Social and Evolutionary Influences,
A. B. Cohen (Editor)

be considered a different culture. In this way, cross-temporal differences can be thought of as akin to cross-cultural differences with the defining element being time rather than region. We use the term *akin*, however, because, as we discuss, the comparison is not always so straightforward.

In this chapter, we focus directly on how cross-temporal changes can be conceptualized through the lens of cultural psychology. We break this discussion into three interrelated sections. In the first section, we discuss the theoretical issues surrounding cross-temporal research and how they can be resolved by using cultural psychological theory as a basis for linking individual-level changes to cultural-level changes over time. In the second section, we discuss the specific methodological approaches used to examine cross-temporal change at both the level of individuals and the level of culture. Last, in the third section, we present selected findings from past research and draw some conclusions about how individuals have changed over time.

THEORY

Cross-temporal research hinges on the notion that individual development is influenced by an ever-changing cultural environment. This idea goes back to the sociologist Karl Mannheim (1928/1952), who theorized that individuals growing up in a culture during a specific time would be exposed to common experiences that would shape their development and ultimately produce similar views and behaviors. As culture changed over time, so too would individuals. Although cultural change is a continuous process leading to small modifications in each new cohort of individuals, over a long enough span of time, generations—groups of individuals sharing similar birth cohorts—can appear distinct from one other. The result is that people born at different points in time may diverge in their beliefs, values, and behaviors as a consequence of the cultural environment in which they grew up.

To understand how cross-temporal changes arise, it is necessary to first conceptualize the interaction between individuals and culture. Understanding this interaction is a primary contribution of cultural psychology. The field of social psychology, which is concerned with how individuals behave in social situations, has tended to exclude culture from its analyses, focusing more closely on immediate situational determinants of behavior (Oishi, Kesebir, & Snyder, 2009). In contrast, cultural psychology views the individual and the culture as inextricably bound. As stated by Shweder (1991), the two "live together, require each other, and dynamically, dialectically, and jointly make each other up" (p. 73). In this view, individuals are in large part a product of their cultural environment. They are shaped by culture as they actively integrate the shared cultural meanings and practices they observe in the environment into their psychological processes (e.g., Kitayama, Duffy, & Uchida, 2007; Kitayama, Markus, Matsumoto, & Norasakkunkit, 1997; Lawrence & Valsiner, 1993; Markus & Hamedani, 2007). Conversely, culture is itself a product of individuals past and present who transmit, modify, and adopt cultural elements.

The coconstructive relationship between individuals and culture is further elucidated by the mutual constitution model (Fiske, Kitayama, Markus, & Nisbett, 1998), which is essentially a positive feedback loop in which the self and social system mutually constitute one another. The main values of a culture are reflected in its social institutions (e.g., schools, families, universities, government, workplaces), which influence interpersonal situations (e.g., everyday social transactions) and ultimately individual psychological processes (e.g., personality, motivations, values). These psychological processes in turn reinforce the cultural system. This description of a self-reinforcing relationship between the culture and the individuals in it is useful for understanding the alignment seen in cultures between individual psychology and cultural values. For example, the collectivistic culture in many parts of Asia is linked to collectivistic social systems (e.g., Confucianism), interdependent self-construals among members of the culture, and even a tendency toward more holistic perceptual processes (Markus & Kitayama, 1991; Masuda & Nisbett, 2001).

The trick when applying self-reinforcing models such as the mutual constitution model to understanding cross-temporal change is the issue of change itself. To begin with, one needs to assume that culture is not static but changes continually over time. This assumption is not a stretch because history has shown that it takes tremendous effort to stabilize a culture in the face of outside contact and technology, with Japan's isolation from the rest of the world in the 1600s being a classic example (Simonton, 1997). At the same time, one also needs to assume that, consistent with the mutual constitution model, stabilization will exist within the process of cultural change. Each component of the system is mutually reinforcing, so change in any one area should be reflected throughout. Thus, cultural changes should be reflected in corresponding changes to psychological processes.

To make this clearer, we use the example of an individual growing up in the United States in the 2010s versus the 1950s. Both individuals would be exposed to a specific cultural context and, consistent with the mutual constitution model, would have an individual psychological system that was consistent with that cultural experience. However, the two individuals would differ in several ways, with the modern individual being more individualistic, more casual in dress and appearance, more anxious, more technologically connected, and so forth. The mutual constitution model falls short of being

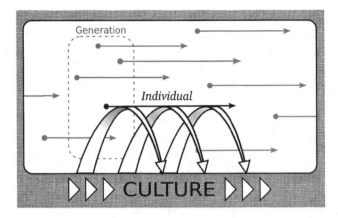

Figure 2.1. The generational change model. To simplify the model, we show only one individual–culture interaction in detail. Other individuals are shown as gray arrows in the background and, although not depicted, the same process is occurring for every individual in the culture.

a sufficient explanation for this cross-temporal change because it operates largely at one point in time. In other words, we can use the model to discuss the individual–culture interaction equally well today or 60 years ago, but we cannot use it to describe how that interaction evolved over time to produce differences in these individuals. To rectify this, we developed the generational change model (Gentile, Campbell, & Twenge, 2011) to better depict cross-temporal cultural and individual change (for ease of explanation, we include Figure 2.1 to provide a window into the process of a single individual interacting with the culture over the course of his or her life span).

The generational change model contains three major components. First, individual developmental changes occurring over the course of the life span are represented by the *individual* arrow. Although a person can change in many ways over the life course, we are mainly concerned with developmental facets that show cohort differences. According to Baltes (1987), these facets should be stable within the individual but not across individuals via genetic or cultural evolution. We should expect, then, to see the majority of cohort differences in traits that develop in conjunction with the sociocultural context in early life and remain stable throughout adulthood (e.g., personality, self-views, attitudes), which is a major distinction between the cross-temporal and the cross-cultural. Not all aspects of culture have the same rate of change, and whereas cross-temporal research is interested in traits that are responsive to cultural change, cross-cultural research is generally more concerned with traits that are endemic to a culture, having been reinforced over time (i.e., individual or communal orientation, cognitive processes). Deepening the divide is the fact that cross-cultural research's focus on stable traits often leads to a divergent view of culture. The culture-as-system view characterizes culture as a system of meanings and assumes stability within a historical period to allow for broad cross-cultural comparisons (Kashima, 2000). In contrast, by virtue of focusing on more variable traits, cross-temporal research is more closely aligned with the culture-as-practice (or culture-as-process; Kashima, 2002) view that characterizes culture as a meaning-making process and assumes culture is continually constructed and altered by individual interactions. Although the latter is more conducive to conceptualizing cultural change over time, both views are really two sides of the same coin because both stability and change are necessary to fully understand cultural dynamics (McIntyre, Lyons, Clark, & Kashima, 2004) and the means by which generations arise.

Second, cultural evolution is represented by the series of small arrows along the bottom of Figure 2.1 because it changes continuously over time. Culture can change as a result of many forces. Most people assume that cultural change occurs sporadically as a result of singular events or grand innovations. In such cases, the culture experiences rapid, sweeping change. Recent theories, however (i.e., Boyd & Richerson, 1985, 2005; Dawkins, 1976/1989), argue for steady continuous changes. These theories allow for large-scale cultural change but propose that it occurs as a result of accumulated small changes made as individuals interact with the culture, adopting some cultural variants (i.e., culturally relevant values, beliefs, attitudes, behaviors, and skills) and modifying others. This process is similar to what McIntyre et al. (2004) termed the "microgenesis of culture" (p. 228). When many people make the choice to adopt the same cultural variant, it can diffuse through the culture, producing large-scale change (Rogers, 1995). In these theories, culture is represented as an accumulation of knowledge that individuals contribute to and sample from (Boyd & Richerson, 1985). Another significant way culture can change is via contact with other cultures through globalization (Giddens, 2003), which likewise influences the available cultural variants.

Third, the model proposes a two-part pathway that links the individual to the culture. This process is essentially as that described in greater detail by the mutual constitution model. Culture begins influencing individuals early in life via socialization and enculturation as shown by the first portion of the pathway (Figure 2.1). During these processes, individuals learn the meanings and practices of their culture in everyday interactions. Culture can be transmitted by a number of different sources (e.g., parents, peers, teachers, media; Cavalli-Sforza & Feldman, 1981) that help structure such interactions. Rather than being passive recipients, however, individuals actively process and negotiate this input, transforming it for their own understanding

(Bugental & Goodnow, 1998). Culture thus becomes "internalized" as it is incorporated into people's individual psychology (Lawrence & Valsiner, 1993). Via a reciprocal process, it is likewise possible for individuals to influence culture, as shown by the second portion of the pathway. As discussed earlier, individuals reconstruct culture through their interactions with it. Once these modified aspects are put back into the culture, externalization is said to have occurred (Valsiner & Lawrence, 1997). Because culture exerts a much greater influence on the individual than does the individual on culture, the first part of the pathway in the model is wider than the second. This interaction occurs throughout the individual's life span, as represented by the recurring pathways.

The generational change model sets the mutually constitutive relationship between individuals and the culture into motion. Cross-temporal changes arise from the repetition of the process depicted in Figure 2.1 across individuals and across time. Because culture is continually being modified and added to by the individuals living in it, each new individual born into the culture experiences it as the accumulated knowledge of previous generations. In sum, each person builds off what came before in an ever-evolving dynamic system. A generation (represented as the group of individuals within the dashed line in Figure 2.1) is produced from the interaction between the component parts of the model across individuals of a cohort. The result is that groups of similar-aged individuals develop within a shared sociocultural context and, when culture has changed to a sufficient degree, they will appear distinct from those of earlier and later generations. We should note that the model does not specify when these distinctions will arise because cultural change sets the pace. The more rapidly culture changes, the faster sharp distinctions between cohorts will appear.

To summarize, cultural psychology provides a theoretical framework for resolving the theoretical issues associated with generational differences. Specifically, it offers a way to conceptualize the coconstructive relationship between individuals and culture. Using this as a starting point, we can extend the theory to understand how individuals living in a culture change over time as a result of cultural dynamics.

METHODS

Cross-temporal research has largely focused on change at two levels: the individual and the culture. By measuring how cohorts of individuals and aspects of the culture change over time, one can begin to draw connections between the micro and the macro. Fortunately, several methods make this type of work possible.

Examining Change in Individuals Over Time

At the level of individuals, cross-temporal changes are generally studied by tracking responses on self-report measures across birth cohorts. The challenge for early psychology researchers interested in how cohorts changed over time was how best to disentangle age and cohort effects. This task cannot be accomplished using traditional cross-sectional and longitudinal methods of examining change because these methods are limited to answering developmental questions (Baltes, 1968; Buss, 1974; Schaie, 1965). Instead, time-lag methods are used. The ideal time-lag design—a cohort-sequential design—follows multiple cohorts longitudinally over time beginning at a young age (Schaie, 1965). This design allows the researcher to examine longitudinal (i.e., developmental) changes within a cohort as well as to examine differences between cohorts. However, the difficulty of collecting such data has largely made this method unfeasible. More common is a simplified time-lag design of collecting samples of the same age at different time points. This approach controls for age effects such that differences between samples can be attributed to cohort and time period effects. Even with a straightforward time-lag design, the problem of collecting data that span a significant period of time—cross-temporal data—has been a central problem in the research. These data can be collected directly by researchers using prospective designs, but such an approach is time intensive and is obviously unable to assess historical changes. As a result, it has rarely been used. Instead, national data sets and previous research have become the primary sources of data used in cross-temporal research. Fortunately, technological advances have made it possible to access these sources relatively easily.

National Data Sets

The most frequently used national data sets for examining generational change are Monitoring the Future, the American Freshman Survey, and the General Social Survey. The first of these, Monitoring the Future, has surveyed high school seniors from across the United States since 1976, as well as eighth and 10th graders since 1991. Researchers have used the data set to investigate change over time in self-esteem, environmental beliefs, drug use, and work attitudes (e.g., Johnston, O'Malley, Bachman, & Schulenberg, 2009; Twenge & Campbell, 2008; Twenge, Campbell, Hoffman, & Lance, 2010; Wray-Lake, Flanagan, & Osgood, 2010). The American Freshman Survey, which has surveyed freshmen at 4-year universities yearly since 1966 through the Cooperative Institutional Research Program, represents a much larger national study and has been used to look at trends in agentic self-views and sex role attitudes (Jacobs, 1986; Twenge, Campbell, & Gentile,

2012). Last, the General Social Survey, conducted by the National Opinion Research Center, has surveyed noninstitutionalized adult populations in the United States since 1972, focusing largely on attitudinal and behavioral questions. Although primarily used by sociologists, this data set has been used to track changes in happiness, sex role attitudes, political views, and goal focus (e.g., A. S. Miller & Nakamura, 1997; Stolte, 2000; Thornton & Young-DeMarco, 2001; Yang, 2008).

These national databases have several notable strengths. They are relatively simple to access, the samples are designed to be representative of the populations studied, and they have a wide range of items to examine within the same sample. However, using a national data set to examine cross-temporal change also presents several limitations. First, the data sets are limited in terms of the years available for study, making it impossible to look at changes that occurred before the 1st year of data collection. Second, conclusions that can be drawn about changes over time are limited to the characteristics inquired about in the survey, and their presentation is not always consistent from year to year. For instance, Twenge and Campbell (2010) noted that Monitoring the Future does not present all 10 Rosenberg Self-Esteem Scale items in order, but rather presents some items mixed together with locus of control and other items on the survey and has changed the item order several times over the years. Last, cohort changes can only be assessed for the age groups included in any given survey, limiting generalizability for those with more restricted age ranges such as Monitoring the Future and the American Freshman Survey.

Cross-Temporal Meta-Analysis

In addition to national data sets, previous research studies can be used to examine generational change via cross-temporal meta-analysis (CTMA). Twenge (1997, 2000; Twenge & Campbell, 2001) developed this method across several studies as a way of assessing mean-level changes over time. CTMA differs from traditional meta-analysis in that it focuses on sample means and year of data collection rather than correlations, ds, or other effect-size metrics. Data are weighted by sample size and analyzed using regression methods. To remove the potential confound of age, separate analyses are performed for each age group (i.e., elementary, middle school, high school). Using this method, it is possible to see not only whether a trait has increased or decreased over time via the correlations between the mean scores and year, but also the proportion of variance accounted for by birth cohort at the individual level. This is accomplished by using the regression equation to calculate the difference between mean scores for the first and last year of data collection and dividing it by the average standard deviation of the individual samples. CTMA has been used examine changes over time in many traits including self-esteem, narcissism, Big Five personality traits, and psychopathology (Gentile, Twenge, & Campbell, 2010; Twenge, 2000, 2001a; Twenge & Campbell, 2001; Twenge, Gentile, et al., 2010; Twenge, Konrath, Foster, Campbell, & Bushman, 2008).

In contrast to national data sets, this method is often able to look at a greater period of time and include a larger number of age groups. It also enables the examination of many measures (and uses full measures, which are often not included in national databases in the interests of space). However, CTMA is not without its own limitations, similar to those of any meta-analysis involving the use of previously conducted research. For instance, interpretations of results are limited to the samples available, so generalizing results to the broader population is problematic. In particular, the majority of psychological research is conducted with children, adolescents, and college students, and thus it is rarely possible to draw conclusions about older adult samples. Another caveat of conducting CTMA is that enough studies using the self-report measure of interest must be available and they must span a significant portion of time. Thus, the traits that can be examined are limited to those with well-established measures. Finally, the samples used in CTMA are typically not nationally representative, meaning that CTMA is not appropriate for answering epidemiological questions (e.g., "What is the average level of self-esteem in the population?") but is appropriate for relational questions (e.g., "What is the nature and direction of the relationship between the trait and birth cohort?")

Examining Change in Culture Over Time

As we have discussed, we view culture as a collective process. Defined in this way, culture necessarily has an existence of its own above and beyond the specific elements that compose it (Durkheim, 1897/1951). As such, it is not possible to study the whole of culture directly and examine how it is changing. However, cultural changes are often the work of individuals; culture evolves as individuals interact with and modify it (Boyd & Richerson, 1985, 2005). Thus, one can study how culture is changing by examining how representations of culture, in the form of cultural products, are changing. Past research with cultural products has largely been devoted to examining cross-cultural differences (for a review, see Morling & Lamoreaux, 2008). Such studies have used a wide variety of products to represent culture, including advertisements, architecture, song lyrics, and books (e.g., Kim & Markus, 1999; Miyamoto, Nisbett, & Masuda, 2006; Snibbe & Markus, 2005; Tsai, Louie, Chen, & Uchida, 2007). Many of these same products can also be used to examine cross-temporal differences if data on them are available for a significant portion of time.

Several studies have used this approach to assess cultural change via changes in cultural products. For instance, researchers have uncovered changes in cultural products in the United States that link to increasing individualism, self-focus, need for uniqueness, and concern with fame. Such trends include a decrease in children receiving popular names (Twenge, Abebe, & Campbell, 2010), an increase in first-person singular pronouns and antisocial themes in song lyrics (DeWall, Pond, Campbell, & Twenge, 2011), an increase in fame values in tween-age television shows (Uhls & Greenfield, 2011), and an increase in home sizes and number of specific rooms (Twenge & Campbell, 2009). We should note that much of this research is relatively recent and has only tapped the surface of potential cultural products, which range from a variety of print and media forms to material objects such as technological and consumer goods. Future research should further explore the how cross-temporal psychological changes are reflected in cultural products.

An additional way cultural products can be used is in examining large-scale cultural shifts. Recent technological advances have made possible the creation of large databases that store information on millions of cultural products and allow them to be analyzed quantitatively. The first such database to be created was Google nGram, a corpus of more than five million digitized books or about 4% of all published books going back to 1800 (Michel et al., 2011). By searching for single or multiword phrases, it is possible to analyze changes in a number of cultural facets computationally, a new area of study that Michel et al. (2011) termed *culturomics*. Michel et al. proposed several applications of nGram, including shifts in commonly used language, interest in historical events, the adoption of technology, the fleeting nature of fame, and suppression or censorship of people and ideas. Ultimately, however, these represent only a fraction of the cultural trends that can be investigated via this method. Currently, nGram is limited to searching books with one- to five-word phrases, but as noted by Michel et al., the future of culturomics lies in extending the technology to other forms of media (e.g., artwork, maps, films, music). Although one of the first of its kind, Google nGram represents a burgeoning avenue of research in cultural dynamics.

RESEARCH ON GENERATIONAL CHANGES IN CULTURE

Cross-temporal research has investigated change over time in a number of attitudes, beliefs, and traits. Although discussing all the ways in which individuals have changed over time is not possible, we present data here on one major shift that is occurring, namely, a shift toward a culture of entitled individualism. In the context of this discussion, we define *individualism* as a focus on the self, and in particular the needs of the self over the group. As a Western country, the United States, where the majority of cross-temporal data are collected, is typically considered to be individualistic. However, in the past few decades there has been an increase in self-admiring traits and behaviors, resulting in a population that is now more self-focused than ever.

Personality

The cultural shift toward entitled individualism is most clearly displayed in rising narcissism levels. Twenge et al. (2008) conducted a CTMA on the best-known measure of trait narcissism, the Narcissistic Personality Inventory. Results showed that from the early 1980s to 2006, narcissism increased by a third of a standard deviation among college students. In other words, by the mid-2000s two thirds of students had higher narcissism scores than the average student in the 1980s. Although some studies reported no change in narcissism (Trzesniewski, Donnellan, & Robins, 2008), further research showed that these samples also showed an increase in narcissism when the confound of campus was removed (Twenge & Foster, 2010).

Rising narcissism levels correspond to increases in several related constructs. Twenge (2001a) found increases in extraversion during the years 1966–1993, a personality trait that is correlated with narcissism (J. D. Miller & Campbell, 2008). During this time period, levels of assertiveness and agentic traits also increased, particularly among women (Twenge, 1997, 2001b), as did levels of self-esteem as measured by the Rosenberg Self-Esteem Scale (Twenge & Campbell, 2001). Recently, an updated CTMA (Gentile et al., 2010) found that levels of self-esteem continued to rise beyond 1994, despite already high levels. By 2008, levels of self-esteem were higher than ever before and rapidly approaching the upper limit of the scale. Thus, positive shifts are occurring across a broad range of personality traits related to individualistic self-focus.

Self-Views

A potential consequence of individuals feeling better about themselves than ever before is a shift toward having inflated self-views. Twenge, Campbell, and Gentile (2012) examined the percentage of respondents to the American Freshman Survey who reported being in the "highest 10%" or "above average" on a number of attributes (e.g., academic ability, drive to achieve, understanding of others) between 1966 and 2009. Among more recent cohorts, a larger percentage claimed to be above average in ability compared with their peers of previous eras. However, the increases were limited to agentic attributes (e.g., drive to achieve, leadership ability), whereas communal attributes (e.g., cooperativeness, understanding of others) showed no change. These trends were not associated with increased ability or effort but were related to grade inflation as measured by grade-point average. In sum, younger cohorts are much more likely than older cohorts to self-enhance on individualistic traits, and these shifts are independent of increased competence.

Not only do people today feel overconfident about their present abilities, they also hold unrealistic expectations for the future. Using Monitoring the Future data, Reynolds, Stewart, Sischo, & MacDonald (2006) found that in 2000, 51% of high school seniors expected to earn graduate or professional degrees compared with 27% in 1976); by 2010, this figure had risen to 59%. Additionally, 63% expected that by age 30 they would hold a professional job, compared with 41% of their peers in 1976. These estimates appear particularly overconfident considering that the actual percentage of high school graduates ages 25 to 34 with advanced degrees and professional jobs are 9% and 18%, respectively, and this figure has not changed since the 1970s. Thus, not only are self-views becoming inflated over time, they are also accompanied by an increasingly individualistic desire to stand out.

Values

Consistent with changes to personality and self-views, people's values are likewise becoming more individualistic. College freshmen today are much more likely to value becoming well-off financially as an important life goal than were their peers of previous generations and less likely to value developing a meaningful philosophy of life (Twenge, Campbell, & Freeman, 2012). Similarly, a 2006 report on the attitudes of Millennials ages 18 to 25 found that 81% believed getting rich to be their generation's most important goal, and 51% said it was getting famous (Pew Research Center, 2007). This agentic drive for success is accompanied by a decline in empathy. A recent study by Konrath, O'Brien, and Hsing (2011) found that between 1979 and 2009, young adults' ability to feel empathy for others and take another's perspective declined. Another study found that Finnish adolescents' fears shifted from global social issues in the 1980s to more personal concerns in the 2000s (Lindfors, Solantaus, & Rimpela, 2012). Thus, it seems that as individuals are becoming more concerned with themselves and their own success, they are becoming increasingly out of touch with others.

Behaviors

In addition to psychological changes, the drive for individualism has created observable changes in behaviors. Now more than ever, people are trying to get noticed. One indicator of this drive is the growing number of people undergoing plastic surgery (American Society for Aesthetic Plastic Surgery, 2011). The desire to stand out is not limited to the self, but extends to one's children as well. A recent study by Twenge, Abebe, and Campbell (2010) found that from 1880 to 2007, the number of traditional names people gave to their children decreased dramatically in favor of unique, uncommon names. The effect remained even after controlling for immigration and examining the trends in ethnically homogeneous states.

Cultural Products

As we discussed earlier, changes in cultural products can be used as indicators of larger changes in the culture. Many cultural products begin as behaviors (e.g., writing a song), and often no distinct line separates the two. Here, however, we distinguish cultural products as intentionally shared representations of culture (e.g., the song itself). The most overt cultural barometers are often forms of media. DeWall et al. (2011) collected lyrics from the 10 most popular songs in the United States every year from 1980 to 2007. Compared with songs in 1980, more recent songs were more self-focused, featuring more first-person singular pronouns such as *I* and *me* to the exclusion of first-person plural pronouns such as *we* and *our*. Newer songs were also less likely to feature positive emotions (e.g., *love, nice*) or words related to social interaction but more likely to include aggressive or antisocial words (e.g., *kill, hate*) indicative of growing social disconnection. The importance of elevating the self above others is likewise communicated by television shows. Uhls and Greenfield (2011) asked adult raters to code the values implicit in popular shows from 1967 to 2007 aimed at tween audiences (i.e., ages 9–11). Results showed that recent shows were more likely to promote the values of fame and achievement over community feeling and tradition. This trend was reflected in the main characters of the shows who over time were rated as being more desirous of fame. Consistent with cross-temporal research using self-report data, younger raters more readily picked up on individualistic values in shows, indicating a greater familiarity with these concepts.

CONCLUSION

Cross-temporal cultural difference can be productively thought of as a special case of cultural differences. Doing so makes the tools and models of cultural psychology available to those interested in cultural or generational changes. However, to effectively study cultural change, models that incorporate change directly, such as the generational change model (Gentile et al.,

2011), are useful. Likewise, specific cross-temporal methods, such as CTMA, open the door to understanding change in many psychological variables. In short, cross-temporal cultural difference is an exciting and constantly changing area of inquiry in the field of cultural psychology.

REFERENCES

American Society for Aesthetic Plastic Surgery. (2011). *Statistics*. Retrieved from http://www.surgery.org/media/statistics

Baltes, P. B. (1968). Longitudinal and cross sectional sequences in the study of age and generation effects. *Human Development, 11*, 145–171. doi:10.1159/000270604

Baltes, P. B. (1987). Theoretical propositions of life-span developmental psychology: On the dynamics between growth and decline. *Developmental Psychology, 23*, 611–626. doi:10.1037/0012-1649.23.5.611

Boyd, R., & Richerson, P. J. (1985). *Culture and the evolutionary process*. Chicago, IL: University of Chicago Press.

Boyd, R., & Richerson, P. J. (2005). *The origin and evolution of cultures*. New York, NY: Oxford University Press.

Bugental, D. B., & Goodnow, J. J. (1998). Socialization processes. In W. Damon (Series Ed.) & N. Eisenberg (Vol. Ed.), *Handbook of child psychology: Vol. 3. Social, emotional, and personality development* (5th ed., pp. 389–462). New York, NY: Wiley.

Buss, A. R. (1974). Generational analysis: Description, explanation, and theory. *Journal of Social Issues, 30*(2), 55–71. doi:10.1111/j.1540-4560.1974.tb00715.x

Cavalli-Sforza, L. L., & Feldman, M. W. (1981). *Cultural transmission and evolution: A quantitative approach*. Princeton, NJ: Princeton University Press.

Dawkins, R. (1989). *The selfish gene* (new ed.). New York, NY: Oxford University Press. (Original work published 1976)

DeWall, C. N., Pond, R. S., Jr., Campbell, W. K., & Twenge, J. M. (2011). Tuning into psychological change: Linguistic markers of psychological traits and emotions over time in popular U.S. song lyrics. *Psychology of Aesthetics, Creativity, and the Arts, 5*, 200–207. doi:10.1037/a0023195

Durkheim, E. (1951). *Suicide: A study in sociology* (J. A. Spaulding & G. Simpson, Trans.). New York, NY: Free Press. (Original work published 1897)

Fiske, A., Kitayama, S., Markus, H. R., & Nisbett, R. E. (1998). The cultural matrix of social psychology. In D. Gilbert, S. Fiske, & G. Lindzey (Eds.), *The handbook of social psychology* (4th ed., pp. 915–981). San Francisco, CA: McGraw-Hill.

Gentile, B., Campbell, W. K., & Twenge, J. M. (2011). *A generational change model: How individuals and the culture interact to produce changes over time*. Unpublished manuscript.

Gentile, B., Twenge, J. M., & Campbell, W. K. (2010). Birth cohort differences in self-esteem, 1988–2008. *Review of General Psychology, 14*, 261–268. doi:10.1037/a0019919

Giddens, A. (2003). *Runaway world: How globalization is reshaping our lives*. New York, NY: Routledge.

Jacobs, J. A. (1986). The sex-segregation of fields of study: Trends during the college years. *Journal of Higher Education, 57*, 134–154. doi:10.2307/1981478

Johnston, L. D., O'Malley, P. M., Bachman, J. G., & Schulenberg, J. E. (2009). *Monitoring the Future national survey results on drug use, 1975-2008: Vol. I. Secondary school students* (NIH Pub. No. 09-7402). Bethesda, MD: National Institute on Drug Abuse.

Kashima, Y. (2000). Conceptions of culture and person for psychology. *Journal of Cross-Cultural Psychology, 31*, 14–32. doi:10.1177/0022022100031001003

Kashima, Y. (2002). Culture and self: A cultural dynamical analysis. In Y. Kashima, M. Foddy, & M. Platow (Eds.), *Self and identity: Personal, social, and symbolic* (pp. 207–226). Mahwah, NJ: Erlbaum.

Kim, H., & Markus, H. R. (1999). Deviance or uniqueness, harmony or conformity? A cultural analysis. *Journal of Personality and Social Psychology, 77*, 785–800. doi:10.1037/0022-3514.77.4.785

Kitayama, S., Duffy, S., & Uchida, Y. (2007). Self as cultural mode of being. In S. Kitayama & D. Cohen (Eds.), *Handbook of cultural psychology* (pp. 136–174). New York, NY: Guilford Press.

Kitayama, S., Markus, H. R., Matsumoto, H., & Norasakkunkit, V. (1997). Individual and collective processes in the construction of the self: Self-enhancement in the United States and self-criticism in Japan. *Journal of Personality and Social Psychology, 72*, 1245–1267. doi:10.1037/0022-3514.72.6.1245

Konrath, S. H., O'Brien, E. H., & Hsing, C. (2011). Changes in dispositional empathy in American college students over time: A meta-analysis. *Personality and Social Psychology Review, 15*, 180–198. doi:10.1177/1088868310377395

Lawrence, J. A., & Valsiner, J. (1993). Conceptual roots of internalization: From transmission to transformation. *Human Development, 36*, 150–167. doi:10.1159/000277333

Lindfors, P., Solantaus, T., & Rimpela, A. (2012). Fears for the future among Finnish adolescents in 1983–2007: From global concerns to ill health and loneliness. *Journal of Adolescence, 35*, 991–999.

Mannheim, K. (1952). The problem of generations. In K. Mannheim (Ed.), *Essays on the sociology of knowledge* (pp. 276–322). London, England: Routledge & Kegan Paul. (Original work published 1928)

Markus, H. R., & Hamedani, M. G. (2007). Sociocultural psychology: The dynamic interdependence among self systems and social systems. In S. Kitayama & D. Cohen (Eds.), *Handbook of cultural psychology* (pp. 3–39). New York, NY: Guilford Press.

Markus, H. R., & Kitayama, S. (1991). Culture and the self: Implications for cognition, emotion, and motivation. *Psychological Review, 98,* 224–253. doi:10.1037/0033-295X.98.2.224

Masuda, T., & Nisbett, R. E. (2001). Attending holistically vs. analytically: Comparing the context sensitivity of Japanese and Americans. *Journal of Personality and Social Psychology, 81,* 922–934. doi:10.1037/0022-3514.81.5.922

McIntyre, A., Lyons, A., Clark, A., & Kashima, Y. (2004). The microgenesis of culture: Serial reproduction as an experimental simulation of cultural dynamics. In M. Schaller & C. S. Crandall (Eds.), *The psychological foundations of culture* (pp. 227–258). Mahwah, NJ: Erlbaum.

Michel, J.-B., Shen, Y. K., Aiden, A. P., Veres, A., Gray, M. K., The Google Books Team, . . . Aiden, E. L. (2011). Quantitative analysis of culture using millions of digitized books. *Science, 331,* 176–182. doi:10.1126/science.1199644

Miller, A. S., & Nakamura, T. (1997). Trends in American public opinion: A cohort analysis of shifting attitudes from 1972-1990. *Behaviormetrika, 24,* 179–191. doi:10.2333/bhmk.24.179

Miller, J. D., & Campbell, W. K. (2008). Comparing clinical and social-personality conceptualizations of narcissism. *Journal of Personality, 76,* 449–476. doi:10.1111/j.1467-6494.2008.00492.x

Miyamoto, Y., Nisbett, R. E., & Masuda, T. (2006). Culture and the physical environment: Holistic versus analytic perceptual affordances. *Psychological Science, 17,* 113–119. doi:10.1111/j.1467-9280.2006.01673.x

Morling, B., & Lamoreaux, M. (2008). Measuring culture outside the head: A meta-analysis of individualism-collectivism in cultural products. *Personality and Social Psychology Review, 12,* 199–221. doi:10.1177/1088868308318260

Oishi, S., Kesebir, S., & Snyder, B. H. (2009). Sociology: A lost connection in social psychology. *Personality and Social Psychology Review, 13,* 334–353. doi:10.1177/1088868309347835

Pew Research Center. (2007). *How young people view their lives, futures and politics: A portrait of "Generation Next."* Washington, DC: Pew Research Center for the People and the Press.

Reynolds, J., Stewart, M., Sischo, L., & MacDonald, R. (2006). Have adolescents become too ambitious? High school seniors' educational and occupational plans, 1976 to 2000. *Social Problems, 53,* 186–206. doi:10.1525/sp.2006.53.2.186

Rogers, E. M. (1995). *Diffusion of innovations* (4th ed.). New York, NY: Free Press.

Schaie, K. W. (1965). A general model for the study of developmental problems. *Psychological Bulletin, 64,* 92–107. doi:10.1037/h0022371

Shweder, R. A. (1991). *Thinking through cultures: Expeditions in cultural psychology.* Cambridge, MA: Harvard University Press.

Simonton, D. K. (1997). Foreign influence and national achievement: The impact of open milieus on Japanese civilization. *Journal of Personality and Social Psychology, 72,* 86–94. doi:10.1037/0022-3514.72.1.86

Snibbe, A. C., & Markus, H. R. (2005). You can't always get what you want: Educational attainment, agency, and choice. *Journal of Personality and Social Psychology, 88,* 703–720. doi:10.1037/0022-3514.88.4.703

Stolte, J. F. (2000). The value of socially extrinsic vs. intrinsic outcomes: An exploration of Americans from 1974–1994. *Social Behavior and Personality, 28,* 387–391. doi:10.2224/sbp.2000.28.4.387

Thornton, A., & Young-DeMarco, L. (2001). Four decades of trends in attitudes toward family issues in the United States: The 1960s through the 1990s. *Journal of Marriage and Family, 63,* 1009–1037. doi:10.1111/j.1741-3737.2001.01009.x

Trzesniewski, K. H., Donnellan, M. B., & Robins, R. W. (2008). Is "Generation Me" really more narcissistic than previous generations? *Journal of Personality, 76,* 903–918. doi:10.1111/j.1467-6494.2008.00508.x

Tsai, J. L., Louie, J. Y., Chen, E. E., & Uchida, Y. (2007). Learning what feelings to desire: Socialization of ideal affect through children's storybooks. *Personality and Social Psychology Bulletin, 33,* 17–30. doi:10.1177/0146167206292749

Twenge, J. M. (1997). Changes in masculine and feminine traits over time: A meta-analysis. *Sex Roles, 36,* 305–325. doi:10.1007/BF02766650

Twenge, J. M. (2000). The age of anxiety? Birth cohort change in anxiety and neuroticism, 1952–1993. *Journal of Personality and Social Psychology, 79,* 1007–1021. doi:10.1037/0022-3514.79.6.1007

Twenge, J. M. (2001a). Birth cohort changes in extraversion: A cross-temporal meta-analysis 1966-1993. *Personality and Individual Differences, 30,* 735–748. doi:10.1016/S0191-8869(00)00066-0

Twenge, J. M. (2001b). Changes in women's assertiveness in response to status and roles: A cross-temporal meta-analysis, 1931–1993. *Journal of Personality and Social Psychology, 81,* 133–145. doi:10.1037/0022-3514.81.1.133

Twenge, J. M., Abebe, E. M., & Campbell, W. K. (2010). Fitting in or standing out: Trends in American parents' choices for children's names, 1880-2007. *Social Psychological and Personality Science, 1,* 19–25. doi:10.1177/1948550609349515

Twenge, J. M., Campbell, S. M., Hoffman, B. J., & Lance, C. E. (2010). Generational differences in work values: Leisure and extrinsic values increasing, social and intrinsic values decreasing. *Journal of Management, 36,* 1117–1142. doi:10.1177/0149206309352246

Twenge, J. M., & Campbell, W. K. (2001). Age and birth cohort differences in self-esteem: A cross-temporal meta-analysis. *Personality and Social Psychology Review, 5,* 321–344. doi:10.1207/S15327957PSPR0504_3

Twenge, J. M., & Campbell, W. K. (2008). Increases in positive self-views among high school students: Birth-cohort changes in anticipated performance, self-satisfaction, self-liking, and self-competence.. *Psychological Science, 19,* 1082–1086. doi:10.1111/j.1467-9280.2008.02204.x

Twenge, J. M., & Campbell, W. K. (2009). *The narcissism epidemic: Living in the age of entitlement*. New York, NY: Free Press.

Twenge, J. M., & Campbell, W. K. (2010). Birth cohort differences in the Monitoring the Future dataset and elsewhere: Further evidence for Generation Me. *Perspectives on Psychological Science, 5*, 81–88. doi:10.1177/1745691609357015

Twenge, J. M., Campbell, W. K., & Freeman, E. C. (2012). Generational differences in young adults' life goals, concern for others, and civic orientation, 1966–2009. *Journal of Personality and Social Psychology, 102*, 1045–1062.

Twenge, J. M., Campbell, W. K., & Gentile, B. (2012). Generational increases in self-evaluations among American college students, 1966-2009. *Self and Identity, 11*, 409–427.

Twenge, J. M., & Foster, J. D. (2010). Birth cohort increases in narcissistic personality traits among American college students, 1982–2009. *Social Psychological and Personality Science, 1*, 99–106. doi:10.1177/1948550609355719

Twenge, J. M., Gentile, B., DeWall, C. N., Ma, D. S., Lacefield, K., & Schurtz, D. R. (2010). Birth cohort increases in psychopathology among young Americans, 1938-2007: A cross-temporal meta-analysis of the MMPI. *Clinical Psychology Review, 30*, 145–154. doi:10.1016/j.cpr.2009.10.005

Twenge, J. M., Konrath, S., Foster, J. D., Campbell, W. K., & Bushman, B. (2008). Egos inflating over time: A cross-temporal meta-analysis of the Narcissistic Personality Inventory. *Journal of Personality, 76*, 875–902. doi:10.1111/j.1467-6494.2008.00507.x

Uhls, Y. T., & Greenfield, P. M. (2011). The rise of fame: An historical content analysis. *Cyberpsychology: Journal of Psychosocial Research on Cyberspace, 5*(1), Article 1.

Valsiner, J., & Lawrence, J. A. (1997). Human development in culture across the life span. In J. W. Berry, Y. H. Poortinga, J. Pandey (Series Eds.), J. W. Berry, P. R. Dasen, & T. S. Saraswathi (Vol. Eds.), *Handbook of cross-cultural psychology: Vol. 2. Basic processes and human development* (2nd ed., pp. 69–106). Boston, MA: Allyn & Bacon.

Wray-Lake, L., Flanagan, C. A., & Osgood, D. W. (2010). Examining trends in adolescent environmental attitudes, beliefs, and behaviors across three decades. *Environment and Behavior, 42*, 61–85. doi:10.1177/0013916509335163

Yang, Y. (2008). Social inequalities in happiness in the United States, 1972-2004: An age-period-cohort analysis. *American Sociological Review, 73*, 204–226. doi:10.1177/000312240807300202

3

CULTURE AND SOCIAL CLASS

P. J. HENRY

Ever since the transition of human societies from hunter–gatherer groups to surplus-producing civilizations, social classes have been dictating the division of labor. Ancient Egyptian, Greek, Indian, and Mayan cultures each divided their societies into nobility and rulers, priests, warriors, artisans, professionals, merchants, farmers, laborers, construction workers, and slaves. Later, during the Industrial Revolution, Marx (1867/2008) identified divisions on the basis of owners of production versus laborers. Social classes throughout time have been determined and defined by various combinations of occupation, land ownership, wealth, income, and education. In modern economies, they are given a variety of classifications; one version in common use in the United States divides classes into upper class, middle class, working

I thank Mark Brandt, Niobe Way, Suzanne Quadflieg, the Prejudice Research Laboratory at New York University—Abu Dhabi, and the students of the Fall 2011 Prejudice class and the Spring 2012 Culture and Context class at New York University—Abu Dhabi for their useful comments on an earlier version draft of this chapter.

http://dx.doi.org/10.1037/14274-003
Culture Reexamined: Broadening Our Understanding of Social and Evolutionary Influences,
A. B. Cohen (Editor)

class, and a class at the bottom, called variously the underclass, lower class, or poor (Argyle, 1994).

Throughout history, people who belong to different social classes have clustered in neighborhoods and regions, either as dictated by law, as in many ancient societies, or by economic circumstances, as in most modern societies. Studies have shown that an important association with social class is where a person lives (Reid, 1998), and wherever clusters of people live, one will find culture. Yet, at least in psychology, social class has been neglected as a source of culture (A. B. Cohen, 2009). In this chapter, I address this lacuna and pose questions about how the introduction of a study of the culture of social class may change how psychologists think both about culture and about social class.

This chapter has two main sections. I devote the first half of the chapter to situating the study of social class in the culture literature and demonstrating some of the ways social class creates what can be seen as culture. Rather than focusing on more material or tangible differences that might be the domain of economists, anthropologists, or sociologists, in this section I focus more on subjective or intangible differences between social classes that are of more interest to psychologists. I devote the second half of the chapter to an examination of how situating the study of social class in a culture literature raises questions about how researchers think about both social class and culture as heretofore mostly separate literatures.

SITUATING SOCIAL CLASS IN THE LITERATURE ON CULTURAL PSYCHOLOGY

Culture has been defined in myriad ways across multiple disciplines. For the sake of simplicity, the definition used here is taken from a cultural psychology perspective, specifically Triandis's (2010), paraphrased as follows: Culture is a human adaptation to an environment, composed of shared practices and meanings that are transmitted to future generations. These practices and meanings can be concrete, as in the diet, clothing, and leisure activities of a people, or abstract, as in the attitudes and beliefs of a people.

Social class is a way of categorizing people into groups. The measures that social scientists have used in research to capture social class also reflect aspects of this composite, including occupation (e.g., Lipset, 1959; Reid, 1998), income (e.g., Henry, 2009; Oakes & Rossi, 2003), education (e.g., Lipset, 1959), or various combinations of these (Argyle, 1994). As with the definition of culture, the characterization of social class is rich with complexity and easy to oversimplify (Reid, 1998), and at the risk of presenting a construct that is too vague, my characterization of social class draws on the composite of these and related socioeconomic indicators: income, accumulated wealth, education, employment status, and occupational prestige.

Social class is a social construction, a way of grouping people within a broader culture, much as with ethnicity and caste, in a way that differs from society to society. As with any other group-based identification scheme, including ethnicity or caste, it largely benefits those of higher status (Lott, 2002). However, the construction of social classes has also helped theorists of the social sciences understand social structures and hierarchies and how they perpetuate themselves. As early as Marx (1867/2008), groups of workers and owners of production were identified as social classes to theorize about the forces that operate between the two. Today, social class distinctions are helpful for determining the distribution (and redistribution) of resources in a society, for example, through union activities, graded tax laws, unemployment and welfare assistance, and scholarships devoted to first-generation and low-income college students.

Social class operates much as other sources of culture, such as ethnicity, nationality, and caste, in at least two ways. First, it shapes *identity*, a feature central to concepts of culture (Brewer & Yuki, 2010) that includes being able to identify oneself as a member of one culture as well as identifying others as part of one's own or other cultures (Côté & Levine, 2002). The identity aspect of culture involves an ownership of particular beliefs and practices as part of the self, presumably an identity one is proud of and has a goal to consciously pass on to future generations. Social class, too, can serve as a part of one's social identity. British and U.S. citizens willingly provide their social class when asked this question in surveys and interviews (Jackman, 1979; Reid, 1998), even if their subjective identification does not always match objective indicators (e.g., one poll showed that more than a third of sampled U.S. participants earning less than $20,000 annually identified as middle class, as well as a third earning more than $150,000; Pew Research Center, 2008). Nevertheless, social class involves group categories that a person can belong to and identify with. This identification can include a variety of labels depending on the historical context. For example, the peerage system in England included labels for those born into wealthy families within the system, such as *lord, baron,* and *duke*. The title *doctor* given to those completing a PhD, MD, or JD is used today to identify the highly educated classes. Pride of identity, however, can also extend to those of the lower classes. Several hundred years ago, for example, members of the lower classes were especially tied to their professions as part of their identity. Many English-language family names are derived from working-class crafts and occupations: Hunter, Miller, Cooper, Baker, Brewer, Carpenter, Cook, Smith, Forester, Gardner, Potter, Weaver, and so forth (Reaney & Wilson, 2005). The tradition of pride in the working class continued through the Soviet glorification of the worker in postrevolutionary propaganda posters; through 19th century European art that broke from traditions of higher class portraiture and classical themes to focus on, if not celebrate, the everyday worker; to today's beer and truck advertisements praising the everyday hardworking American.

Second, social class divisions, much as do ethnicity and nationality, represent a way of breaking down a broader culture into groups that result in subcultures that have markers specific to them. Social class cultural markers can be identified in the clothing, speech and dialects, food, and so forth that differ along class lines. Individuals can identify others' social class with good reliability, even on the basis of a 1-minute clip of an interaction (Kraus & Keltner, 2009). American English is peppered with phrases that indicate whether a cultural practice is associated with a particular class: *classy*, *posh*, and *high end* are used to reflect upper class tastes and practices, whereas *ghetto* or *white trash* are used to reflect lower class tastes. Concerning higher class tastes, the rules of civility and good manners have been passed along the generations as the markers of higher-class culture, documented in relics such as the nearly 1,000-page tome *Miss Manners' Guide to Excruciatingly Correct Behavior* (Martin, 2005) or *The Official Preppy Handbook* (Birnbach, 1980). Historically, class divisions on these cultural markers have been enforced by law, as in the class-based sumptuary laws of Europe that prohibited individuals of the lower classes from wearing clothes that would indicate a higher class standing, laws that continued in some parts of Europe even through the early days of the Industrial Revolution (Freudenberger, 1963).

CULTURAL DIFFERENCE BASED ON SOCIAL CLASS: A SAMPLER

What are some of the dimensions along which one may observe markers of culture based on social class? What are those aspects of socioeconomic status (SES) that transcend ethnic and nationality differences to manifest themselves as culture? This type of exploration could take up an entire volume, and so it is necessary to limit the analysis here. One distinction is between material versus subjective cultural differences (Herskovits, 1955; Triandis, 1972), with material differences reflecting those that are tangible, visible to the eye, and clearly manifest, such as differences in clothing or food consumption, and subjective differences reflecting more intangible qualities of culture, such as values and beliefs. Because I am approaching this chapter from a psychological perspective, my focus here is on those subjective, intangible differences. This analysis is not meant to be exhaustive or even comprehensive, but a sampler of research on class differences that could be interpreted as cultural.

A caveat: In general, the discussion of cultural differences walks a line between culture and stereotyping, and exploring social class differences is thus especially dangerous because members of the lower classes are, partly by definition, less powerful and are often the victims of prejudice and discrimination (Saegert et al., 2007). Complicating matters is that being a member of the lower classes is seen as a controllable (and therefore more harshly judged) stigma, at least in the United States (Weiner, 1995), and is especially stigmatizing for those who rely on government assistance (Gilens, 1999; Henry, Reyna, & Weiner, 2004). Furthermore, a cultural explanation has been used to describe the perpetuation of poverty among the underclass (Marks, 1991), blaming the cause of poverty on poor individuals themselves and the cultures they perpetuate, including the values people who are poor teach their children and share with their peers. This approach is at the expense of understanding factors of poverty caused by the broader society or otherwise outside of the control of the underclass. An examination of cultural differences based on class thus risks a value judgment that validates those in power and rejects those without it. This is not my intention here. Instead, what follows is only documentation of some of what social scientists have observed about differences based on social class.

A second caveat: Another theme that becomes evident throughout this summary is that research on the differences between the lower and upper classes focuses its explanations on attitudes and beliefs of the lower classes rather than those of the higher classes. Scientists typically ask, for example, why the working classes are more authoritarian, religious, and collectivistic, yet do not ask why the middle and upper classes are less so. This approach risks problematizing the lower classes, putting them in a position that is not normal and that requires explanation while implying that the higher classes are normal and do not require explanation. This criticism of isolating analyses to those who are disenfranchised in a society has had a long history in the social sciences, at least since Simone de Beauvoir (1949) famously raised similar questions about problematizing women as a group requiring explanation. The analysis of ethnicity has been similarly criticized (Perry, 2001). A similar lesson could be applied here with respect to social class.

Environmental Cultivation and Perpetuation of Class Cultures

Different workplaces are imbued with different cultural values (Sanchez-Burks & Lee, 2010), and these values may differ systematically depending on the social class associated with the modal worker. For example, the culture of white-collar institutions such as marketing and investment firms is different from that of blue-collar institutions such as factories. As an anecdote, while working in a factory in Madison, Wisconsin, I brought in a book of poetry with the intention of studying a couple of lines between the timed arrival of plastic office supplies on a conveyer belt. The supervisor noticed and told me with some disdain, "We do not read here." Whether the reprimand was out of concern for my safety, concern for my productivity, or a transmission of cultural norms and expectations, the result was the same: One does not read in a factory. The country music in the background completed the working-class picture (cf. Snibbe & Markus, 2005). It is reasonable to expect that exposure to this setting 8 hours a day, 5 days a week—what would effectively amount to nearly half of an employee's waking life—would influence the psychology of the individual as much as any aspect of culture that an individual is exposed to. Whether the setting of a factory is a source of working-class culture or simply a reflection of the tastes of the working class is beside the point because the setting reinforces the norms of the class of the modal worker.

As early as Karl Marx (1867/2008), social scientists were considering how a person's and a culture's values can be influenced by modes of production, including the monotony of most laborers' activities throughout their long workday. Later empirical studies explored the relationship between social class and values (Kohn, 1959), and one oft-cited study considered specifically those elements of the workplace that can influence the values of the people who work there (Kohn & Schooler, 1983). In this study, those in working-class occupations in the United States had less opportunity for self-direction in the workplace (including less complex and more routine work with closer supervision), which was associated with valuing self-direction less for themselves, for their children, and even for their wives (Pearlin & Kohn, 1966). This effect has been replicated cross-nationally, including in samples from Italy, Poland, and Japan (Schooler, 2010), hinting that these class effects are not restricted to any one society and may be part of fundamental human social processes.

Qualities of self-direction are also transmitted and reinforced in schools. A study examining four types of schools (working class, middle class, affluent professional, and executive elite) showed that lower class schools reinforce conformity, dependency on the teacher, and little self-direction, whereas higher class schools reinforce creativity, autonomy, and self-direction (Anyon, 1980). Put another way, the classroom environment socializes and prepares students for lives as unskilled laborers or CEOs, depending on the class base of the school.

Empirical work in psychology has validated these findings. Unlike sociologists, psychologists are typically not concerned about the sources of these relationships but nevertheless have confirmed that members of the working class have less outward-directed agency and engage in less self-promotion (e.g., Snibbe & Markus, 2005; Stephens, Markus, & Townsend, 2007).

Altogether, evidence has shown that the environments in which people of different social classes find themselves help to shape beliefs and attitudes, specifically in this case beliefs about self-direction. However, one should not assume that members of the working classes are inherently uninterested in self-direction. Research has just as easily suggested that lack of self-direction may be a function of the futility of asserting self-direction at school or in the workplace for those of the lower classes, a consequence of their disempowered positions in their environments. If people change their work environments, they may change their sense of the utility of self-direction. Nevertheless, this is one example of a robust difference between the social classes in terms of beliefs and attitudes.

Authoritarianism

Strongly related to self-directedness is the broader construct of *authoritarianism,* or the value in conforming to authorities and rules at the expense of individual expression (Feldman, 2003; Stenner, 2005). Social scientists have long considered the relationship between social class and authoritarianism, starting most conspicuously with Lipset's (1959) classic article on working-class authoritarianism. In his cross-cultural review of a multitude of studies, Lipset showed that people who were less educated or had less prestigious occupations were inclined to oppose civil liberties and to endorse a more black-and-white approach to politics, signs of authoritarian-type beliefs. A later cross-national survey confirmed, across nine countries and using a different measure of authoritarianism, that working-class parents were far more punitive toward their misbehaving children than were middle-class parents (Lambert, Hamers, & Frasure-Smith, 1979).

Classic explanations for the working-class–authoritarianism link have focused the source of authoritarianism within working-class individuals themselves. These explanations include the greater economic insecurity (akin to a kind of frustration or aggression) and lack of social and political sophistication among members of the working classes (Lipset, 1959). This perspective is consistent with approaches that have shown that authoritarianism may be explained in part by a narrow worldview (Gabennesch, 1972) or a lack of exposure to multiple perspectives (Kelman & Barclay, 1963) that a good education would redress.

An alternative hypothesis focuses more on the context in which people of lower class find themselves. Working-class endorsement of authoritarianism may be more related to their stigmatized condition in a society, something that those of lower SES may feel acutely. Unpublished data using the World Values Survey reveal that in countries in which education is valued more, the relationship between social class (as measured by education) and authoritarianism increases (Brandt & Henry, 2012b). Put another way, uneducated people are especially likely to endorse authoritarianism in places in which their lack of education is devalued and situates them more firmly in the lower classes.

Cultures of Honor

Several characteristics identify *cultures of honor,* in particular, the type found in Mediterranean Europe (Rodriguez Mosquera, Manstead, & Fischer, 2002), the U.S. South (Nisbett & Cohen, 1996), and inner-city gangs in the United States (Horowitz & Schwartz, 1974), where issues of interpersonal respect, social value, and reputation loom large. People from cultures of honor are especially likely to react harshly, if not violently, to violations of personal respect and dignity, such as insults (Nisbett & Cohen, 1996).

The leading explanation for the roots of a culture of honor has been the economic patterns in a region, notably the presence of a herding economy (Nisbett, 1993). Cultures of honor are said to emerge in herding communities because herders have to be especially vigilant in protecting their property from threats in the form of wolves and thieves, for example, and such vigilance embeds itself into the protection of the self against interpersonal threats as well.

This perspective was further elaborated on and clarified by the theory of stigma compensation, also called low-status compensation (Henry, 2009), which offers an alternative explanation for the prevalence of cultures of honor in herding communities. Rather than emerging from a response to realistic threats to people's herds, cultures of honor instead emerge from groups of people who are lower in social status, including SES. Those who compose the lower social classes find themselves in psychological circumstances that differ from those of the middle and upper classes, which include being targets of devaluation and stigmatization (Saegert et al., 2007). Because very few people want to be devalued or treated as second-class citizens, those who are treated in this way need to manage, psychologically, their marginalization and devalued sense of social worth. One way may be through increasing vigilance and defense of one's existing social worth, which may include reacting aggressively to those who further threaten that social worth with insults and verbal rejection. Recent evidence has indicated that those who are socially rejected on the basis of their group membership behave similarly to those who are rejected in an interpersonal manner (Smart Richman & Leary, 2009), including the aggressive defense of the self against insults. More important, gaining reassurance of one's sense of social worth may ameliorate this aggressive defensiveness. In one study, participants from low-income families were more likely to endorse a willingness to

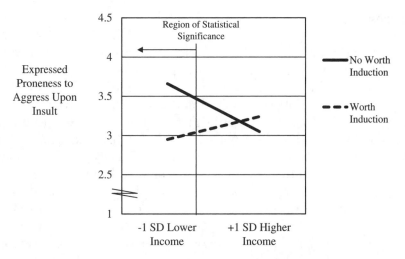

Figure 3.1. Expressed willingness to aggress as a function of socioeconomic status, with and without affirmation manipulations. From "Low-Status Compensation: A Theory for Understanding the Role of Status in Cultures of Honor," by P. J. Henry, 2009, *Journal of Personality and Social Psychology, 97,* p. 463. Copyright 2009 by the American Psychological Association.

react with violence in the face of insults relative to participants from higher income families, but when they were given the opportunity to reflect on their sense of social worth (through a kind of affirmation manipulation), that endorsement dropped to match that of participants from higher income families (see Figure 3.1; Henry, 2009, Study 4).

How are these patterns related to herding cultures, then? Herding cultures may lead to cultures of honor because herding economies are associated with greater inequality than other economic systems (Bradburd, 1990; Fratkin & Roth, 1990; Galaty & Bonte, 1992), and greater inequality typically means a larger and more marginalized lower class. The theoretical perspective of stigma compensation is, however, especially useful because in addition to explaining cultures of honor that emerge from herding societies, it also explains cultures of honor that emerge in places where herding is not a plausible explanation for its roots, such as inner-city gangs (Horowitz & Schwartz, 1974) and prisons (Jenness, Maxson, Matsuda, & Sumner, 2007).[1]

---

[1]A culture of honor among members of lower social classes is not inconsistent with findings that have shown that people of lower socioeconomic status may show more prosocial behavior under other circumstances (Piff, Kraus, Côté, Cheng, & Keltner, 2010). When seeing someone in need, people of lower socioeconomic status may be more likely than their higher status counterparts to seize the opportunity to exercise compassion. Although on the surface this behavior may seem contradictory to the impulsive aggressiveness suggested by a culture-of-honor perspective, the motivations may be the same. In the case of helping, the behavior provides a sense of value in a world that otherwise devalues them, whereas aggressing in the face of insults protects against further devaluing.

Religiosity

At this point, empirically, it is clear that people of lower SES are more likely to be religious than their higher class counterparts, a finding observed across the social sciences (e.g., Coreno, 2002; Norris & Inglehart, 2004; Ruiter & van Tubergen, 2009; Smith & Faris, 2005; Taylor, Mattis, & Chatters, 1999). One explanation is that religiosity provides comfort as a means of dealing with realistic financial hardships that accompany poverty (Norris & Inglehart, 2004; see also Ruiter & van Tubergen, 2009). Another explanation, also informed by stigma compensation theory, is that members of the lower classes are psychologically defensive because of their devalued and marginalized social position, and religiosity provides psychological protection irrespective of realistic financial threats (Brandt & Henry, 2012a). What is certain at this point is that regardless of the cause of religiosity among members of the lower classes, it seems to be an important component of lower class experience and culture.

Conversely, members of the middle and upper classes may cultivate more of a culture of agnosticism or of practicing their religious beliefs less devoutly. Perhaps the decreased value of religion among those groups is rooted in beliefs that religious devotion is for people who are superstitious, bored, or uneducated and easily duped. These explanations are speculative, however: Research on the relationship between social class and religious practices and beliefs has not sought an explanation for patterns of beliefs among the higher classes.

Individualism Versus Collectivism

Social class "may be the major variable that distinguishes individualists and collectivists" (Triandis, 1995, p. 82; see also Hofstede, 1980), and many psychological patterns of members of lower social classes resemble psychological patterns of those from collectivistic cultures. People of lower SES have been shown to be more likely to consider contextual aspects of their environment (Kraus, Piff, & Keltner, 2009), much as do their collectivistic counterparts (Morris & Peng, 1994). Working-class Americans show less emphasis on autonomy and individual choice (Snibbe & Markus, 2005), or at least their choices reflect pressures to conform to others' choices (Stephens et al., 2007), similar to results found with collectivistic cultures (Iyengar & Lepper, 1999; Kim & Markus, 1999). Other research has reflected the other-directed nature of the lower classes: People of lower SES have more nonverbal engagement with others (Kraus & Keltner, 2009) and tend to be more accurate in judging others' emotions (Kraus, Côté, & Keltner, 2010). Note here again the focus on trying to understand and explain lower class patterns of behavior rather than higher class patterns. Few social scientists have tried to explain the greater individualism of the middle and upper classes.

However, these similar kinds of patterns of attitudes and thoughts between the lower classes and collectivistic cultures need not be caused by similar mechanisms. One explanation is that those of lower SES require interdependence as an economically based survival mechanism (Triandis, 1995). Another suggests that a lack of control in the environment of the lower classes may drive the focus on context as a means of recapturing that control (Kraus et al., 2009). Yet another suggests that the lack of emphasis on individual choice among those who are less educated may be a function of different strategies of agency that help protect against the adversities of the outside world (Snibbe & Markus, 2005). These explanations are notably different from the explanations for collectivistic cultures that are otherwise steeped in a rich political, economic, ecological, and social history, including mass media exposure, modernization, and immigration patterns (Kitayama, Ishii, Imada, Takemura, & Ramaswamy, 2006; Triandis, 1995).

WHAT CAN THE STUDY OF SOCIAL CLASS GAIN FROM A CULTURAL APPROACH

I devote the second part of this chapter to an analysis of how the study of social class and the study of cultural psychology, heretofore largely separate literatures, may inform each other by considering social class as a form of culture. In this first section, I consider two ways in which social class culture can help inform and possibly change some preconceptions of social class. In the next section, I do the reverse, considering how a study of social class culture can inform and influence approaches in cultural psychology. These sections self-consciously raise more questions than they answer, but the intention is to consider how the study of social class culture can open the study of both social class and culture to broader ways of understanding and studying each separate phenomenon.

Separating Social Class From Overlapping Categories

Social class differences have been observed in an otherwise relatively homogeneous population of people of the same ethnicity or nationality, such as parts of England a few decades ago (Reid, 1998). However, in most societies the identifiers of social class, such as income, wealth, education, occupation, and employment status, overlap considerably with other social divisions and sources of culture, including ethnicity, nationality, and caste. In the United States, those of the higher classes tend to be predominantly White, and those who are working class and poor tend to be ethnic minorities. In Europe, the higher classes are typically nationals, and the lower classes are typically immigrants. In India, the caste system has theoretically been occupationally based: The highest castes have, at least historically, been priests and nobles and the lowest castes, waste collectors and disposers of the dead.

Yet ethnicity, nationality, and caste each has its own influences on culture that transcend social class. For example, many people across the socioeconomic spectrum in the United States identify with and celebrate U.S. culture, such that Americans of all social classes can be found celebrating the Fourth of July; enjoying apple pie, burgers, and beer; and watching American football. Similarly, the African American subculture is embraced by African Americans across the socioeconomic spectrum, from financially struggling rural families in the South to successful Black celebrities and entrepreneurs such as those interviewed on CNN's documentary series *Black in America* (see http://inamerica.blogs.cnn.com/).

The tight relationship between these overlapping categories of ethnicity, nationality, and caste and social class, raises the question of the utility of separating out the unique influence of social class on culture independent of these other influences. Is it even possible to separate out these influences? The situation of caste is instructive of the complexities of this endeavor. The relationship between caste and class has historically been so tight that it has been claimed that classes cannot form in the caste system and that caste is synonymous with socioeconomic class (Argyle, 1994). Another suggestion has been that "to look at caste and class separately would be an artificial exercise" (Jaffrelot, 2011, p. 610). Even fictionalized, futuristic visions of caste, as in Aldous Huxley's (1932/2008) *Brave New World,* have conceptualized it as inescapable, birth-determined occupations that are inextricably intertwined with a social class hierarchy.

Yet, despite the fact that caste is almost entirely permanent from birth, class mobility has been shown even within caste systems, with income and education fluctuating considerably among those in a particular caste (Biswas & Pandey, 1996). Although it is true that caste historically constrained one to a specific occupation, today the relationship no longer holds. For example, the Indian government program of reservations, a kind of affirmative action for underrepresented castes and tribes, helps to ensure that occupation and education are distributed more equitably across the castes. Caste culture also has cultural markers that operate separately from SES, including diet, dress, and rituals that, similar to ethnicity, can and do transcend the social classes (Bayly, 2001). Caste, unlike SES, is also rich with religious meaning, including the concept of reincarnation that imbues caste with a sense of legitimacy that even those of the lowest castes accept (Keay, 2011); social class is independently not religion based. All of these aspects of caste layer into the concept of SES extra factors that are not generalizable cross-culturally. It appears that even caste and class are distinguishable.

Because social class is distinguishable from these other overlapping categories of ethnicity, nationality, and caste, is it worth making the distinction for the purposes of developing a theory of the universal influences of social class on culture? One example of the benefits of this endeavor is Kohn and Schooler's (1983; Schooler, 2010) cross-cultural research, described earlier, that considered the influences of working-class conditions on working-class attitudes. This work was conducted across multiple countries and with otherwise homogeneous samples so that social class could be considered more precisely. Other social scientists, too, have controlled for the effects of these overlapping categories by isolating the effects of social class within a homogeneous ethnic group (e.g., Whites in the United States; Murray, 2012) to useful effect. This research has arguably shed light on the universal nature of these working conditions in the development of different attitudes between the social classes, making a case for influences on social class culture that are independent of overlapping categories of ethnicity, nationality, and caste and that are generalizable.

An alternative solution could be to have class indicate a larger category that encompasses, rather than removes, the categories of ethnicity, nationality, and caste. Here, class-based cultures would describe the cultural markers of any groups that are disenfranchised versus enfranchised. This broader category of class-based cultures would be based on all the factors that contribute to one's overall status in a society, including not just socioeconomic indicators such as occupation, income, wealth, and education but also nationality, ethnicity, religion, caste, and so forth. This exercise would allow an examination of similarities across disenfranchised versus privileged groups across different cultures, to track similarities in cultural effects despite the wide range of contributors to what makes a group disenfranchised or privileged cross-culturally.

The overall point here, though, is to recognize that research on social class culture opens the possibility of considering universal effects of social class on culture, a question that has heretofore not received much theoretical or empirical attention. This question of examining universals could refer to similarities in the content of the markers of class culture cross-nationally (e.g., do members of the higher social classes uniformly endorse individualistic values more than their lower class counterparts cross-nationally?) or similarities in the roots of class differences (e.g., do members of the higher classes cross-nationally experience greater freedoms than their lower class counterparts in a way that affects their beliefs and attitudes?). The approach one would use, whether examining social class within a homogeneous ethnic, national, or caste group or by examining social class across a range of its manifestations cross-culturally, would depend on the scope of the analysis and the ambition of the investigator. The utility of this endeavor is an open question, but I believe that researchers could better understand the universal aspects of social class culture.

Considering Cross-Class Identifications

A second way in which the study of social class can be informed by situating it within culture research is the examination of cross-cultural influences. A common assumption for more than a century has been that members of the lower classes imitate members of the higher classes or that considerable pressure is put on the lower classes to adopt higher class tastes, customs, and goods (Bourdieu, 1984; Veblen, 1899/2007). However, an examination of cultural exchanges throughout the centuries has shown that even less powerful, colonized, or oppressed cultures can influence the cultures of dominant societies. Might the same be true of social class, that the lower classes can influence upper class culture?

At first glance, plenty of evidence appears to show that the lower classes adopt higher-class cultural practices. A typical kind of study identifies the delay—or "cultural lag"—that occurs in the lower classes as they become aware of and later adopt higher class practices, often after the higher classes have abandoned those practices. One study examined how the nouveau riche of one Greek village would adopt higher class practices that were already passé and replaced by other practices, such as the use of outdated speech forms (Friedl, 1964). Economists (Leavitt & Dubner, 2005) have also shown that members of the lower classes adopt names for their children that have a higher class (and presumably successful) sound; however, by the time these children are older, their names are already outdated among higher class communities. A higher class name "starts working its way down the socioeconomic ladder" (Leavitt & Dubner, 2005, p. 204) as these names are adopted less by those from higher classes and more by those from the lower classes.

The lower classes not only adopt higher class practices but also higher class ideologies. The problem of the adoption of dominant ideologies by the working classes goes back to Marxist thought (Gasper, 2005) but has gained currency and empirical validation among psychologists through concepts of legitimizing ideologies as found in social dominance theory (Sidanius & Pratto, 1999) and especially system justification theory (Jost & Banaji, 1994). One idea behind these theories is that members of lower status groups tend to disproportionately adopt beliefs and practices of the higher classes (rather than the reverse), especially in a way that serves to further disadvantage them and keep them in their lower status position in society (Jost, Banaji,

& Nosek, 2004; Jost, Pelham, & Carvallo, 2002). For example, in representative samples of U.S. respondents, low-income respondents were even more likely than higher income respondents to endorse the idea that large pay differences are important for encouraging motivation in people and that economic inequality is legitimate (Jost, Pelham, Sheldon, & Sullivan, 2003).

Literary depictions of attempts by lower classes to adopt higher class practices abound, most classically in George Bernard Shaw's play *Pygmalion*, in which Professor Henry Higgins teaches a cultured, higher class demeanor to Eliza Doolittle, a brash, cockney, working-class woman. However, here the upper class standards are imposed on Eliza, not sought by her. The blockbuster Hollywood film *Pretty Woman* is based on a similar premise: A prostitute is transformed, successfully, into a cultured beauty queen worthy of the attentions of a multimillionaire businessman and socialite, this time with her approval. A typical comedic device in these plays and films involves people of the lower classes slipping back into lower class speech and behaviors when in higher class company. The television show *The Beverly Hillbillies* rested almost entirely on this comedic device, in which the Clampetts, a formerly poor family (presumably Southern), strike oil and move to Beverly Hills but continue to hand-churn butter, spin thread on a spinning wheel, and eat sorghum and hog jowls. This resistance to adopting higher class cultural practices despite their access to wealth would not be so funny were it not so unexpected. Higher class culture seems to be an ideal to strive toward, not resist.

It would be a mistake, though, to deny that the opposite influence occurs as well. Higher classes adopt lower class practices, too, and this phenomenon, although widespread, has gone understudied in the social sciences despite the fact that examples abound going back at least 500 years. In 17th century Europe, men of the higher classes were known to adopt the relaxed jackets common among the peasantry, and lower-class prostitutes, mistresses, and actresses were highly influential in setting high fashion (Freudenberger, 1963). In the 19th century, blue jeans originated as durable working wear for those hunting gold in California, but they have since become the classic symbol of U.S. fashion, even among the upper classes of society willing to pay premium prices (Sullivan, 2006). The modern fashion of sagging pants originated with ill-fitting prisoner outfits (Christian, 2007) and was eventually adopted by rap and hip-hop artists in the 1990s before spreading across the broader U.S. fashion landscape. Dance forms such as tango, martial arts forms such as capoeira, and musical forms such as jazz, blues, country, and folk all have origins in the lower and working classes but have been embraced by people of all walks of life. Some of the greatest composers of classical music have adopted countryside folk tunes in their oeuvre, including Mozart, Grieg, Copeland, Dvorak, and Mahler. Food practices that have originated in the working classes can now be found in higher class establishments. A chopped liver sandwich goes for more than $11 at Katz Deli on the Lower East Side of Manhattan, and meatloaf, tripe soup, and burritos have appeared in Michelin-starred restaurants. Even the hot dog has its high-end, costly versions, such as at Hot Doug's in Chicago, where for $10 one can order a foie gras and sauternes duck hot dog, complete with truffle aioli and fleur de sel. Each of these examples serves to demonstrate that customs that originated in the lower classes can influence the higher classes.

These kinds of examples are well known in the anecdotal and historical record, but they have not been rigorously studied as a social class phenomenon. Their existence raises some interesting questions concerning the adoption of lower class practices by the higher classes. Under what circumstances would the higher classes adopt lower class practices? What are the consequences of this kind of approach to the lower classes? In adopting these practices, do those of the upper classes see them as quaint? practical? cool? Do they see themselves as being respectful? open-minded? ironic?

This kind of cultural influence is an open area for further investigation and could even be broadened for understanding not only the cultural influences of the lower social classes but also any group in society that is generally of lower status. For example, who might be most responsible for setting trends in language use and vocal inflections in U.S. culture—powerful, middle-aged White male public speakers? Wrong: Teenage girls (Quenqua, 2012).

WHAT CAN THE STUDY OF CULTURE GAIN FROM A SOCIAL CLASS APPROACH

The definition and concept of culture has developed almost exclusively in the context of studying how culture operates among ethnic groups and nationalities. However, the concept of culture may need to be rethought with an increasing understanding of broader influences on culture, including those represented throughout this book and, specifically here, social class. Just as situating the study of social class within the culture literature may help inform and broaden how researchers think of social class, the same exercise may also help inform and broaden how researchers think of culture. The following sections describe some examples.

Examining the "Mutual" in Mutual Constitution

One way in which the study of social class culture may inform culture research concerns the concept of *mutual constitution*, or the assumption that individuals influence their culture at least as much as culture influences individuals (Markus & Hamedani, 2010).[2] The concept of mutual constitution is potentially important and useful but nonetheless murky and untested. Taken at its strongest and most literal, the idea that individuals can influence culture as much as cultures can influence individuals is provocative but highly speculative.

The empirical record on social class and culture may give reason to question a strong version of mutual in the mutual constitution of culture or the idea that culture and individuals influence each other equally. The direction of influence between members of a social class and their culture may not be entirely reciprocal. In one classic study that examined workplace conditions, although the conditions of the workplace and the workers' personalities did mutually influence each other, a demonstrable lag was seen in the direction of the workers influencing their environment (Kohn & Schooler, 1983). That is, the culture of the workplace seemed to influence the workers' personalities more quickly than the workers influenced their workplace environment. Furthermore, this lag may be exaggerated for the lower classes compared with the upper classes: Politicians, for example, tend to be more responsive to their wealthier constituents than to their lower class constituents (Bartels, 2010), suggesting that more time and energy may be needed from members of the lower classes to effect social change, at least politically.

This research from the social class literature illustrates the need for more research to understand the relative influence of culture on individuals versus individuals on culture. Whether the findings of a cultural lag of influence in the social class literature can be generalized to other forms of culture, including ethnicity- and nationality-based cultures, is a currently untested empirical question. How easily an individual can influence a culture, and who one needs to be to do so, are important questions for those interested in making changes to any culture, whether for epidemiological reasons (e.g., changing cultural eating patterns that can affect diabetes rates), social justice reasons (e.g., increasing awareness of the importance of equality for women), environmental reasons (e.g., introducing recycling norms and behaviors to a culture), or other social and political reasons.

Understanding the Formation of Culture Via Adaptations

Research in cultural psychology typically starts with culture as a given and considers the consequences of being situated within a culture. For example, given that a person is situated within a culture that emphasizes

---

[2]Note that mutual constitution here is different from the preceding discussion concerning the mutual influence of cultures. Lower class culture influencing higher class culture, and vice versa, is not mutual constitution as it has been defined in the literature but is instead a kind of cross-cultural influence.

individualistic versus collectivistic values, how might that culture influence that person's thoughts, beliefs, and interpersonal relations? Psychologists typically do not investigate what is at the root of cultures: what forms them, perpetuates them, and changes them. These factors are often environmental, geographical, meteorological, economic, political, and social structural, factors that psychologists typically leave to the domain of anthropologists and sociologists (although a number of exceptions of psychologists tackling these questions about origins have occurred; e.g., D. Cohen, 2001; Henry, 2009; Kitayama et al., 2006; Nisbett & Cohen, 1996; Oishi & Graham, 2010).

Part of the definition of culture is that it emerges out of adaptations to an environment. In general, culture researchers have considered three types of adaptation to environment that result in cultural patterns, which I label *evolutionary vestiges*, *postevolutionary vestiges*, and *current society-level adaptations* and discuss next. However, I propose a fourth adaptation that has not been considered as much of an influence but that comes to light in an analysis of social class.

Evolutionary Vestiges

The types of adaptations that culture researchers have considered include, first, human adaptations over a million years of biological evolution, particularly during the environment of evolutionary adaptedness that predates agriculture and in which current human beings no longer live but for whom behaviors, even maladaptive vestiges, still exist. Evolved preferences may influence culture, such as the foods people are biologically prepared to eat (Konner, 2010; Rozin, 2010).[3]

Postevolutionary Vestiges

A second adaptation is also a vestigial one but does not involve biological evolution. Groups may have developed practices that at one point in their history were adaptive to their environment but that are no longer necessary. Nevertheless, the practice may continue despite its lack of utility (D. Cohen, 2001). For example, in my home city of Abu Dhabi, the Arabian *dishdasha* is a common way for local Emirati men to identify each other in an otherwise exceptionally international and multicultural city. The dishdasha is a uniformly white, full-body covering that at one time protected men from the sun

---

[3]This argument is different from that which states that humans have evolved the flexibility of adaptation to environments that results in cultural differences (a cultural acquisition device; Konner, 2010), which is intended to explain the general existence of cultural variability in the human species but not the existence of specific manifestations of culture.

and blowing sands of the desert while simultaneously reflecting sunlight and ensuring good ventilation. Many Emirati men nevertheless continue to wear this clothing in their everyday life that is spent largely in the air conditioned, sun- and sand-free indoors.

Current Society-Level Adaptations

Third are collective adaptations to a society's immediate environment, such as features of one's current climate, economics, and so forth, that are reflected in culture. Some examples include the skins and furs traditionally worn by Inuit cultures living in cold northern Canadian climates or the Spanish siesta taken to escape the midday heat. Similarly, the food choices of a culture may simply be a function of what grows in a certain region (Rozin, 2010).

Aggregations of Individual-Level Adaptations

I argue for a fourth type of adaptation—not considered carefully by culture researchers to this point—that results accidentally as a function of the collective acts of individuals. This adaptation is not the same as a collective adaptation to the broader environment of individuals' immediate geography, climate, and so forth. Rather, this sort of adaptation does not affect everyone in a region but only those individuals affected by particular circumstances, including individuals adapting to their socioeconomic condition. These adaptations develop into beliefs, attitudes, and practices that can be passed on to others in similar circumstances and from generation to generation. One might not intuitively think of a group of people coincidentally doing the same thing as culture, and cultural psychologists have cautioned against assuming that there is a correspondence between individual psychological experiences and culture (Na et al., 2010). However, the aggregation of individuals' beliefs and practices can be seen and experienced as culture by outsiders. A study of social class cultures may illuminate two ways in which these kinds of adaptations can manifest as culture: as a function of adaptation to realistic economic conditions and as a function of the psychological conditions of their immediate surroundings.

Adaptations to Realistic Economic Hardships. People who compose the lower classes find themselves in realistically difficult material circumstances that differ from those of people in the upper classes and that eventually result in beliefs and practices that can in and of themselves become culture (Markus & Hamedani, 2010). For example, people who are poor generally lack access to supermarkets and healthy foods (Crister, 2000; Zenk et al., 2005). The difficulty of accessing healthy foods might be responsible for the kinds of food choices made by those of lower socioeconomic status, including opting for more readily available junk foods and fast food. These forced choices result in a heavier lower class, something that could develop into a marker of working-class culture.

Adaptations to Psychological Devaluing and Social Rejection. As discussed earlier, people who are of lower socioeconomic status also face psychological devaluing and social rejection compared with their higher status counterparts, an experience that may lead to cultures of honor. However, in this case, these cultures of honor develop where an aggregate of people are individually and coincidentally responding to their psychological condition of social marginalization. Cultures of honor emerge from these aggregates even though the individuals do not share a common fate or consciously pass along a practice of reactive aggression to future generations. The aggregate of individual-level adaptations may then appear as culture even though its origins are based on individual adaptations, not group adaptations.

Raising Questions About the Definition of Culture

To summarize this section, social class may contribute to researchers' understanding of how culture may form, not based on a collective adaptation to an environment but based on the aggregate of individual, coincidental practices. This pattern, however, raises a question concerning definitions of culture, which often have the transmission of culture as central to the definition (e.g., Triandis, 2010). If cultures can form accidentally and coincidentally, then how necessary is it to the definition of culture to have it consciously and deliberately transmitted across generations? Although basic social learning processes, such as modeling behavior, are sufficient, are they necessary? It may be possible that, for example, working-class children eventually adopt working-class beliefs and practices as adults not because the ideas have been transmitted to them but because they happen to find themselves in the same circumstances as their parents and thus acquire the same adaptations.

Understanding Social Class Culture at Multiple Levels of Analysis

A final point of consideration concerning how social class can inform the study of culture is related to multiple levels of analysis. Culture is often considered the broadest level of social analysis (e.g., Kruglanski & Higgins, 2007); however, the cultural level of analysis may itself be further divided into different levels of analysis.

People typically understand social class in terms of how society is divided into groups on the basis of varying economic conditions. Social class culture has been studied in places in which people of a certain social class cluster in specific neighborhoods (e.g., Kusserow, 2004). However, society can be considered creatively as operating at multiple levels of analysis that go beyond the upper, middle, and working classes that operate at a national level of analysis. Class may operate on a global level. Karl Marx (1867/2008) identified the division of labor that occurs across countries and that "converts one part of the globe into a chiefly agricultural field of production, for supplying the other part which remains a chiefly industrial field" (p. 274).In other words, undeveloped countries supply the raw materials for production by wealthier countries, forming the economic basis of colonialism. This division across societies mirrors the division of labor that occurs within a society to produce class differences.

Today, countries have been given labels according to their resources and state of modernization, including *developed* or *industrialized* versus *developing* countries, which are modern versions of the *First World* versus *Third World* designations that emerged during the Cold War. These kinds of global class distinctions are likely to shape cultural differences. One can sense cultural differences, for example, between Stockholm, the capital of the very modern country of Sweden, and Khartoum, the capital of the developing country of Sudan, that are based on the state of modernization of the country alone. Compare other capital cities, such as Brussels with Guatemala City, Paris with Kolkata, Tokyo with Cairo, and the cultural distinctions clearly go beyond mere differences of region or ethnicity.

Class-cultural differences may be observed between cities within a country, too. In terms of a city's education level, compare Boston or San Francisco (among the most educated cities in the United States; Zumbrun, 2008) with Detroit or Cleveland. These education differences may manifest in cultural differences such as frequency and accessibility of bookstores, coffee shops, artistic venues, and performance outlets, as well as differences in politics and values.

Is it useful to understand other types of culture as they operate at multiple levels of analysis? Past commentators on culture have thought so. Edward Said (1979) famously understood the global level of analysis of culture in *Orientalism*, his critique of Western approaches to the Middle East. African American culture is an important aspect of U.S. culture, but pan-African culture is also a global phenomenon, as espoused by Black civil rights activists such as Marcus Garvey and Malcolm X. Religious cultures exist within societies but also on a global scale, with the Vatican representing global Catholic culture and Mecca representing global Islamic culture. As the world becomes increasingly globalized, identification of such global forms of culture will become harder to ignore.

CONCLUSION

Psychologists can no longer ignore the forms of culture that go beyond the familiar bases of ethnicity and nationality, including culture based on social class (A. B. Cohen, 2009). Given the complexity of social class across different economic systems and different societies, this task is no easier than isolating the antecedents and consequences of any plausible influence on a culture. Nevertheless, considerable value may be found in considering social class as a form of culture, including the ways in which research on both social class and culture can mutually inform each other by considering social class as leading to a set of beliefs and practices that are in and of themselves culture.

The foundation is just being laid, however. If the study of cultural psychology in general is young relative to that of other cultural approaches, the study of the psychology of class-based culture is in its infancy. It will therefore be important to continue to draw from sociological and anthropological influences in laying its foundation. Combined with the knowledge of social and cultural psychologists, these interdisciplinary perspectives can help build a theoretically rich understanding of culture and social class.

REFERENCES

Anyon, J. (1980). Social class and school knowledge. *Curriculum Inquiry, 11*, 3–42. doi:10.2307/1179509

Argyle, M. (1994). *The psychology of social class.* New York, NY: Routledge.

Bartels, L. (2010). *Unequal democracy.* Princeton, NJ: Princeton University Press.

Bayly, S. (2001). *Caste, society and politics in India from the eighteenth century to the modern age.* Cambridge, England: Cambridge University Press.

Birnbach, L. (Ed.). (1980). *The official preppy handbook.* New York: Workman.

Biswas, U. N., & Pandey, J. (1996). Mobility and perception of socioeconomic status among tribal and caste group. *Journal of Cross-Cultural Psychology, 27*, 200–215. doi:10.1177/0022022196272004

Bourdieu, P. (1984). *Distinction: A social critique of the judgment of taste* (R. Nice, Trans.). Cambridge, MA: Harvard University Press.

Bradburd, D. (1990). *Ambiguous relations: Kin, class, and conflict among Komachi pastoralists.* Washington, DC: Smithsonian Institution Press.

Brandt, M., & Henry, P. J. (2012a). Psychological defensiveness as a mechanism explaining the relationship between low socioeconomic status and religiosity. *International Journal for the Psychology of Religion, 22*, 321–332.

Brandt, M. J., & Henry, P. J. (2012b, July). *A society's value of education increases the relationship between education and authoritarianism.* Paper presented at the 35th annual meeting of the International Society for Political Psychology, Chicago.

Brewer, M. B., & Yuki, M. (2010). Culture and social identity. In S. Kitayama & D. Cohen (Eds.), *Handbook of cultural psychology* (pp. 307–322). New York, NY: Guilford Press.

Christian, M. A. (2007). The facts behind the saggin' pants craze. *Jet, 111*(18), 16.

Cohen, A. B. (2009). Many forms of culture. *American Psychologist, 64*, 194–204. doi:10.1037/a0015308

Cohen, D. (2001). Cultural variation: Considerations and implications. *Psychological Bulletin, 127*, 451–471. doi:10.1037/0033-2909.127.4.451

Coreno, T. (2002). Fundamentalism as a class culture. *Sociology of Religion, 63*, 335–360. doi:10.2307/3712473

Côté, J. E., & Levine, C. G. (2002). *Identity formation, agency, and culture: A social psychological synthesis.* Mahwah, NJ: Erlbaum.

Crister, G. (2000, March). Let them eat cake. *Harper's Magazine*, pp. 41–47.

de Beauvoir, S. (1949). *The second sex.* New York, NY: Vintage Books.

Feldman, S. (2003). Enforcing social conformity: A theory of authoritarianism. *Political Psychology, 24*, 41–74. doi:10.1111/0162-895X.00316

Fratkin, E., & Roth, E. A. (1990). Drought and economic differentiation among Ariaal pastoralists in Kenya. *Human Ecology, 18*, 385–402.

Freudenberger, H. (1963). Fashion, sumptuary laws, and business. *Business History Review, 37*, 37–48. doi:10.2307/3112091

Friedl, E. (1964). Lagging emulation in post-peasant society. *American Anthropologist, 66*, 569–586. doi:10.1525/aa.1964.66.3.02a00040

Gabennesch, H. (1972). Authoritarianism as world view. *American Journal of Sociology, 77*, 857–875.

Galaty, J. G., & Bonte, P. (1992). *Herders, warriors, and traders: Pastoralism in Africa.* Boulder, CO: Westview Press.

Gasper, P. (Ed.). (2005). *The communist manifesto: A road map to history's most important political document.* Chicago, IL: Haymarket Books.

Gilens, M. (1999). *Why Americans hate welfare: Race, media and the politics of antipoverty policy.* Chicago, IL: University of Chicago Press. doi:10.7208/chicago/9780226293660.001.0001

Henry, P. J. (2009). Low-status compensation: A theory for understanding the role of status in cultures of honor. *Journal of Personality and Social Psychology, 97*, 451–466. doi:10.1037/a0015476

Henry, P. J., Reyna, C. E., & Weiner, B. (2004). Hate welfare but help the poor: How the attributional content of stereotypes explains the paradox of reactions to the destitute in America. *Journal of Applied Social Psychology, 34*, 34–58.

Herskovits, M. J. (1955). *Cultural anthropology.* New York, NY: Knopf.

Hofstede, G. (1980). *Culture's consequences: International differences in work-related values.* Newbury Park, CA: Sage.

Horowitz, R., & Schwartz, G. (1974). Honor, normative ambiguity and gang violence. *American Sociological Review, 39*, 238–251.

Huxley, A. (2008). *Brave new world*. New York, NY: Harper Perennial. (Original work published 1932)

Iyengar, S. S., & Lepper, M. R. (1999). Rethinking the value of choice: A cultural perspective on intrinsic motivation. *Journal of Personality and Social Psychology, 76*, 349–366. doi:10.1037/0022-3514.76.3.349

Jackman, M. (1979). The subjective meaning of social class identification in the United States. *Public Opinion Quarterly, 43*, 443–462. doi:10.1086/268543

Jaffrelot, C. (2011). *Religion, caste and politics in India*. New York, NY: Columbia University Press.

Jenness, V., Maxson, C. L., Matsuda, K. N., & Sumner, J. N. (2007). *Violence in California correctional facilities: An empirical investigation of sexual assault*. Report submitted to the California Department of Corrections and Rehabilitation, Sacramento.

Jost, J. T., & Banaji, M. R. (1994). The role of stereotyping in system-justification and the production of false consciousness. *British Journal of Social Psychology, 33*, 1–27. doi:10.1111/j.2044-8309.1994.tb01008.x

Jost, J. T., Banaji, M. R., & Nosek, B. A. (2004). A decade of system justification: Accumulated evidence of conscious and unconscious bolstering of the status quo. *Political Psychology, 25*, 881–919. doi:10.1111/j.1467-9221.2004.00402.x

Jost, J. T., Pelham, B. W., & Carvallo, M. (2002). Non-conscious forms of system justification: Cognitive, affective, and behavioral preferences for higher status groups. *Journal of Experimental Social Psychology, 38*, 586–602. doi:10.1016/S0022-1031(02)00505-X

Jost, J. T., Pelham, B. W., Sheldon, O., & Sullivan, B. N. (2003). Social inequality and the reduction of ideological dissonance on behalf of the system: Evidence of enhanced system justification among the disadvantaged. *European Journal of Social Psychology, 33*, 13–36. doi:10.1002/ejsp.127

Keay, J. (2011). *India: A history*. New York, NY: Grove Press.

Kelman, H. C., & Barclay, J. (1963). The F scale as a measure of breadth of perspective. *Journal of Abnormal and Social Psychology, 67*, 608–615.

Kim, H. S., & Markus, H. R. (1999). Deviance or uniqueness, harmony or conformity? A cultural analysis. *Journal of Personality and Social Psychology, 77*, 785–800. doi:10.1037/0022-3514.77.4.785

Kitayama, S., Ishii, K., Imada, T., Takemura, K., & Ramaswamy, J. (2006). Voluntary settlement and the spirit of independence: Evidence from Japan's "northern frontier." *Journal of Personality and Social Psychology, 91*, 369–384. doi:10.1037/0022-3514.91.3.369

Kohn, M. L. (1959). Social class and parental values. *American Journal of Sociology, 64*, 337–351.

Kohn, M. L., & Schooler, C. (1983). *Work and personality: An inquiry into the impact of social stratification*. Norwood, NJ: Ablex.

Konner, M. (2010). Evolutionary foundations of cultural psychology. In S. Kitayama & D. Cohen (Eds.), *Handbook of cultural psychology* (pp. 77–106). New York, NY: Guilford Press.

Kraus, M. W., Côté, S., & Keltner, D. (2010). Social class, contextualism, and empathic empathy. *Psychological Science, 21*, 1716–1723. doi:10.1177/0956797610387613

Kraus, M. W., & Keltner, D. (2009). Signs of socioeconomic status: A thin-slicing approach. *Psychological Science, 20*, 99–106. doi:10.1111/j.1467-9280.2008.02251.x

Kraus, M. W., Piff, P. K., & Keltner, D. (2009). Social class, sense of control, and social explanation. *Journal of Personality and Social Psychology, 97*, 992–1004. doi:10.1037/a0016357

Kruglanski, A., & Higgins, E. T. (Eds.). (2007). *Social psychology: Handbook of basic principles* (2nd ed.). New York, NY: Guilford Press.

Kusserow, A. S. (2004). *American individualism: Child rearing and social class in three neighborhoods.* New York, NY: Palgrave MacMillan.

Lambert, W. E., Hamers, J. F., & Frasure-Smith, N. (1979). *Child-rearing values: A cross-national study.* New York, NY: Praeger.

Leavitt, S. D., & Dubner, S. J. (2005). *Freakonomics: A rogue economist explores the hidden side of everything.* New York, NY: Harper Collins.

Lipset, S. M. (1959). Democracy and working-class authoritarianism. *American Sociological Review, 24*, 482–501. doi:10.2307/2089536

Lott, B. (2002). Cognitive and behavioral distancing from the poor. *American Psychologist, 57*, 100–110. doi:10.1037/0003-066X.57.2.100

Marks, C. (1991). The urban underclass. *Annual Review of Sociology, 17*, 445–466. doi:10.1146/annurev.so.17.080191.002305

Markus, H. R., & Hamedani, M. G. (2010). Sociostructural psychology: The dynamic interdependence among self systems and social systems. In S. Kitayama & D. Cohen (Eds.), *Handbook of cultural psychology* (pp. 3–39). New York, NY: Guilford Press.

Martin, J. (2005). *Miss Manners' guide to excruciatingly correct behavior, freshly updated.* New York, NY: Norton.

Marx, K. (2008). *Capital: An abridged edition* (D. McLellan. Trans.). Oxford, England: Oxford University Press. (Original work published 1867)

Morris, M. W., & Peng, K. (1994). Culture and cause: American and Chinese attributions for social and physical events. *Journal of Personality and Social Psychology, 67*, 949–971. doi:10.1037/0022-3514.67.6.949

Murray, C. (2012). *Coming apart: The state of White America, 1960–2010.* New York, NY: Crown Forum.

Na, J., Grossmann, I., Varnum, M. E. W., Kitayama, S., Gonzalez, R., & Nisbett, R. E. (2010). Cultural differences are not always reducible to individual differences. *Proceedings of the National Academy of Sciences of the United States of America, 107*, 6192–6197. doi:10.1073/pnas.1001911107

Nisbett, R. E. (1993). Violence and regional U.S. culture. *American Psychologist, 48,* 441–449. doi:10.1037/0003-066X.48.4.441

Nisbett, R. E., & Cohen, D. (1996). *Culture of honor: The psychology of violence in the South.* Boulder, CO: Westview Press.

Norris, P., & Inglehart, R. (2004). *Sacred and secular: Religion and politics worldwide.* Cambridge, England: Cambridge University Press. doi:10.1017/CBO978 0511791017

Oakes, J. M., & Rossi, R. H. (2003). The measurement of SES in health research: Current practice and steps toward a new approach. *Social Science & Medicine, 56,* 769–784. doi:10.1016/S0277-9536(02)00073-4

Oishi, S., & Graham, J. (2010). Social ecology: Lost and found in psychological science. *Perspectives on Psychological Science, 5,* 356–377. doi:10.1177/ 1745691610374588

Pearlin, L. I., & Kohn, M. L. (1966). Social class, occupation, and parental values: A cross-national study. *American Sociological Review, 31,* 466–479.

Perry, P. (2001). White means never having to say you're ethnic. *Journal of Contemporary Ethnography, 30,* 56–91. doi:10.1177/089124101030001002

Pew Research Center. (2008). *Middle class, by the numbers.* Retrieved from http:// pewresearch.org/pubs/983/middle-class-by-the-numbers

Piff, P. K., Kraus, M. W., Côté, S., Cheng, B. H., & Keltner, D. (2010). Having less, giving more: The influence of social class on prosocial behavior. *Journal of Personality and Social Psychology, 99,* 771–784. doi:10.1037/a0020092

Quenqua, D. (2012, February 12). They're, like, way ahead of the linguistic currrrve. *New York Times,* p. D1. Retrieved February 28, 2012, http://www.nytimes.com/ 2012/02/28/science/young-women-often-trendsetters-in-vocal-patterns.html? pagewanted=all&_r=0

Reaney, P. H., & Wilson, R. M. (2005). *A dictionary of English surnames.* Oxford, England: Oxford University Press.

Reid, I. (1998). *Class in Britain.* Cambridge, England: Polity Press.

Rodriguez Mosquera, P. M., Manstead, A. S. R., & Fischer, A. H. (2002). Honor in the Mediterranean and Northern Europe. *Journal of Cross-Cultural Psychology, 33,* 16–36. doi:10.1177/0022022102033001002

Rozin, P. (2010). Food and eating. In S. Kitayama & D. Cohen (Eds.), *Handbook of cultural psychology* (pp. 391–416). New York, NY: Guilford Press.

Ruiter, S., & van Tubergen, F. (2009). Religious attendance in cross-national perspective: A multilevel analysis of 60 countries. *American Journal of Sociology, 115,* 863–895. doi:10.1086/603536

Saegert, S. C., Adler, N. E., Bullock, H. E., Cauce, A. M., Liu, W. M., & Wyche, K. F. (2007). *Report of the APA Task Force on Socioeconomic Status.* Washington, DC: American Psychological Association.

Said, E. W. (1978). *Orientalism.* New York, NY: Random House.

Sanchez-Burks, J., & Lee, F. (2010). Cultural psychology of workways. In S. Kitayama & D. Cohen (Eds.), *Handbook of cultural psychology* (pp. 346–369). New York, NY: Guilford Press.

Schooler, C. (2010). Culture and social structure: The relevance of social structure to cultural psychology. In S. Kitayama & D. Cohen (Eds.), *Handbook of cultural psychology* (pp. 370–388). New York, NY: Guilford Press.

Sidanius, J., & Pratto, F. (1999). *Social dominance: An intergroup theory of social hierarchy and oppression*. New York, NY: Cambridge University Press.

Smart Richman, L., & Leary, M. (2009). Reactions to discrimination, stigmatization, ostracism, and other forms of interpersonal rejection: A multimotive model. *Psychological Review, 116*, 365–383. doi:10.1037/a0015250

Smith, C., & Faris, R. (2005). Socioeconomic inequality in the American religious system: An update and assessment. *Journal for the Scientific Study of Religion, 44*, 95–104. doi:10.1111/j.1468-5906.2005.00267.x

Snibbe, A. C., & Markus, H. R. (2005). You can't always get what you want: Educational attainment, agency, and choice. *Journal of Personality and Social Psychology, 88*, 703–720. doi:10.1037/0022-3514.88.4.703

Stenner, K. (2005). *The authoritarian dynamic*. New York, NY: Cambridge University Press. doi:10.1017/CBO9780511614712

Stephens, N. M., Markus, H. R., & Townsend, S. S. M. (2007). Choice as an act of meaning: The case of social class. *Journal of Personality and Social Psychology, 93*, 814–830. doi:10.1037/0022-3514.93.5.814

Sullivan, J. (2006). *Jeans: A cultural history of an American icon*. New York, NY: Gotham Books.

Taylor, R. J., Mattis, J., & Chatters, L. M. (1999). Subjective religiosity among African Americans: A synthesis of findings from five national samples. *Journal of Black Psychology, 25*, 524–543.

Triandis, H. C. (1972). *The analysis of subjective culture*. New York, NY: Wiley.

Triandis, H. C. (1995). *Individualism and collectivism*. Boulder, CO: Westview Press.

Triandis, H. C. (2010). Culture and psychology: A history of the study of their relationship. In S. Kitayama & D. Cohen (Eds.), *Handbook of cultural psychology* (pp. 59–76). New York, NY: Guilford Press.

Veblen, T. (2007). *The theory of the leisure class*. Oxford, England: Oxford University Press. (Original work published 1899)

Weiner, B. (1995). *Judgments of responsibility*. New York, NY: Guilford Press.

Zenk, S. N., Schulz, A. J., Israel, B. A., James, S. A., Bao, S., & Wilson, M. L. (2005). Neighborhood racial composition, neighborhood poverty, and the spacial accessibility of supermarkets in metropolitan Detroit. *American Journal of Public Health, 95*, 660–667. doi:10.2105/AJPH.2004.042150

Zumbrun, J. (2008, November 24). America's best- and worst-educated cities. *Forbes*. Retrieved from http://www.forbes.com/2008/11/24/economics-education-colorado-biz-beltway-cx_jz_1124educated.html

4

REGIONAL CULTURE

JOSEPH A. VANDELLO, VANESSA E. HETTINGER,
AND KENNETH MICHNIEWICZ

If you have ever taken a road trip across the United States, you may
have noticed that just as the physical landscape can change dramatically
from Piedmont to plains to mountains, from open rural vistas to congested
urban freeways, the people—the psychological landscape—can vary from
region to region as well. Those raised in the Midwest are often taken aback
by the directness of those from the East Coast, who can at times seem intrusive or even rude; conversely, Easterners sometimes find Midwesterners frus-
tratingly obtuse. Southerners are renowned for their hospitality, those from
the Mountain West for their rugged individualism. Californians are typified
by their laid-back attitudes, New Englanders by their obdurate pragmatism.
Although some of the regional stereotypes are well-known enough to be
clichés, how much do they reflect real psychological differences versus superficial and perhaps exaggerated or inaccurate stereotypes?

http://dx.doi.org/10.1037/14274-004
Culture Reexamined: Broadening Our Understanding of Social and Evolutionary Influences,
A. B. Cohen (Editor)

In this chapter, we make the case for within-nation geographical region as an important but underappreciated unit of cultural variation with the potential to inform research in cultural psychology. Researchers have documented distinct regional cultures in many nations. For example, in relatively collectivist Japan, the northern island of Hokkaido is highly individualistic (Kitayama, Ishii, Imada, Takemura, & Ramaswamy, 2006), and southern Italy is more collectivistic than northern Italy (Putnam, 1994). Our focus is on regional cultural variation within the United States.

At first blush, it seems to go without saying that different geographical regions of the United States have different cultures. Regional variations in cuisines (think of the regional variations in barbeque or pizza), speech dialects, music, and pastimes are often pronounced. Are these merely superficial local variations in preferences that conceal deeper universals or do they reflect fundamental differences in the way people think? Do people from these different regions have different psychologies—that is, do they think about the world differently, operating under different norms, attitudes, and cognitive processes? If distinct regional psychologies exist (for which we make the case), how does geography shape psychology?

We begin by providing evidence from recent work in cultural psychology establishing that distinct regional cultures exist within the United States across attitudes, cognitions, well-being, and personality. We then speculate on some theoretical approaches that link ecologies to culture, showing how distinct regional cultures emerge, change, and persist. Next, we present some methodological and conceptual challenges to the study of regional culture. Finally, we speculate about the future of regional cultural differences within the United States and advocate for the continued development of a psychology of geographical regions as a valuable approach to cultural psychology.

EXAMPLES OF REGIONAL CULTURE WITHIN THE UNITED STATES

Evidence from a diverse body of research over the past 20 years has provided a picture of substantial regional variation within the United States across a number of psychological domains. Much of this research has focused on differences relating to the orientation of the self to others, both in general (e.g., individualism vs. collectivism) and more specifically (norms about honor and retribution). Still other research has focused on variations in intrapersonal qualities, such as personality and subjective well-being. Before reviewing this work, two points are important to emphasize. First, the various studies discussed here have characterized regions somewhat differently (e.g., Texas may accurately be classified as part of the South, the Southwest, or the West South

Central), which is to be expected because geographical regions have no firm borders but overlap. Second, regions that may be very similar on one dimension may be very different on another dimension. These two factors can make it difficult to pin down consistent psychological profiles of various regions.

Individualism and Collectivism

Within cultural psychology, perhaps the most important, and certainly the most widely studied, dimension of cultural variation is individualism versus collectivism. The United States is the prototypical individualist culture (Hofstede, 1980; Triandis, 1994), prioritizing an independent self, personal choice, autonomy, and uniqueness. Despite being at the far end of the individualism–collectivism dimension compared with other nations, substantial regional variation also exists within the United States. Vandello and Cohen (1999) examined regional differences in individualism and collectivism by creating a state-level collectivism index. They used data on family living arrangements (e.g., percentage of households with grandchildren in them, percentage of people living alone [reverse scored]), religion (e.g., percentage of people with no religious affiliation [reverse scored]), politics (e.g., percentage of people voting Libertarian [reverse scored]), and behaviors (e.g., percentage of people carpooling to work; percentage of self-employed workers [reverse scored]) to create an eight-item index on which higher scores reflect greater emphasis on collectivism and lower scores reflect greater individualism. What emerged was a map of distinct regional clustering. In general, southern states emerged as relatively collectivistic. After Hawaii, the most collectivist state, eight of the top 12 collectivist states were southern as defined by U.S. Census classification. The Great Plains and Mountain West were the most individualistic (Utah, with its unique Mormon culture, was a notable exception). States in the Great Lakes, Northeast, and Southwest tended to fall in between.

Vandello and Cohen's (1999) index correlated strongly with data from the National Election Survey measuring individualism, providing evidence of the index's validity. In addition, they used the index to test various hypotheses. For example, as predicted, individualism was associated with suicide and binge drinking but also with racial and gender equality. Collectivism was associated with poverty, population density, and ethnic diversity. Vandello and Cohen also tested some speculative hypotheses about the origins of individualism and collectivism using state-level historical records. For example, they predicted that the rise of the South's plantation economic system required large groups of field workers, social stratification, and hierarchy, conditions that should foster collectivism. Indeed, slavery (percentage of slaves per state) was associated with collectivism. In contrast, the prevalence of small homestead farms (typical of migrants to the Plains and West) correlated with individualism. Although caution must be taken in drawing causal conclusions from this type of correlational data, the data suggest a model linking historical ecological patterns to cultural outcomes, a topic we flesh out in more detail later in the chapter.

Other recent work has also linked state-level individualism and collectivism to various outcomes. For instance, Conway, Sexton, and Tweed (2006) explored the link between regional individualism and collectivism and government-initiated restrictions on daily life. Using Vandello and Cohen's (1999) state-level collectivism index, they tested for an association between individualism–collectivism and indices measuring the degree of government restrictions on individual freedoms. As predicted, relatively individualistic states were less accepting of government restrictions on daily life (e.g., gun prohibitions, sales taxes, speed limits). Presumably, individuals in more collectivistic states see legislation as an acceptable means of collective norms (rather than individual attitudes) guiding human behavior.

In other work, Conway, Ryder, Tweed, and Sokol (2001) linked state-level collectivism to pace of life and to helping. In the case of pace of life, they reasoned that collectivist states would focus more on affiliation than achievement and so would favor a more leisurely pace of life. Using creative behavioral measures of pace of life drawn from earlier work across U.S. cities by Levine and colleagues (Levine, Lynch, Miyake, & Lucia, 1989; Levine, Martinez, Brase, & Sorenson, 1994), Conway et al. found that collectivist regions did indeed have a slower pace of life, as reflected in behaviors such as walking and talking speeds and percentage of people wearing watches. Interestingly, the same focus on affiliation over achievement that promotes a more leisurely pace of life in collectivist regions may also stifle prosocial behavior. Regarding helping, they found that the helping of strangers (e.g., picking up a dropped pen, helping a blind person cross a street) was negatively associated with the U.S. collectivism index, a finding that makes sense when remembering that the strong social ties promoted by collectivism are usually reserved for a small ingroup of family members and close others. In fact, the sociologist Brent Simpson (2006) argued that collectivist value orientations promote high levels of mistrust. He found that the relatively collectivistic U.S. South is characterized by a poverty of trust that may impede civic engagement. Supporting this argument, Kemmelmeier, Jambor, and Letner (2006) also linked state-level individualism to prosocial behaviors such as volunteerism and charitable giving. Interestingly, and as one would expect, the link tends to be strongest for causes that are most compatible with individualistic values but not for religiously based charities.

Kemmelmeier, Wieczorkowska, Erb, and Burnstein (2002) also used Vandello and Cohen's (1999) state-level collectivism index to explore the link between individualism–collectivism and attitudes toward assisted suicide. Reasoning that individualism champions self-determination and the pursuit of self-interest, they predicted and found that regional levels of individualism were positively associated with patterns of support for assisted suicide.

Well-Being

Cultural work on subjective well-being has found various predictors of happiness that appear to be universal; however, predictors of happiness also have substantial cross-cultural variation (Diener & Suh, 2003; Oishi & Diener, 2003). Within the United States, Plaut, Markus, and Lachman (2002) examined a nationally representative survey to uncover shared features in the constitution of American well-being, as well as regional variations. They reasoned that given the high overall individualism of the United States (despite the regional variations in this variable explored in the previous section), wellness would generally be associated with the pursuit of autonomy and personal efficacy. However, given the different ecologies, histories, economies, and ethnic diversity of various regions, the specific route to well-being would also diverge in predictable ways.

Plaut et al. (2002) made several region-specific hypotheses about varieties of well-being, all of which received empirical support. For example, they found that New Englanders' relatively high social class and spirit of independence led to health- and autonomy-focused well-being. The well-being profile of those from the Mountain region emphasized personal autonomy and self-focus. The strong presence of Hispanic culture in the West South Central region emphasized emotion-focused well-being because Mexicans are socialized to express positive affect and suppress negative affect (Triandis, Marin, Lisansky, & Bettancourt, 1984). The profile of the West North Central region, sometimes thought of as the Heartland or America's breadbasket, is that of hardworking, stable people who prefer a simple life. Not surprisingly, elements of well-being such as self-acceptance and self-satisfaction, as well as feeling peaceful and calm, characterized the region. The East South Central, with its relatively high poverty and high collectivism, focused on social responsibility and contributing to the welfare of others. In short, Plaut et al. found that just as regional variation exists in objective measures of well-being (e.g., health, poverty), somewhat distinct regional profiles of subjective well-being also appear to exist.

Honor and Retribution

Sociologists, historians, and cultural anthropologists have long noted disproportionate violence in the South (and, to a lesser extent, in the West) compared with the rest of the country. Researchers have proposed many theories to explain this, ranging from the hot climate to poverty to its defeat in the Civil War. Within psychology, Nisbett and Cohen (1996) proposed that the South's cultural emphasis on honor best explained greater Southern violence. A concern with honor (of self, family, and property) and its defense historically and currently is more central to the ideology of the South and West than to that of the rest of the country. Nisbett, Cohen, and their colleagues have conducted a wide-ranging program of research using multiple methods in support of this theory. Evidence from surveys has indicated that Southerners are more approving than non-Southerners of honor-related violence (Cohen & Nisbett, 1994). Laboratory experiments and fields studies have shown evidence of greater retaliatory aggression after insult and support for such violence (Cohen & Nisbett, 1997; Cohen, Nisbett, Bowdle, & Schwarz, 1996; Cohen, Vandello, Puente, & Rantilla, 1999). Analyses of laws and social policies have indicated that Southern and Western states more strongly endorse capital punishment violence for protection of self and property, and aggressive foreign policy (Cohen, 1996). In short, considerable evidence has suggested that Southerners and Westerners place a greater emphasis on personal reputation and respect and endorse violence in defense of reputation to a greater extent than people in other U.S. regions. In the coming pages, we present some theories about how these differences originated and why they persist.

Personality Trait Profiles

Evidence for distinct regional personality profiles has come from recent work by Rentfrow, Gosling, and Potter (2008). They created state personality profiles on the basis of survey data from a large sample of U.S. residents, using the Big Five Inventory of personality (John & Srivastava, 1999). The data yielded several noteworthy findings. For example, New Yorkers are less warm and dutiful but more high strung and creative than the rest of the country. North Dakotans score the highest in Agreeableness and Extraversion. New Mexicans are the most Conscientious, and West Virginians score highest in Neuroticism. By mapping the state-level scores on each of the five personality factors, Rentfrow et al. were able to uncover some clear geographical clustering. For example, Extraversion was highest in the Midwest, Great Plains, and Southern states; Neuroticism was highest in the Northeast and Southeast; and Openness tended to be highest on the coasts.

In addition, Rentfrow et al. (2008) used state-level scores on the personality traits to predict corresponding behavioral outcomes. For instance, Extraversion was associated with social activities such as attending club meetings, spending time in bars, and entertaining guests at home. Agreeableness was negatively related to crimes such as robbery and homicide. Conscientiousness was associated with religiosity.

The work reviewed in this section highlights the potential for research using regional cultures to test theory-based predictions. Within a single nation, evidence has demonstrated a great deal of variance in psychological profiles across geographical regions.

PROCESSES THAT CREATE AND MAINTAIN REGIONAL CULTURE

In the previous section, we presented a sampling of evidence for regional cultures within the United States. We turn now to a discussion of processes that might give rise to and sustain regional variation. Several theories have emerged to explain processes of cultural evolution, change, and persistence.

One perspective recognizes the importance of ecological factors in shaping the emergence and persistence of human culture (Berry, 1979; Oishi & Graham 2010; Triandis, 1994). According to these theories, features of the physical environment (e.g., climate, amount of daylight, terrain, availability of resources) can influence the psychological characteristics of people living in these contexts. Thus, for example, U.S. regional economies that required large-scale cooperation (e.g., Southern plantations) developed norms for greater collectivism, unlike economies less dependent on cooperation (e.g., small homestead farms of the Plains; Vandello & Cohen, 1999). One must be cautious when making causal claims from historical data, however. For example, although Vandello and Cohen (1999) found that the historical presence of large-scale cooperative plantations in the South was associated with present-day collectivism, this account is difficult to reconcile with research reviewed earlier showing that collectivism in the South is associated with mistrust and lack of civic engagement (Kemmelmeier et al., 2006; Simpson, 2006).

Other recent theories have emphasized migration and residential mobility in creating cultures (Kitayama & Bowman, 2009; Kitayama et al., 2006; Oishi, 2010). Migration and mobility are nonrandom. That is, certain types of people choose to migrate, and these people carry with them distinct attitudes, values, and personality profiles that are likely shared by similar others who migrate to the same places. This clustering of like-minded individuals can create and reinforce regional cultures in two ways. First, it creates a restricted gene pool from which further generations of genetically similar people reproduce. Second, it creates an environment that reinforces distinct psychological characteristics through social influence and the development of shared norms (see Rentfrow et al., 2008).

This idea is developed most fully in Kitayama, Conway, Pietromonaco, Park, and Plaut's (2010) production–adoption model. Kitayama, Varnum, and Sevincer provide a fuller description of the model in Chapter 5 of this volume, so we note its relevance to regional cultures within the United States only briefly. The model argues that frontier conditions—that is, harsh, sparsely populated environments—produce a mind-set of individualism. This mind-set may in turn get romanticized and adopted by residents in more developed regions. Oishi (2010) made a similar argument about residential mobility. He provided evidence that in places to which a high percentage of people have moved, the personal self is given primacy over the collective self. Friendships in these areas of high mobility tend to be "duty-free" and transitory. Residential mobility is associated with lower well-being overall, and well-being in these areas tends to derive from personal attributes such as self-esteem and self-verification rather than interpersonal processes such as social support. A focus on residential mobility may have particular relevance to those regions of the United States that have experienced high rates of migration in recent years (e.g., the South and Southwest).

Once cultural norms develop, they can reproduce, spread, and receive reinforcement through several processes. Dynamic social impact theory (Harton & Bullock, 2007; Latané, 1996) describes how social influence processes create geographical clustering of attitudes and norms through communication and socialization. This bottom-up approach emphasizes how microlevel processes at the interpersonal level (e.g., group polarization, conformity, emotional contagion) can produce local or regional cultures.

Individuals who live in close proximity and routinely interact with each other are more likely to influence each other than those who live further apart. Over time, these repeated interactions create regional clustering of attitudes and reduction in attitude variance (consolidation).

Vandello and Cohen (2004) proposed a general four-stage model of cultural evolution and perpetuation that incorporates many of the preceding ideas. In the first (behavioral) stage, behaviors arise as adaptive responses to the physical and social environments. For example, on the Southern frontier, without adequate law enforcement and in herding-based economies, residents adopted prickly stances that made it clear that theft or violations of one's property or family would not be tolerated. In the second (meaning) stage, cultural norms develop in support of these functional behaviors. People communicate norms about the importance of personal honor, which become socialized and imbued with cultural meaning. In the third (internalization) stage, behaviors may lose their adaptive value because of changes (ecological, economic, or demographic) in the environment. However, because the norms have become part of automatic scripts, they may persist. For instance, although the South is no longer a herding-based frontier region, norms about honor have become deeply embedded into the psyche of Southerners and remain. Internalization of norms may also eventually fade, but norms may persist in a fourth (compliance) stage, creating a type of cultural lag. Thus, among present-day Southern males, college men appear no more endorsing of violence in response to insults than their Northern counterparts; however, Southerners mistakenly believe that their peers approve of violence more than they do, a misconception Northerners do not share, and they may behave aggressively to conform to these mistaken norms (Vandello, Cohen, & Ransom, 2008). More generally, this model provides a mechanism for how psychological or behavioral differences may stubbornly persist in the face of external change, even in the absence of strongly internalized regional differences in values or attitudes.

ISSUES AND CHALLENGES IN STUDYING REGIONAL CULTURE

Although the use of geographical regions in cultural psychology provides opportunities, it also presents both methodological and conceptual challenges.

Studies of regional variation are usually not true experiments. One cannot manipulate region, and thus studies comparing regions are typically quasi-experiments. This circumstance is not unique to the study of regional culture; indeed, most cultural psychological research is correlational, which can complicate causal claims and raises the issue of whether any observed regional differences are the result of culture or some demographic variable such as socioeconomic status, racial diversity, religious composition, rural versus urban populations, and so on. Thus, the fact that regions tend to differ on these variables complicates the study of region as culture, and these things (rather than regional culture per se) could account for regional differences. There are no foolproof solutions, but being aware of this issue and using solid methodology are essential.

Statistically controlling for other variables can help to tease out the various contributors to regional differences, but it is an imperfect solution, partly because, even with statistical controls, one cannot establish strong causal conclusions with correlational data and, more important, because these various demographic variables are culture, and simply statistically controlling for them in regional comparisons runs the risk of removing what creates culture in the first place. To say that Southerners are more religious than Westerners or that those on the East Coast are more urban and ethnically diverse than those in the Midwest is to make a statement about the cultures of these regions.

Ideally, one can conduct controlled laboratory experiments in which the researcher manipulates the hypothesized cultural variable of interest (e.g., priming individualism or collectivism). In lieu of manipulations, collecting data on as many of the relevant demographic variables as possible will at least help to tease apart their various influences. Using multiregion (more than two) samples can also help to address the possibility that some demographic variable unique to a single region accounts for a difference. Ultimately, multistudy/multimethod approaches will yield the most robust conclusions.

In the foregoing paragraphs, we discussed the methodological challenges of investigating the cultural psychology of regions, but conceptual difficulties exist as well. For instance, a fundamental issue is defining the boundaries of a region. Researchers often choose some established (but perhaps fairly arbitrary) definition, such as census bureau classifications. This may work well enough, just as treating nations as cultures may work, but formal boundaries usually emerge for reasons other than culture. Alternatively, researchers may want to let the data guide them, but this places them in danger of making a circular argument. For example, a researcher may explore whether the South is more violent than the North by looking at state-level homicide data. She or he may wonder whether Kentucky should be considered a Southern state and note that its murder rate is higher than average, thus classifying it as Southern. Of course, this logic is flawed—it may be true that Southern states are more violent, but the classification of a state as Southern should be independent of the outcome of interest. To guard against this, researchers should classify their regions a priori with strong theoretical reasoning. For example, in Vandello and Cohen's (1999) study of regional patterns of individualism and collectivism in the United States, they predicted that the Mountain West would be relatively individualistic. However, given Utah's unique history and predominantly Mormon population, they also predicted that it would be much more collectivistic than its neighbors, a prediction borne out by the data.

Another conceptual problem when studying regional cultures is the chicken–egg issue: Do regional ecologies create cultures, or do like-minded people with similar attitudes, values, and personalities migrate to similar regions? The answer is probably both, because regions both create and reinforce cultural identities. Indeed, some theorists have developed models that explicitly propose bidirectional causality (Oishi & Graham, 2010; Rentfrow et al., 2008), which again speaks to the limitations of correlational research, which can be partially addressed through multiple methods (experimental and longitudinal designs) as well as strong theoretical models. Ultimately, the study of regional culture, and culture more generally, requires sensitivity to the fact that geography and individual psychological tendencies mutually constitute and reinforce each other in complex ways.

LOOKING AHEAD

In an age of increasing interconnectedness and homogenization through national and international corporations, chain stores, shared media, quick and easy transportation, and increasing migration, characteristics that were once uniquely identified with distinct regions (e.g., Southerners' love of country music and NASCAR, Californians' preference for organic health food) have gone mainstream. One might expect that regional variation will decrease or disappear in the near future. In fact, some have challenged the notion of geographically localized culture given increasing globalization and interconnectedness (Hermans & Kempen, 1998). When cultures intersect and blend together, regional geography should be less important as a marker of cultural identity. However, the eminent cultural geographer Walter Zelinsky (1992) chronicled the various geographical cultures within the United States and argued that regional consciousness and affinity for one's particular geographical area were alive and well and showed no signs of disappearing. Although it is impossible to say with any certainty how important geographical region will be in the future, two psychological mechanisms argue for the continued importance of region at the psychological level.

First, evidence has suggested that when important aspects of a person's identity (including cultural identity) disappear or are threatened, there is often pushback. Optimal distinctiveness theory (Brewer, 1991, 2003) asserts that people seek an optimal balance of opposing needs for assimilation and differentiation from others. People will avoid seeing themselves as either too unique from others or too similar, instead opting to define themselves in ways that strike a balance. Thus, we might predict that the homogenization of culture across regions will be experienced as threatening a valued group identity. People may feel the strongest identification with those self-categorizations that simultaneously provide a sense of regional belonging and a sense of distinctiveness from other regions.

Another force working against the blending of regional culture is inertia. Cultural norms can be stubborn, perpetuating for generations beyond the point of being functional (see the earlier discussion of Vandello and Cohen's, 2004, model of cultural evolution). One psychological process that can perpetuate even outdated or unpopular cultural norms is pluralistic ignorance (Miller & Prentice, 1994; Vandello et al., 2008). When individuals mistakenly assume that they are alone in their opinions and beliefs, they may feel compelled to go along with a norm assumed to be favored by others. As an example, racial segregation in the South probably persisted for years beyond the point at which most Southern Whites privately ceased supporting it, simply because they mistakenly believed it had widespread support among their peers (O'Gorman, 1975). Similarly, as detailed earlier, the Southern culture of honor continues despite the fact that the conditions that gave rise to it no longer exist. It may be driven in part by the mistaken belief that other Southerners endorse honor-protecting violence (Vandello et al., 2008).

In short, although there are influences that signal transformation (including large migrations from the Midwest and Rust Belt to the South and Southwest and immigration from Latin American and Asian countries), regional culture may be quite resistant to change.

CONCLUSION

In this chapter, we have presented evidence that within-nation geographical regions can be effectively examined for cultural psychological differences; however, regional cultures remain a largely unstudied area. For those researchers intimidated by the many challenges of cross-cultural research, studying regions presents several advantages and opportunities. From a methodological perspective, using within-nation regions helps to eliminate or minimize some of the challenges of finding comparable cross-cultural samples. For instance, cross-national cultural studies must often use samples that vary dramatically in language, economic prosperity, education, and other variables that are incidental to the cultural variables of interest. Focusing on regions within nations can mitigate the variance on these variables, helping to rule out rival hypotheses, or at least permit the use of a standardized set of materials across groups. In addition, a focus on regions often makes possible a sample size that would be difficult to achieve in a traditional cross-national sample. For example, an ambitious cross-national study may include samples from six or even a dozen countries (and materials might require translation into a different language for each sample). In contrast, many of the regional cultural studies described in this chapter used data from each of the United States, allowing for a sample size of 50 when the states are the unit of analysis. With a sample of this size, moderate-sized relationships will be statistically significant.

Perhaps one of the most important advantages of a psychology of geographical region is that such a focus reminds researchers that using broad labels such as *American culture* obscures significant regional variation. This is not to say that nations cannot be perfectly adequate units of analysis in cultural investigations. However, unpacking nations into smaller meaningful aggregates can yield important insights. We are excited by the increased attention given to geographical region in recent years, and we suspect many further insights await.

REFERENCES

Berry, J. W. (1979). A cultural ecology of social behavior. In L. Berkowitz (Ed.), *Advances in experimental social psychology* (Vol. 12, pp. 177–207). New York, NY: Academic Press.

Brewer, M. B. (1991). The social self: On being the same and different at the same time. *Personality and Social Psychology Bulletin, 17,* 475–482. doi:10.1177/0146167291175001

Brewer, M. B. (2003). Optimal distinctiveness, social identity, and the self. In M. Leary & J. Tangney (Eds.), *Handbook of self and identity* (pp. 480–491). New York, NY: Guilford Press.

Cohen, D. (1996). Law, social policy, and violence: The impact of regional cultures. *Journal of Personality and Social Psychology, 70,* 961–978. doi:10.1037/0022-3514.70.5.961

Cohen, D., & Nisbett, R. E. (1994). Self-protection and the culture of honor: Explaining Southern violence. *Personality and Social Psychology Bulletin, 20,* 551–567. doi:10.1177/0146167294205012

Cohen, D., & Nisbett, R. E. (1997). Field experiments examining the culture of honor: The role of institutions in perpetuating norms about violence. *Personality and Social Psychology Bulletin, 23,* 1188–1199. doi:10.1177/01461672972311006

Cohen, D., Nisbett, R. E., Bowdle, B. F., & Schwarz, N. (1996). Insult, aggression, and the southern culture of honor: An "experimental ethnography." *Journal of Personality and Social Psychology, 70,* 945–959. doi:10.1037/0022-3514.70.5.945

Cohen, D., Vandello, J. A., Puente, S., & Rantilla, A. K. (1999). "When you call me that, smile!" How norms for politeness, interaction styles, and aggression work together in Southern culture. *Social Psychology Quarterly, 62,* 257–275. doi:10.2307/2695863

Conway, L. G., III, Ryder, A. G., Tweed, R. G., & Sokol, B. W. (2001). Intranational cultural variation: Exploring further implications within the United States. *Journal of Cross-Cultural Psychology, 32,* 681–697. doi:10.1177/0022022101032006003

Conway, L. G., III, Sexton, S. M., & Tweed, R. G. (2006). Collectivism and governmentally initiated restrictions: A cross-sectional and longitudinal analysis across nations and within a nation. *Journal of Cross-Cultural Psychology, 37,* 20–41. doi:10.1177/0022022105282293

Diener, E., & Suh, E. M. (Eds.). (2003). *Culture and subjective well-being.* Boston, MA: MIT Press.

Harton, H. C., & Bullock, M. (2007). Dynamic social impact: A theory of the origins and evolution of culture. *Social and Personality Psychology Compass, 1,* 521–540. doi:10.1111/j.1751-9004.2007.00022.x

Hermans, H. J. M., & Kempen, H. J. G. (1998). Moving cultures: Perilous problems of cultural dichotomies in a globalizing society. *American Psychologist, 53,* 1111–1120. doi:10.1037/0003-066X.53.10.1111

Hofstede, G. (1980). *Culture's consequences.* Beverly Hills, CA: Sage.

John, O. P., & Srivastava, S. (1999). The Big Five trait taxonomy: History, measurement, and theoretical perspectives. In L. A. Pervin & O. P. John (Eds.), *Handbook of personality: Theory and research* (2nd ed., pp. 102–138). New York, NY: Guilford Press.

Kemmelmeier, M., Jambor, E., & Letner, J. (2006). Individualism and good works: Cultural variation in giving and volunteering across the United States. *Journal of Cross-Cultural Psychology, 37,* 327–344. doi:10.1177/0022022106286927

Kemmelmeier, M., Wieczorkowska, G., Erb, H.-P., & Burnstein, E. (2002). Individualism, authoritarianism and attitudes toward assisted death: Cross-cultural, cross-regional and experimental evidence. *Journal of Applied Social Psychology, 32,* 60–85. doi:10.1111/j.1559-1816.2002.tb01420.x

Kitayama, S., & Bowman, N. A. (2009). Cultural consequences of voluntary settlement in the frontier: Evidence and implications. In M. Schaller, A. Norenzayan, S. Heine, T. Yamagishi, & T. Kameda (Eds.), *Evolution, culture, and the human mind* (pp. 205–227). New York, NY: Psychology Press.

Kitayama, S., Conway, L. G., Pietromonaco, P. R., Park, H., & Plaut, V. C. (2010). Ethos of independence across regions in the United States: The production-adoption model of cultural change. *American Psychologist, 65,* 559–574. doi:10.1037/a0020277

Kitayama, S., Ishii, K., Imada, T., Takemura, K., & Ramaswamy, J. (2006). Voluntary settlement and the spirit of independence: Evidence from Japan's "northern frontier." *Journal of Personality and Social Psychology, 91,* 369–384. doi:10.1037/0022-3514.91.3.369

Latané, B. (1996). Dynamic social impact: The creation of culture by communication. *Journal of Communication, 46,* 13–25. doi:10.1111/j.1460-2466.1996.tb01501.x

Levine, R. V., Lynch, K., Miyake, K., & Lucia, M. (1989). The type A city: Coronary heart disease and the pace of life. *Journal of Behavioral Medicine, 12,* 509–524. doi:10.1007/BF00844822

Levine, R. V., Martinez, T. S., Brase, G., & Sorenson, K. (1994). Helping in 36 U.S. cities. *Journal of Personality and Social Psychology, 67,* 69–82. doi:10.1037/0022-3514.67.1.69

Miller, D. T., & Prentice, D. A. (1994). Collective errors and errors about the collective. *Personality and Social Psychology Bulletin, 20,* 541–550. doi:10.1177/0146167294205011

Nisbett, R. E., & Cohen, D. (1996). *Culture of honor.* Boulder, CO: Westview Press.

O'Gorman, H. (1975). Pluralistic ignorance and White estimates of White support for racial segregation. *Public Opinion Quarterly, 39,* 313–30.

Oishi, S. (2010). The psychology of residential mobility: Implications for the self, social relationships, and well-being. *Perspectives on Psychological Science, 5,* 5–21. doi:10.1177/1745691609356781

Oishi, S., & Diener, E. (2003). Culture and well-being: The cycle of action, evaluation and decision. *Personality and Social Psychology Bulletin, 29,* 939–949. doi:10.1177/0146167203252802

Oishi, S., & Graham, J. (2010). Social ecology: Lost and found in psychological science. *Perspectives on Psychological Science, 5*, 356–377. doi:10.1177/1745691610374588

Plaut, V. C., Markus, H. R., & Lachman, M. E. (2002). Place matters: Consensual features and regional variation in American well-being and self. *Journal of Personality and Social Psychology, 83*, 160–184. doi:10.1037/0022-3514.83.1.160

Putnam, R. D. (1994). *Making democracy work: Civic traditions in modern Italy*. Princeton, NJ: Princeton University Press.

Rentfrow, P. J., Gosling, S. D., & Potter, J. (2008). A theory of the emergence, persistence, and expression of geographic variation in psychological characteristics. *Perspectives on Psychological Science, 3*, 339–369. doi:10.1111/j.1745-6924.2008.00084.x

Simpson, B. (2006). The poverty of trust in the southern United States. *Social Forces, 84*, 1625–1638. doi:10.1353/sof.2006.0066

Triandis, H. C. (1994). *Culture and social behavior*. New York, NY: McGraw-Hill.

Triandis, H. C., Marin, G., Lisansky, J., & Bettancourt, H. (1984). *Simpatia* as a cultural script of Hispanics. *Journal of Personality and Social Psychology, 47*, 1363–1375. doi:10.1037/0022-3514.47.6.1363

Vandello, J. A., & Cohen, D. (1999). Patterns of individualism and collectivism across the United States. *Journal of Personality and Social Psychology, 77*, 279–292. doi:10.1037/0022-3514.77.2.279

Vandello, J. A., & Cohen, D. (2004). When believing is seeing: Sustaining norms of violence in cultures of honor. In M. Schaller & C. Crandall (Eds.), *The psychological foundations of culture* (pp. 281–304). New York, NY: Erlbaum.

Vandello, J. A., Cohen, D., & Ransom, S. (2008). U.S. Southern and Northern differences in perceptions of norms about aggression: Mechanisms for the perpetuation of a culture of honor. *Journal of Cross-Cultural Psychology, 39*, 162–177. doi:10.1177/0022022107313862

Zelinsky, W. (1992). *The cultural geography of the United States*. New York, NY: Prentice Hall.

5

FRONTIER SETTLEMENT AND CULTURAL CHANGE

SHINOBU KITAYAMA, MICHAEL E. W. VARNUM,
AND A. TIMUR SEVINCER

Innovations and inventions, whether in technology, in science, or in business—or more generally, as we argue in this chapter, in culture—involve the active production of new ideas, as well as the effort to make them work and to promote them so that they are successful. These efforts can eventually lead to payoffs in economic, political, and symbolic terms. If these ideas are successful economically, politically, and symbolically, then they are likely to be adopted by many other people and thus become widely disseminated. Equally important, however, is that any serious innovation or invention entails a variety of risks. The new ideas may not work. The technologies or novel business models may not receive much support from consumers, colleagues, or fellow group members. One may go bankrupt or have one's reputation tarnished. Because of these risks, people who are highly successful in

We thank Keiko Ishii and Kosuke Takemura for their helpful comments on an earlier version of this chapter. The writing of this chapter was supported by National Science Foundation Grant BCS 0717982 and National Institute on Aging Grant RO1 AG029500-01.

http://dx.doi.org/10.1037/14274-005
Culture Reexamined: Broadening Our Understanding of Social and Evolutionary Influences,
A. B. Cohen (Editor)

the mainstream may have little incentive to try out anything that is radically new. Moreover, their mode of thinking may be so entrenched in old, existing ways of thought that it may well be very hard for them to think in new ways. All innovations and inventions may then be expected to emerge in the periphery of any given domain under consideration.

In the domain of business, for example, firms that are highly successful with major technologies or business models often fail to catch up to innovations that arise elsewhere. For example, up until the 1980s and even into the 1990s, Kodak and Sony were at the cutting edge in the areas of camera film and music players, respectively. However, in the past decade or so these companies have undergone severe setbacks caused by new technologies and emerging cultural trends. These latter technologies and cultural trends are what define the completely new, emerging standards. Similar considerations apply to the history of psychology. For example, the new ideas that formed the cognitive revolution in the 1950s came not from psychology itself but from the neighboring fields of linguistics and computer science. Looking at social psychology—the subdiscipline that requires careful and astute observations of daily social life—it is evident that many of the early pioneers, such as Muzafer Sherif, Fritz Heider, and Kurt Lewin, were all immigrants from Europe (Sherif from Turkey, Heider from Austria, and Lewin from Germany). As immigrants, these scholars were not fully embedded in the mainstream of U.S. society. As a result, they may well have been freer in their thinking, more open to new possibilities, and more willing to take chances to see whether their innovative ideas might work. More generally, much of innovation in both science and technology in the previous century occurred in the United States. It is probably no coincidence that the United States happened to be a country that had been relatively recently established by voluntary settlers.

Our goal in this chapter is to explore the idea that voluntary immigration to and subsequent settlement in the frontier is linked to the ethos of independence. This thesis has been examined under the rubric of the voluntary settlement hypothesis (e.g., Kitayama, Conway, Pietromonaco, Park, & Plaut, 2010). We use *frontier* as a term that broadly encompasses all geographic regions (e.g., Western states in the 18th century United States) and spheres of human activity (e.g., cutting-edge science, technology, fashion, art) that are at the periphery of existing social entities such as existing countries or regions (and the values, practices, and ways of thinking that are common to them), as well as the conventions and common practices in given technological and business circles. By *ethos*, we mean a complex of beliefs, values, and practices that as a whole is grounded in certain key ontological ideas and ultimate values such as freedom, community, purity, democracy, and the like. The *ethos of independence*, then, is defined by a complex of meanings and practices that are based on independence as a value and ultimate goal.

This chapter consists of four main parts. First, we consider contemporary U.S. culture through the theoretical lens of the voluntary settlement hypothesis. We evaluate the merit of the hypothesis by examining existing survey research and cross-cultural experimental findings as well as census data with respect to cross-cultural variations. Second, we apply a comparable analysis to within-U.S. regional variations. Third, we turn to Japan and examine its northern island, Hokkaido, which has a settlement history that is analogous to that of the United States—particularly the Western frontier of the United States. As such, Hokkaido provides an extremely important test case of the voluntary settlement hypothesis.

Fourth, we switch gears and argue that especially in the 21st century, the frontier in science, fashion, art, and business has come to increasingly be defined vis-à-vis human activities within a respective domain of technology, art, or business. We argue that cosmopolitan city centers (e.g., Berlin, London, New York) constitute one prominent case of this sort. Such city centers embrace a wide range of activities, including not only those that may best be seen as the mainstream of the society at large but also those that do not fit neatly into the existing cultural models—activities that are more experimental, unconventional, even countercultural and avant garde in both the spirit of the people who engage in them and the outputs they generate. In other words, these latter aspects of city centers are analogous to the geographical frontiers that existed historically. Those frontierlike elements are much rarer, if not completely absent, in more rural and provincial areas. We thus hypothesize that settlement in cosmopolitan cities is likely to be linked to independence. After examining these three domains of empirical work, we conclude the chapter by suggesting some new future directions for research.

VOLUNTARY SETTLEMENT AND THE CONTEMPORARY UNITED STATES

How can one define the American mentality? In the beginning of the 19th century, Alexis de Tocqueville, the French historian and diplomat, toured the United States and left behind a rich array of observations that illustrate how the society he saw there was strikingly different from his native France in terms of its passion for equality and freedom. For example, he noted, "Democracy [which is taking roots in America] seeks equality in liberty" (de Tocqueville, 1864, p. 546). He contrasted this idea of equality with equality that is guaranteed by "restraint and servitude" (p. 546), which he attributed to socialism. At the same time, de Tocqueville (1862/1969) also identified Christianity as the central moral or spiritual guiding force in the new continent. In another section of the book, de Tocqueville (1862/1969) stated,

"All the sects of the United States are comprised within the great unity of Christianity, and Christian morality is everywhere the same" (p. 359).

In short, de Tocqueville (1862/1969) highlighted both individualism (equality and freedom) and religiosity as fundamental constitutive facets of U.S. society—a point that is very much consistent with a recent observation by Cohen, Hall, Koenig, and Meador (2005). Cohen et al. contended that the notion of religiosity as intrinsically and personally motivated and as separate from social, extrinsic forces is uniquely individualistic. Far from being universal, this idea is linked most closely to Protestant denominations in the United States (see also Li et al., 2012). Indeed, in recent decades, social and behavioral science research has recapitulated this same theme by noting the remarkable degree to which Americans as a whole are both highly individualistic and religious.

Explicit Independence

Traditionally, social scientists have used survey methods to investigate cultural values. By examining responses to questions designed to assess values, they have examined how cultures and societies may vary in explicit endorsement of various values.

Explicit Values Across the World

One important source of insight into the nature of contemporary U.S. culture comes from the World Value Survey (e.g., Inglehart & Baker, 2000). On the basis of a comprehensive survey covering more than 60 countries, Inglehart and Baker (2000) identified two value dimensions. One is a dimension defined by traditional versus secular values. Items defining this dimension include "God is very important in my life" and "I favor more respect to authority." Affirmative answers to these items define traditional values, and negative answers define secular values. Another of the two dimensions that were identified in the survey is the dimension of survival versus self-expression values. Items defining this dimension include "I give priority to economic and physical security over self-expression and quality of life" and "You have to be very careful trusting other people." Affirmative answers to these items define survival values, and negative answers define self-expression values.

Figure 5.1 illustrates the pertinent results (Inglehart & Baker, 2000). Country means are computed for each of the two dimensions and plotted in a two-dimensional space. It is evident that poor countries in South Asia, Africa, and Latin America tend to occupy the quadrant defined by traditional and survival values. Ex-communist countries tend to be quite secular and yet survival oriented, reflecting the fact that many of these countries faced (and still

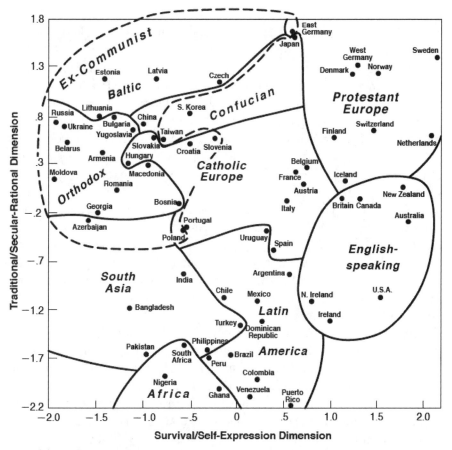

Figure 5.1. Locations of 65 societies on two dimensions of traditionalism versus secularism and survival versus self-expression orientation. From "Modernization, Cultural Change, and the Persistence of Traditional Values," by R. F. Inglehart and W. E. Baker, 2000, *American Sociological Review, 65,* p. 29. Copyright 2000 by the American Sociological Association. Adapted with permission.

do face) enormous economic challenges. Asian Confucian societies are similarly secular, and yet they are substantially less survival oriented, more strongly endorsing self-expression values. Western European countries, especially those with Protestant traditions, strongly endorse both secular values and self-expression values. Relative to Protestant Europe, Western European countries with Catholic traditions are substantially less oriented toward self-expression values, and in this regard they are similar to Confucian Asia.

It is notable that within this schema, the United States is an outlier. It is quite high in self-expression values—as high as its Western European cousins. However, it is extremely low in secular values or, conversely, rather high in traditional and largely religious values. As Inglehart and Baker (2000) themselves noted, "The United States seems to be a deviant case. . . . Its people hold more traditional values and beliefs than any equally prosperous society" (p. 49).

It makes sense that economic development and prosperity essentially erase any values placed on survival concerns. Instead, people in prosperous countries tend to emphasize happiness, life satisfaction, and expressiveness of the self. Another overall trend is that as a function of economic prosperity, people tend to be less traditional and more secular. However, herein lies a paradox of American exceptionalism. Why is the most prosperous country in the world so traditional and religious—forming a clear exception to the general trend toward secularism?

It may be the case that traditional values in general and religious values in particular tend to be endorsed more under conditions of ontological threat. In support of this analysis, Inglehart and Baker (2000) documented that a substantial increase in traditionalism in general, and religiosity in particular, occurred after the collapse of the Soviet Union in most countries in Eastern Europe. Various threats that caused fundamental insecurity in meaning, values, and national defense may have caused this systematic cultural change. In this regard, it is important to bear in mind that the United States has a long history of massive immigration and settlement over the course of its establishment as a nation and that it has undergone territorial expansion over the course of several hundred years. Insofar as frontier environments are replete with a variety of threats that endanger one's basic sense of security, the history of settlement might be crucial in understanding the extraordinarily high levels of religiosity evident in the contemporary United States.

For the purposes of this chapter, the World Value Survey has one important limitation. It does not focus on independence per se. Although self-expression values are likely to form a facet of independence, these values are defined primarily in terms of reduced needs for survival and increased desires for better life in general and self-expression in particular. For this reason, one might expect that nations will tend to be high on self-expression as long as they are prosperous regardless of whether they value equality, freedom, and other values that are linked to independence, and it may explain why East Asian countries are just as high in self-expression values as are some Western European countries (see Figure 5.1).

Explicit Attitude Toward Independence and Interdependence

Over the past 2 decades or so, many cross-cultural psychologists have used measures of independent versus interdependent self-construal (Singelis, 1994) or, correspondingly, measures of individualism versus collectivism (Triandis & Gelfand, 1998) to see whether the country means of attitudes toward these two values or value clusters might vary systematically. One problem with existing scales of independence versus interdependence is that these scales have very few reverse-coded items. Hence, interdependence is nearly completely confounded with acquiescence (Schimmack, Oishi, & Diener, 2005). Although acquiescence itself could be an integral part of interdependence (or collectivism; Smith & Fischer, 2008), this fact still raises concerns and should call for caution in interpreting results using these measures. Nevertheless, the emerging pattern is still informative.

About a decade ago, Oyserman, Coon, and Kemmelmeier (2002) reviewed existing data that were based on the scales of independence versus interdependence (or individualism vs. collectivism). The results were twofold. First, when global regions of the world were considered as a whole, collapsing all data across individual studies conducted within each region, the results were highly systematic. As shown in Figure 5.2, North America (including both the United States and Canada) is the most independent region and the least collectivistic. Second, however, this conclusion was mitigated by the fact that substantial within-region variation was present. Thus, the effect sizes associated with the comparisons of cultural regions were often small.

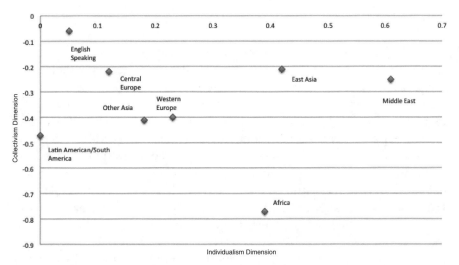

Figure 5.2. Relative locations of major world regions (vis-à-vis North America, including both the United States and Canada) on the dimensions of individualism (or independence) and collectivism (or interdependence). Positive scores on the individualism dimension (*x*-axis) mean less individualism indicated by survey responses from primarily college student samples, and negative scores on the collectivism dimension (*y*-axis) mean more collectivism. From "Rethinking Individualism and Collectivism: Evaluation of Theoretical Assumptions and Meta-Analyses," by D. Oyserman, H. M. Coon, and M. Kemmelmeier, 2002, *Psychological Bulletin, 128,* p. 23. Copyright 2002 by the American Psychological Association.

In understanding why cultural variations are quite systematic and yet can appear rather weak, it is important to note that when reporting their own attitudes, participants are likely to use their knowledge about others as a reference point, which means that in judging whether they are independent (or interdependent), people will use the average level of independence (or interdependence) within their culture as an anchor and will judge whether they are more or less independent (or interdependent) relative to this anchor (Heine, Lehman, Peng, & Greenholtz, 2002). Note that people in any given cultural group are likely to use people in their own group, especially when their group is geographically separated from other cultural groups (as in Japan in comparison with, say, the United States). If reference group effects are strong, they can eliminate all cultural variation in the mean country levels of independence or interdependence. Although the fact that global cultural variation arises when a large amount of data are collapsed shows that a real cultural difference is likely to exist, the present consideration implies that a substantial amount of noise should stem from idiosyncratic and cross-culturally disparate choices of reference groups. In part to address this concern, researchers have examined more implicit forms of independence and interdependence and sought to determine whether clearer cultural differences might be observed.

Implicit Independence

Implicit independence (or interdependence) implies a style of cognition, emotion, and motivation that is grounded in the corresponding value of independence (or interdependence). When certain values (e.g., independence or interdependence) predominate in a given region over a reasonably extended period of time, these values are used to generate a variety of behavioral routines, conventions, and scripts or, simply, cultural practices. Once born into the cultural world composed of, or constituted by, these practices, people necessarily perform these practices again and again, insofar as these practices define the way of life within their cultural world. Kitayama and colleagues (Kitayama, Park, Sevincer, Karasawa, & Uskal, 2009; Kitayama & Uskul, 2011) have pointed out that repeated engagement in cultural practices is likely to foster a variety of psychological processes including cognition, emotion, and motivation in such a way that these processes are attuned to the practices that are available in the particular cultural world. Recent work has suggested that this socialization process entails substantial changes in neural connectivity in the brain (Kitayama & Uskul, 2011). The emerging psychological processes are likely to be automatic because they are well practiced. Automatic processes are often unconscious or subconscious as well, although they can also be highly contingent on situational cues. Thus, these processes have been called *implicit* in contrast to the explicit values, attitudes, and beliefs assessed in the survey studies we reviewed earlier. Several dimensions of implicit independence have been proposed.

Certain cognitive characteristics are likely to be linked to the cultural values of independence (vs. interdependence), for example:

1. *Focused attention:* People who are attuned to a variety of independent (vs. interdependent) practices that emphasize self-focus, personal goals, and self-realization (simply called *independent people* hereinafter) are likely to focus their attention on what they want or what they seek to accomplish, whereas interdependent people are likely to be more holistic, attending more broadly to the goals and expectations of others. Hence, independent (vs. interdependent) people are likely to be more focused (or less holistic) in their patterns of attention (Kitayama, Duffy, Kawamura, & Larsen, 2003; Masuda & Nisbett, 2001).

2. *Dispositional bias:* Independent people may be expected to project their own schema of the self as internally motivated to other people, thereby inferring another person's internal dispositions when observing that person's behavior. An important note is that this tendency toward dispositional inference may occur even when there is a clear situational constraint on the behavior (Choi, Nisbett, & Norenzayan, 1999; Miller, 1984).

3. *Socially disengaged (vs. engaged) emotions:* Emotions can also reflect implicit independence. The hypothesized focus on one's goals and desires among independent (vs. interdependent) people may result in a greater propensity to experience both socially disengaged positive emotions, such as pride and feelings of self-confidence, that arise when these goals and desires have been accomplished and socially disengaged negative emotions, such as anger and frustration, that arise when such personal goals and desires have been compromised or interfered with.[1] Conversely, independent people are unlikely to experience socially engaged positive emotions, such as friendly feelings and respect for others, that arise when interdependent goals are accomplished or socially engaged negative emotions, such as guilt and feelings of indebtedness, that arise when interdependence is threatened or compromised (Kitayama, Mesquita, & Karasawa, 2006).

---

[1]Although all emotions are inherently social, socially disengaged emotions motivate the self to express one's internal attributes (as in pride) while asserting one's interests and goals when they are interfered with or compromised (as in anger).

4. *Happiness stemming from personal achievement (vs. social harmony):* Evidence for this prediction is found in a series of studies by Kitayama and colleagues (Kitayama, Ishii, Imada, Takemura, & Ramaswamy, 2006; Kitayama, Markus, & Kurokawa, 2000; Uchida & Kitayama, 2009). Independent (vs. interdependent) people will be most happy when they achieve goals that reflect independence (vs. interdependence). Independent people are more likely to feel happy when they experience socially disengaged (vs. engaged) positive emotions, whereas interdependent people are more likely to feel happy when they experience socially engaged (vs. disengaged) positive emotions.

5. *Personal (vs. social) goals:* As already implied, motivation constitutes the core of implicit independence. Independent people are more likely than interdependent people to hold personal (vs. social) goals and to feel motivated to achieve them. Oishi and Diener (2001) have shown this to be the case.

6. *Symbolic significance of the self:* Relative to interdependent people (who value significant others), independent people place the utmost significance on the personal self, which may be reflected in the size of mental representations of the self (vs. others). When asked to draw their own social network by using circles to designate people in the network, independent people use larger circles to designate the self (vs. others; Kitayama et al., 2009).

7. *Self-uniqueness:* Independent people define themselves in terms of unique internal attributes such as abilities, personality traits, and interests, whereas interdependent people do so in terms of social roles and categories that are shared with others. Hence, independent people may be expected to view the self as more unique and to take actions to reflect that belief more than do interdependent people (Kim & Markus, 1999).

United States–Asia Comparisons

Nearly all of these measures of implicit independence have been developed in a large number of studies comparing European Americans with East Asians. This body of research has provided compelling evidence that compared with East Asians, European Americans are more focused in their patterns of attention (e.g., Kitayama et al., 2003; Masuda & Nisbett, 2001), more dispositional in person perception (Kitayama et al., 2009; Miller, 1984), more disengaged in terms of their emotional experiences (Kitayama, Mesquita, & Karasawa, 2006), more oriented toward personal (vs. social) happiness (Kitayama, Mesquita, & Karasawa, 2006), more inclined toward personal (vs. social) goals (Oishi & Diener, 2001), larger in their symbolic selves (Kitayama et al., 2009), and higher in preference for self-uniqueness (Kim & Markus, 1999). Although much of this literature is based on data from college undergraduates in the respective countries, the pattern remains the same when nonstudent samples from a wide age range are tested (Kitayama et al., 2012).

United States–Western European Comparisons

If the mentality of Americans is shaped by the United States' history of frontier settlement, Americans should be expected to be more independent even when compared with their Western European cousins. Kitayama et al. (2009) found that compared with both the British and Germans, European Americans are more focused in their patterns of attention, are more disengaged in their emotional experiences, have a more personal sense of happiness, and are larger in their symbolic representations of the self. The only measure that did not show the predicted difference concerned dispositional bias in attribution. In all cases, Western Europeans were significantly more independent than an Asian group (Japanese). The average effect size between European Americans and Western Europeans was small to moderate (Cohen's $d = 0.29$), indicating that the two regions are relatively similar, although the United States is consistently more independent. More important, virtually no difference exists between the two Western European groups (Cohen's $d = 0.02$). Asians (as represented by Japanese participants) are substantially less independent (or more interdependent) relative to Western Europeans (Cohen's $d = 0.59$). The amount of difference that separates Asia from Western Europe is roughly twice as much as the amount of difference that separates Western Europe from the United States. In addition, the effect size associated with the United States–Japan comparison is quite substantial. The average Cohen's d was 0.87, which in fact qualifies as large in accordance with current statistical convention.

Baby Names

One important aspect of independence that is particularly important in frontier settlement is the value placed on uniqueness of the self (Kim & Markus, 1999). As discussed previously, innovation and novelty are keys to survival in frontiers whether the frontiers are defined geographically or more in terms of activity domains (e.g., business, science). Indeed, uniqueness encourages creative problem solving (Förster, Friedman, Butterbach, & Sassenberg, 2005), which would have been advantageous in frontier conditions in which supply chains and manufacturing were limited and unfamiliar environments might have presented unexpected challenges. In short, frontiers likely both select for and foster uniqueness.

One important behavior that is based on this value concerns the names given to babies (Varnum & Kitayama, 2011). Naming is an act of considerable cultural, familial, and personal significance (Lieberson & Bell, 1992) and has a number of psychological, sociological, and economic consequences (Christenfeld & Larsen, 2008). The choice of a name for one's child is a deliberate act that many view as an expression of their values. Thus, the choice of a relatively popular name may reflect a preference for, or a strong value placed on, conformity versus uniqueness.

As may be predicted from the hypothesis that frontier settlement encourages greater value to be placed on uniqueness of the self (vs. conformity to social conventions), Varnum and Kitayama (2011) recently found that naming practices do in fact differ rather markedly between countries recently founded by Europeans (e.g., the United States) and European countries. In Figure 5.3, the countrywise percentages of baby boys and girls with one of the 10 most common names are plotted against a measure of individualism proposed by Hofstede, Hofstede, and Minkov (2010). As can be seen from this figure, compared with nearly all European nations, settler nations (the United States as well as Canada, Australia, and New Zealand) are substantially more individualistic and, simultaneously, show much weaker preferences for conventional names and, by implication, stronger preferences for unique names. It is worth noting that these frontier societies tend to be more multicultural, hence a greater variety of names may be available. However, within-country analyses of regional variation in naming practices have revealed that frontier status remains a significant predictor of relatively unique names even when controlling for ethnic diversity, suggesting that such differences cannot solely be accounted for by ethnic homogeneity.

CULTURAL VARIATIONS BY REGION WITHIN THE UNITED STATES

Systematic westbound settlement from Europe to North America took place over several centuries. At the same time, during the 18th and 19th centuries, a very much analogous process took place within the United States. People who did not fit in with the emerging cities on the East Coast, as well as those who sought the promise of land and new opportunities for success, migrated to the West. This history of westbound frontier settlement is likely to have left permanent marks in the American mentality. The ontological insecurity and physical danger that are likely associated with frontier settlement may account for the unusually high level of religiosity and conservatism among Americans (relative to other, equally wealthy Western European

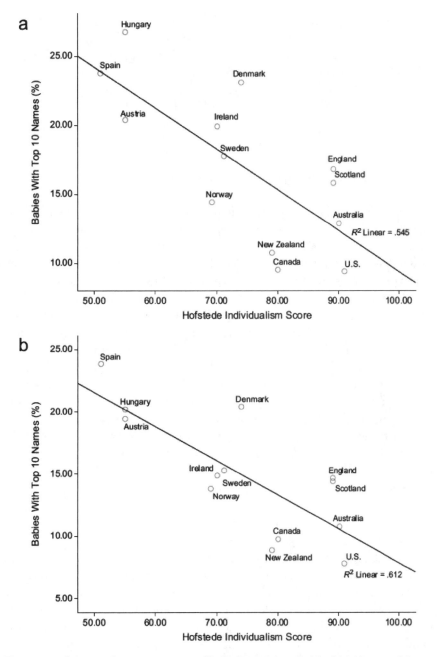

Figure 5.3. Countrywise percentages of baby boys (a) and girls (b) with one of the 10 most common names, plotted as a function of Hofstede, Hofstede, and Minkov's (2010) country-level individualism scores. From "What's in a Name? Popular Names Are Less Common in Frontiers," by M. E. W. Varnum and S. Kitayama, 2011, *Psychological Science, 22,* p. 181. Copyright 2011 by Sage Publications. Adapted with permission.

counterparts; Inglehart & Baker, 2000). More important for the purpose of this chapter, this history may well have been instrumental in increasing the level of independence among Americans. An increasing number of empirical studies on regional variations within the United States can be brought to bear on this discussion. In this section, we first discuss regional variation in explicit values of independence in the United States. We then turn to differences in behaviors that reflect these values. After that, we turn to evidence regarding implicit independence.

Regional Variation in Explicit Independence

Do any regional variations remain within the United States such that Western states are more independent relative to their Eastern counterparts? Park, Conway, Pietromonaco, Plaut, and Kitayama (2009, as cited in Kitayama et al., 2010) examined the value priorities of college undergraduates at four state universities in Massachusetts, Georgia, Michigan, and Montana and observed that independent values such as individualism and antipower values are more strongly endorsed in both Montana and Michigan than in Massachusetts and Georgia. It is important to note that this pattern was evident only for those whose parents and grandparents had all been born and raised in the United States. Supposedly, many of these participants' families had lived in similar regions for generations. Interestingly, Park et al. found no regional variation for those whose families immigrated to the United States relatively recently. Kitayama et al. (2010) noted that because Michigan was on the western frontier of the country until the beginning of the 19th century (and Montana until far more recently), these regions bred strong independent values, which have since been handed down over generations.

Regional Variation in Collectivist and Conformist Behaviors

If explicit values differ across regions, behaviors that are guided by these explicit values should also vary. We may therefore expect that in terms of behaviors that are guided directly by these explicitly endorsed values, residents of Western states should be more independent than those of Eastern states. Vandello and Cohen (1999) used census data to examine several face-valid indicators of individualism, including the percentage of people living alone, the percentage of households without grandchildren, the divorce-to-marriage ratio, the percentage of people voting libertarian in past presidential elections, and the percentage of people who are self-employed. Using these behaviors as an indicator, both the Mountain West and the Pacific Northwest prove to be substantially more individualistic than Eastern and Southern regions of the United States.

Regional variation can also be observed in behaviors that reflect conformity (e.g., the relative prevalence of conventional names). As noted earlier, one may assume that giving uncommon and, thus, relatively unique names to newly born babies is a deliberate expression of independent values such as autonomy, uniqueness, and self-expression. Varnum and Kitayama (2011) found that conventional names are indeed less common in frontiers. More children born in New England received conventional names (either the most popular or one of the 10 most popular in their respective state that year) than children born in the Mountain West and Pacific Northwest. Moreover, Varnum and Kitayama found a strong negative correlation between date of statehood (a proxy for recency of settlement) and the prevalence of conventional names. These results are illustrated in Figure 5.4 for baby boys and girls. This finding held even after controlling for other factors, such as income, population density, and ethnic composition. Varnum and Kitayama found similar results when comparing Western and Eastern Canadian provinces and (as previously noted) when comparing frontier countries (i.e., the United States, Australia, Canada) with European countries.

Beyond reflecting regional differences in values, naming practices might also play a role in maintaining these differences. A reanalysis of data collected as part of the Michigan Wisdom Project (Grossmann et al., 2010) found that people with one of the 10 most popular names nationally in their year of birth scored lower on an adapted version of Singelis's (1994) independence subscale than those who did not have one of the 10 most popular names in their birth year (Varnum, 2011). Although this finding is by no means definitive, it suggests another reason why preferences for uniqueness are important in understanding the effects of voluntary settlement. If having a relatively unique (vs. conventional) name affects how one views oneself and how one is viewed by others, then perhaps differences in naming practices help perpetuate differences in values between frontier and nonfrontier regions.

Might similar patterns also be present for conformity as psychologists have typically measured it? Varnum (2012) recently addressed this question by reanalyzing the data reviewed by Bond and Smith (1996), who had reviewed existing Asch-style (1952) conformity studies and found significant variation in the strength of these effects as a function of culture. Varnum performed an analysis of 91 studies included in Bond and Smith's meta-analysis and found regional variation in these effects within the United States as well. Conformity effect sizes were smaller in frontier regions of the United States than in areas with a longer history of settlement. Further state-level conformity effect sizes were positively correlated with the frequency of conventional names.

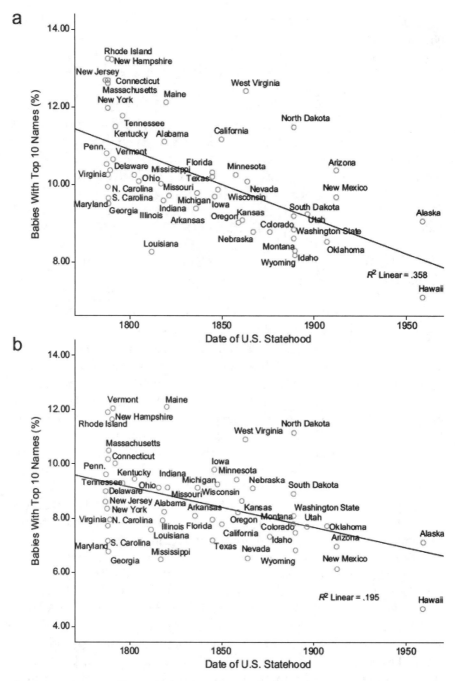

Figure 5.4. Statewise percentages of baby boys (a) and girls (b) with the 10 most common names in the United States, plotted as a function of date of U.S. statehood. From "What's in a Name? Popular Names Are Less Common in Frontiers," by M. E. W. Varnum and S. Kitayama, 2011, *Psychological Science, 22,* p. 179. Copyright 2011 by Sage Publications. Adapted with permission.

Regional Variation in Implicit Independence

So far, we have considered regional variation in explicit independence. All measures we considered pertain to endorsement of explicit values of independence and behaviors that are directly conditional on these values, such as divorce (Vandello & Cohen, 1999), naming of one's own babies (Varnum & Kitayama, 2011), and conformity (Varnum, 2012), which raises an important question of what we might find in terms of implicit independence.

Recall that a work discussed earlier (Kitayama et al., 2009) found that relative to their Western European counterparts, European Americans have more narrowly focused attention, experience more socially disengaged emotions, have a more personal sense of happiness, and have a symbolically inflated view of the self. These differences on the whole can be attributed to the United States' history of frontier settlement during the past several hundred years and the absence thereof in Western Europe during the same period. Following this line of thought, it might seem reasonable to anticipate that residents of the Western United States would be higher in implicit independence than those of the Eastern United States.

In the aforementioned study that demonstrated regional variation in explicit independence, Park et al. (2009) also examined four different measures of implicit independence: dispositional bias, salience of socially disengaged (vs. engaged) emotions, personal (vs. social) happiness, and inflated symbolic self-views. Using these measures, the researchers tested residents in Massachusetts, Michigan, Georgia, and Montana and found absolutely no regional variation in implicit independence regardless of whether their parents and grandparents were born in the United States.

Production and Adoption Processes of Cultural Values and Practices in the United States

At first glance, it would seem quite puzzling that no regional variation existed in implicit independence within the contemporary United States especially because evidence is very clear that the expected regional variation is present for endorsement of explicit independent values. Addressing this dissociation, however, may help in understanding some peculiarities associated with the frontier history of the United States. Kitayama et al. (2010) hypothesized (a) that settlers in the frontier were likely to hold explicit values of independence and, moreover, (b) that they generated a variety of practices that are rooted in these values in their efforts to survive and prosper on the frontier.

Kitayama et al. (2010) further hypothesized that explicit values and practices are likely to be transmitted very differently because to understand

and develop a deep appreciation for values such as freedom and democracy or, alternatively, tradition and social harmony requires extensive and systematic inculcation in terms of examples, role models and, most of all, convincing stories and discourses (McAdams, 2006). Culturally variable public representations such as children's books and texts for moral education (Imada, 2012; Tsai, Miao, & Seppala, 2007; see Morling & Lamoreaux, 2008, for a review) serve this important function. What this means, among other things, is that values are likely to be transmitted vertically through generations by explicit education and inculcation of children by caregivers in any given culture (Knafo & Schwartz, 2009; Schönpflug, 2009). One may therefore expect that values do not travel very well across space, which, in the present context, explains why sizable regional differences still remain in value profiles across regions of the United States (as previously noted) even though the Western geographic frontier disappeared more than a full century ago.

Practices are very different in this regard, however. Independent practices that are generated, such as expressing one's own views or seeking one's personal goals or uniqueness, constitute the new, emerging folkways of the frontier. Unlike values, practices are observable action routines or scripted behaviors and, as such, they can easily be imitated and adopted by others. Since Bandura (1977), social psychologists have investigated the significant role played by automatic imitation in transmission of behavioral routines (Chartrand & Bargh, 1999). Automatic mimicry is especially likely when the model is higher in status and coming from one's own group (Cialdini, 2001; Lakin, Chartrand, & Arkin, 2008; Thelen & Kirkland, 1976). Hence, practices can be disseminated quickly across time and space to different regions—especially when they are associated with high status, prestige, or visible success—as long as these regions fall in the same political category (e.g., the United States).

Kitayama et al. (2010) pointed out that one important feature of the Western frontier of the United States was that it was economically highly successful, at least in the eyes of East Coast residents. Moreover, the expansion of the territory, and thus, the western extension of the frontier, was fully endorsed by the federal government. In combination, then, it would seem sensible that frontier practices were imitated and adopted by East Coast residents who either observed or heard about various frontier practices. Remember that various forms of implicit independence are likely shaped through active engagement in independent action scripts, routines, and practices. The adoption process under discussion here might then be responsible for the absence of differences in implicit independence across regions.

Our account may also explain why Western Europeans remain less independent in implicit mentality as well as in explicit value endorsement or why Japanese are also less independent even though they have had, overall, positive attitudes toward Westerners during the past 100 years. Is it possible that imitation opportunities might simply be very limited when regions (e.g., North America and Europe vs. Asia) are separated by major barriers such as oceans and languages? Is it also possible that imitation of behavioral routines might not occur across national boundaries?

HOKKAIDO: JAPAN'S NORTHERN FRONTIER

Our understanding of the settlement process can be informed by similar processes that might be at work in other regions of the world. One important test case is Hokkaido—a northern island of Japan that was a wilderness until the middle of the 19th century. Ethnic Japanese—mostly farmers and peasants— immigrated with the support of the national government to transform the island into a territory of Japan, in part to defend against Russia, which extended its influence in the Far East in the mid-19th century. The settlement was voluntary in the sense that it was often decided in the units of local villages. By no means was it enforced by the government, although it was placed squarely within the governmental policy of national defense. Today, Hokkaido has been assimilated into the national culture of Japan. Yet, evidence is also mounting that its settlement history has left visible marks on the regional culture of Hokkaido and the mentality of the people living there.

Public Behaviors Reflecting Explicit Independence

An examination of census data provides an initial indication that Hokkaido might in fact be quite individualistic even today. Recently, Hitokoto and Uchida (2012), using similar methodology to that used by Vandello and Cohen (1999), examined regional variations in the prevalence of behaviors that are linked to independent values. Among the 47 prefectures of Japan, Hokkaido is ranked quite high in divorce rate and in the proportion of elderly people living alone—in fact, it ranks as highly as the major metropolitan areas of Tokyo and Osaka (Hitokoto, Murabe, Narita, & Tanaka-Matsumi, 2010).

Measuring Implicit Independence in Hokkaido

Are the residents of Hokkaido more independent than the residents of mainland Japan? Kitayama, Ishii, et al. (2006) addressed this question with respect to three aspects of implicit independence: personal happiness, personal dissonance, and dispositional bias.

First, Kitayama, Ishii, et al. (2006) examined predictors of happiness. Previous work showed that for Americans, happiness is predicted more strongly by socially disengaged positive emotions, such as pride and feelings of self-confidence, than by socially engaged positive emotions, such as communal feelings and friendly feelings (Kitayama et al., 2000). This finding was replicated in a new sample of Americans. Previous work also showed that for mainland Japanese, happiness is predicted more strongly by socially engaged positive emotions than by socially disengaged positive emotions. This finding was also replicated. More important, however, the mainland Japanese pattern became somewhat weaker for Hokkaido residents who had grown up on the mainland and, moreover, for Hokkaido-born Hokkaido residents, the pattern was more similar to the pattern for Americans, with socially disengaged positive emotions better predicting their happiness than socially engaged emotions.

Second, Kitayama, Ishii, et al. (2006) also tested cognitive dissonance. It is well known that people justify a choice they have made by increasing their liking of a chosen object while decreasing their liking of a rejected object. This justification supposedly occurs because the individuals feel certain worries about themselves (e.g., "Am I stupid that I have made this choice?" or "What will my boyfriend think about me if he learns of my choice?") when they have made a very difficult choice and, thus, they are motivated to reduce the discomfort—called *cognitive dissonance*—by justifying the choice (Festinger, 1957). Previous cross-cultural studies have shown, however, that mainland Japanese do not show this dissonance effect when their choice is believed to be completely private. The reason is that their selves are quite interdependent, meaning that they are defined more in terms of others' appraisals. Without public scrutiny, they have no worry about their self-images (Kitayama, Snibbe, Markus, & Suzuki, 2004). Private choice, however, is precisely the condition that is required for Americans to show the justification effect. The reason is that choices that are made in private—and, thus, that are formed without any social pressures—are the ones that are most clearly expressive of their internal features such as decision abilities and tastes. It is in this condition that people with independent selves are likely to most worry about a choice they have made. Results from a study Kitayama, Ishii, et al. (2006) conducted in Hokkaido were striking. Hokkaido Japanese showed a pattern quite similar to the pattern for Americans and very different from the pattern for mainland Japanese. Moreover, this was the case regardless of whether the Hokkaido residents had grown up in Hokkaido or on the mainland. This finding has since been replicated (Takemura & Arimoto, 2008).

A third measure tested in the Kitayama, Ishii, et al. (2006) article concerns dispositional bias. As noted earlier, Americans show a quite robust dispositional bias, attributing another person's behavior to that person's internal characteristics, such as attitudes and abilities, while relatively ignoring available situational or contextual reasons for the behavior. This pattern of social inference stems from an independent schema Americans recruit to interpret others' behavior. In contrast, for Asians, including Japanese, this tendency is much attenuated or even absent. Kitayama, Ishii, et al. (2006) replicated this cross-cultural pattern and then sought to find out which pattern Hokkaido Japanese might show. As may be predicted by the voluntary settlement hypothesis, the researchers found that Hokkaido-born Hokkaido residents show a dispositional bias that is just as pronounced as the one shown by Americans. Quite interestingly, the pattern was quite different from that of mainland-born Hokkaido residents. This latter group of participants was highly similar to mainland Japanese, exhibiting very little dispositional bias.

Overall, with respect to Hokkaido-born Hokkaido residents, the results were clear. These individuals tend to be very similar to North Americans on all the three measures tested. Thus, they tend to experience personal happiness; are made anxious by personal, private choices; and, furthermore, show a strong dispositional bias in person perception. Curiously, mainland-born Hokkaido residents show very different patterns depending on the measures under discussion. In particular, they show little or no dispositional bias, which might indicate that cultural knowledge, including pertinent person schemas that are brought to bear on person perception, is acquired relatively early in life and, once obtained, is relatively stable. An important note is that these participants were strikingly independent with respect to the emphasis placed on personal choice (i.e., dissonance) and, to a lesser extent, on the personal form of happiness. Kitayama, Ishii, et al. (2006) interpreted this pattern to suggest that those who grew up to be relatively independent on the mainland might choose to move to Hokkaido, which might explain why mainland-born Hokkaido residents are just as independent as those who have grown up in Hokkaido. This kind of self-selection may prove to be quite pervasive in forming the independent ethos of frontiers. We come back to this point in the next section.

COSMOPOLITAN CITIES AS THE FRONTIER
OF THE 21ST CENTURY

In a geographical sense, at the beginning of the 21st century, frontiers have disappeared almost everywhere across the globe. Yet, it appears that (some) people keep inventing new frontiers in space, in science, in business, and in all other domains of activity. In recent decades, the notion of the frontier is coming to be redefined in terms of the technological, economical, or societal and cultural boundaries of human activity. In this section, we argue that just as the historical frontier in the United States fueled American individualism, the frontier of today may be located in cosmopolitan cities that fuel modern civilization's orientation toward individualism.

By *cosmopolitan cities*, we mean urban metropolitan areas that are characterized by moral commitments to universalistic values associated with a world citizen identity (freedom, autonomy, egalitarianism; Appiah, 2006; Simmel, 1903) and that are often melting pots of diverse ethnic groups (Rentfrow, Mellander, & Florida, 2009). Moreover, cosmopolitan cities are commonly centers of economic development and serve as the headquarters of global financial networks (Florida, 2002; see also global city index, Sassen, 2001). Examples of cosmopolitan cities include New York and San Francisco in the United States, Berlin and London in Europe, and also booming cities in other parts of the world, such as Istanbul, Singapore, and Hong Kong.

In combination with their greater economic resources, the egalitarian, free-spirited ethos of cosmopolitan cities may offer ample economic, personal, and social opportunities to succeed for ambitious, creative, and open-minded people. These opportunities are often associated with the high-tech information industry, research and development, and the arts, fashion, the media, and the music business. At the same time, because these opportunities are independent of people's socioeconomic and ethnic backgrounds and because they are not linked to traditional social networks, the risks involved can be substantial, especially for those who are economically and socially privileged. Cosmopolitan cities often harbor high-risk–high-return enterprises that are open to everyone who dares to take the risk. Just as the historical frontier did, cosmopolitan cities may thus fuel an independent ethos by attracting independently inclined people who are oriented toward self-reliance, personal goal pursuit, novelty, and risk taking.

Residential Mobility

Previous research has provided some initial data pertaining to our thesis that settlement in cosmopolitan cities might be linked to independent mentality. Some existing studies have examined the personality traits of those who migrate or do not migrate to different cities in Finland (Jokela, 2009; Jokela, Elovainio, Kivimäki, & Keltikangas-Järvinen, 2008). Jokela (2009) and Jokela et al. (2008) observed that the likelihood of migration from rural to urban municipalities in Finland over a 9-year period was prospectively predicted by the personality trait sociability. The relevance of this work with respect to our current thesis is uncertain, however, because no clear measures of independence were included. Moreover, the urban municipalities included in this study (Helsinki, Kuopio, and Oulu, among others) might not fully qualify as cosmopolitan centers.

In another relevant line of work, Oishi and colleagues (see Oishi, 2010, for a review) have linked residential mobility (i.e., people's tendency to relocate) to several psychological indices that are often linked to independence, including salience of personal (vs. collective) self, broad (vs. narrow) friendship, and personal (vs. collective) form of well-being. According to Oishi and Kisling (2009), their analysis implies that "residential mobility should give rise to an individualistic way of defining the self and relating with others and communities" (p. 230). Evidence from a series of studies by Oishi and colleagues (for a summary, see Oishi, 2010) appears to be consistent with this proposition. For example, personality traits, rather than group membership, were more central to the self-definitions of frequent movers than to those of nonmovers. For the most part, however, this work does not take into account the destination of residential move (i.e., the move to cosmopolitan vs. noncosmopolitan cities; Oishi, Ishii, & Lun, 2009, Study 3; Oishi, Lun, & Sherman, 2007, Studies 1, 2, and 3). The present analysis implies that the exact destination of residential moves might therefore prove to be more important than the moves themselves.

Fortunately, a few studies have compared cities that vary in residential mobility (Oishi, Rothman, et al., 2007, Studies 1 and 2; Oishi et al., 2009, Study 2). Because some of the mobile cities (e.g., Dallas and Phoenix) are not obviously cosmopolitan, whereas some of less mobile cities (e.g., Chicago and Boston) seem to qualify more as cosmopolitan, it might be possible to determine whether residential mobility or the destination of the move is linked to independence. For example, Oishi, Rothman, et al. (2007, Study 2) found that residents in more mobile cities (operationalized in terms of lower proportion of residents living in the same house over a 5-year period) tended to support their home baseball teams only if they kept a winning record. This phenomenon can be interpreted as a manifestation of independence. One could argue that independent people may appreciate the team only if it does some good to them. Indeed, when we rated the cities included in the Oishi, Rothman, et al. (2007) study in terms of how cosmopolitan they were with criteria used by Sevincer and Kitayama (2012), the cosmopolitan index did not relate to the record-contingent support of home teams.

At first glance, this analysis seems to go against our claim that the destination of the move rather than residential mobility per se is what increases independence. However, the problem here is that the record-contingent support of home teams might simply mean that more mobile people have shorter time perspectives. That is, because mobile people anticipate leaving their city, they may expect their home teams to succeed sooner than do less mobile people. Accordingly, it is far from certain that the record-contingent support of home baseball teams is a valid indicator of independence.

In short, Sevincer and Kitayama (2012) reviewed this literature and observed that when reasonably valid indicators of independence were used, the destination of residential move was not tested separately from residential mobility in general, whereas when the destination of residential move (cosmopolitan vs. regional cities) was examined separately from residential mobility in general, the validity of the dependent variables as an indicator of independence was uncertain.

Urban Versus Rural Comparisons

Our analysis of settlement processes in cosmopolitan cities may be informed by a small but important body of literature documenting greater independence among city dwellers than among residents of more rural areas (Kashima et al., 2004; Matsumoto, Willingham, & Olide, 2009; Yamagishi, Hashimoto, Li, & Schug, 2012). On the basis of these findings, Yamagishi et al. (2012) argued that social constraints are inherently low in urban environments and thus hypothesized that "city air brings freedom" (p. 38).

The finding that urbanites as a whole are more independent than residents of rural areas is beyond dispute. Moreover, in some respects, it is sensible to hypothesize that urban environments are more affording of independence than rural environments. For example, in many parts of the world, rural areas are more agricultural. The evidence is clear that farming requires close interdependence (Berry, 1979; Edgerton, 1965; Uskul, Kitayama, & Nisbett, 2008). Furthermore, some desk jobs—especially managerial jobs, which may be found much more frequently in urban areas—require greater degrees of autonomous decision making, self-direction, and, more generally, independence (Schooler, Mulatu, & Oates, 2004).

Nevertheless, whether all urban environments are less constraining and thus affording of independence is not certain. Whereas some aspects of these environments are surely less constrained and tuned more toward novelty, creativity, and experimentation, as can be seen in cutting-edge science as well as avant-garde movements, some other elements of the same environments, such as business and political establishments, are inherently more conservative and conventional. Thus, perhaps urban environments might be more constrained in these ways than some rural towns and villages.

The urban–rural difference in independence might thus not necessarily mean that urban environments are in general less constraining and thus more affording of independence. Instead, in view of the voluntary settlement hypothesis under discussion here, it might be the case that many urban residents are independent precisely because they are the ones who voluntarily moved to the city at some point in their lives. Urban populations become more independent overall because of these settlers; however, if this were the case, the independent mentality might prove to be most prominent among the settlers. Native residents might not necessarily be high in independence even in urban environments.

Are Voluntary Settlers More Independent

To address this important gap in knowledge, Sevincer and Kitayama (2013) compared matched samples from a cosmopolitan city (Hamburg) and a noncosmopolitan city (Braunschweig) in Germany. Both cities are comparable in many aspects (geographic location, education level, predominant religious denomination), but Hamburg was judged to be more cosmopolitan by German participants in a pretest. As indicators of independence, Sevincer and Kitayama assessed participants' propensity toward personal (vs. social) goal pursuit by asking them to report on the goals they planned to pursue in the near future. The extent to which participants pursued goals primarily aimed at personal success (e.g., "getting a promotion") versus goals aimed at establishing social relationships (e.g., "visit my family") or promoting group welfare (e.g., "do social work") was taken as an indicator of their tendency toward independent goal pursuit. Moreover, participants' propensity toward novelty was assessed using an abstract figures task (Kim & Markus, 1999). As predicted, students who voluntarily moved to Hamburg to attend the university were more independent on both measures than those who voluntarily moved to Braunschweig and students who never moved. No difference was found in level of independence between those native to Hamburg and those native to Braunschweig.

The fact that the Hamburg natives were no more independent than their counterparts in Braunschweig indicates that the "city air" might not inherently be independent (i.e., less constraining). Instead, the critical variable would appear to be settlement of urban areas rather than the nature of urban environments per se. This may be the case because, as we argued earlier, any urban environment is extremely diverse, representing a complex mixture of both the mainstream of the society (which is likely to be highly conventional and even traditional) and elements that are newer, more experimental, less constrained, and avant garde.

Independence and Choosing Where to Live

Data reported by Sevincer and Kitayama (2013) indicate that people's motivation toward independence does affect their residential choices. In one study, participants indicated their goals (personal vs. social) and their connectedness with others. Their preference for cosmopolitan (vs. noncosmopolitan) cities was assessed by means of two measures: First, participants listed the three U.S. cities in which they would most like to live if they were to move out of their current city. These cities were coded for cosmopolitanism by two independent raters. Second, participants were presented with 10 pairs of U.S. cities. The cities in each pair were matched on geographic location, size, and wealth but differed on cosmopolitanism (according to the results of a pretest with another group of Americans). For each pair, participants indicated in which city they would prefer to live. The number of times participants chose the more cosmopolitan city was taken as an indicator of their preference for cosmopolitan cities.

The key finding was that participants' independence correlated positively with their preference for cosmopolitan cities. Of importance, participants' independence did not correlate with their favorite cities' size or wealth. Thus, although cosmopolitan cities are on average bigger and wealthier than less cosmopolitan cities (Florida, 2002), independent people do not simply prefer cosmopolitan cities because of their size or absolute wealth. This finding suggests that it is indeed specific features linked to cosmopolitanism (e.g., available opportunities to achieve success) that attract independently inclined people.

CONCLUSIONS AND FUTURE DIRECTIONS

The frontier attracts independent people. Settlers on frontiers therefore tend to endorse explicit independent values and, moreover, they tend to engage in behaviors that are guided by these values. Furthermore, settlers on frontiers tend to develop cultural practices that reflect these values. Their implicit psychological tendencies will therefore tend to be modified in accordance with their explicit independent values. The different forms of implicit independence discussed earlier in this chapter will thus result. This general thesis has received substantial support from research on contemporary U.S. mentality, within-U.S. regional variations, and Japan's "wild north," as well as research focusing on immigrants to cosmopolitan cities.

Our work is consistent with recent work on the link between residential mobility and independent, individualistic mentality (Oishi, 2010). What we have added to this literature is that it is probably not residential mobility per se, but residential mobility to the frontier broadly defined—both geographic frontiers and cosmopolitan cities—that fosters independent mentality. Moreover, our work is also consistent with urban residents being more independent than rural residents (e.g., Kashima et al., 1995; Yamagishi et al., 2012). We suspect that at least part of the reason for the urban–rural difference in independence might stem from the fact that urban areas attract more independent people. Future work should further address these possibilities.

We have largely left open the specific mechanisms underlying the association between frontier settlement and independence. Our findings, taken together with previous research on residential mobility, suggest that self-selection is one important mechanism. Those who settle on frontiers may tend to be more independent to begin with and tend to be higher on personality traits such as openness to experience. Such differences in personality may be in part genetic, thus those who engage in voluntary settlement on frontiers may differ in genotype from those who do not.

One candidate is *DRD4*, a dopamine receptor gene that has been linked to novelty seeking and risk taking (Munafò, Yalcin, Willis-Owen, & Flint, 2008). In an important study, Chen, Burton, Greenberger, and Dmitrieva (1999) found a close association between the prevalence of the 7-repeat variety of the *DRD4* gene (the variety that is linked to novelty seeking and risk taking) in a given cultural population and the distance the group traveled in the distant past. Moreover, this association cannot be accounted for by chance alone (Matthews & Butler, 2011), suggesting the operation of selective pressures in producing the cross-cultural variations in the prevalence of the gene polymorphisms. Another gene that may be important is *5HTTLPR*, a serotonin transporter gene that has been linked to cross-national variations in individualistic (vs. collectivistic) values (Chiao & Blizinsky, 2010). Future work should test whether genotype might be linked to the decision to migrate to cosmopolitan (vs. provincial) cities or to engage in cutting-edge science (vs. more conventional science). Genes may not only push people to settle on frontiers but may also play a role in the maintenance of regional variations in tendencies such as independence and nonconformity long after geographic frontiers have vanished.

Another important mechanism especially with respect to geographic frontier settlement is selective environmental pressures. One factor that might prove to be important pertains to the prevalence of pathogens. The parasite–stress hypothesis holds that the presence of infectious disease causes behaviors and values to be adopted that reduce the likelihood of transmission of pathogens (Schaller & Murray, 2011). Both collectivist values and conformity have been proposed as adaptations to environments in which infectious disease was (and is) more common. Such tendencies may be adaptive because they promote norms (such as adherence to tradition and avoidance of out-group members) that may reduce disease transmission. Indeed, cross-national variation as well as state-level variation in collectivism have been linked to the prevalence of disease (Fincher, Thornhill, Murray, & Schaller, 2008), as has cross-national variation in conformity (Murray, Trudeau, & Schaller, 2011). Moreover, regional variations in collectivism within the United States have been linked to pathogen prevalence (Fincher & Thornhill, 2012). Pathogens were likely less common in areas of the United States that were more recently frontiers (and indeed are less common today in such regions). Thus, relatively low disease prevalence may be one factor that encouraged independence on the frontier and may perhaps continue to promote related values and practices.

Genes and germs are important, but they are likely not the whole story. Uprooting oneself from family and community to settle on the frontier was likely a more attractive choice for those who feel more comfortable with mobility across different relations. Similarly, those who choose to move to the modern frontiers of cosmopolitan cities also likely find it easier to enter into new friendships and relationships (and to leave behind old ones). Communities that are composed of such people are also probably places in which relational bonds are relatively weak and relational mobility is high. Because relational mobility itself has been linked to independence (Falk, Heine, Yuki, & Takemura, 2009), this may be another mechanism involved in the creation and maintenance of differences between frontier and nonfrontier regions.

Last, but not least, a host of psychological mechanisms likely link frontier settlement to independence. Sevincer and colleagues (Sevincer & Kitayama, 2012; Sevincer, Kitayama, Pradel, & Singmann, 2012) have hypothesized that the frontier symbolizes an independent lifestyle (e.g., freedom, self-realization, nonconformity), and because of this symbolic association, it may activate independent mind-sets. Moreover, this association may also motivate independent people to choose to settle in the frontier via the mechanism of prototype matching between personality and location (Niedenthal, Cantor, & Kihlstrom, 1985). These possibilities deserve more careful scrutiny in the future.

In conclusion, the frontier presents a unique vantage point for cultural psychology theories and research. As we see it, the frontier is key to understanding the mechanisms underlying cultural change. The spirit of independence, nurtured and reinforced in the frontier, may be instrumental in forging new forms of culture, which may subsequently be spread to other regions if they are successful economically, symbolically, and politically. In the process, the initial spirit of independence may sometimes drop out and frontier culture may eventually be assimilated into existing, less independent or more interdependent forms of life. Nevertheless, the frontier will surely leave traces on existing cultural forms and, in fact, our analysis is consistent with the recent worldwide trend toward independence and individualism (Inglehart & Baker, 2000; Hamamura, 2011; Twenge, Abebe, & Campbell, 2010). Given our analysis of production and adoption processes (Kitayama et al., 2010), the dissemination of individualism may have stemmed from the fact that at least during the past several centuries, both cultural freedom and technological innovations did help individualistic cultural, political, and economic entities flourish and succeed. Of course, whether this will continue to be the case in the increasingly globalizing, economically and politically interdependent world has yet to be seen.

Altogether, a much more concerted research effort on the frontier would be well justified. Novel cultural elements are likely to be produced by innovators—and innovators are likely to come from the periphery of any given society or human activity. To the extent that this is the case, the notion of frontier may prove to be indispensable to achieve a reasonably comprehensive theoretical understanding of the processes involved in the production of and change in cultural meanings and practices.

REFERENCES

Appiah, K. A. (2006). *Cosmopolitanism: Ethics in a world of strangers*. New York, NY: Norton.

Asch, S. E. (1952). *Social psychology*. Englewood Cliffs, NJ: Prentice-Hall.

Bandura, A. (1977). *Social learning theory*. New York, NY: General Learning Press.

Berry, J. W. (1979). A cultural ecology of social behavior. In L. Berkowitz (Ed.), *Advances in experimental social psychology* (Vol. 12, pp. 177–206). New York, NY: Academic Press.

Bond, R., & Smith, P. B. (1996). Culture and conformity: A meta-analysis of studies using Asch's (1952b, 1956) line judgment task. *Psychological Bulletin, 119*, 111–137. doi:10.1037/0033-2909.119.1.111

Chartrand, T. L., & Bargh, J. A. (1999). The chameleon effect: The perception–behavior link and social interaction. *Journal of Personality and Social Psychology, 76*, 893–910. doi:10.1037/0022-3514.76.6.893

Chen, C., Burton, M., Greenberger, E., & Dmitrieva, J. (1999). Population migration and the variation of dopamine D4 receptor (DRD4) allele frequencies around the globe. *Evolution and Human Behavior, 20*, 309–324. doi:10.1016/S1090-5138(99)00015-X

Chiao, J. Y., & Blizinsky, K. D. (2010). Culture–gene coevolution of individualism–collectivism and the serotonin transporter gene (5HTTLPR). *Proceedings of the Royal Society B: Biological Sciences, 277*, 529–537. doi:10.1098/rspb.2009.1650

Choi, I., Nisbett, R., & Norenzayan, A. (1999). Causal attribution across cultures: Variation and universality. *Psychological Bulletin, 125*, 47–63. doi:10.1037/0033-2909.125.1.47

Christenfeld, N., & Larsen, B. (2008). The name game. *The Psychologist, 21*, 210–213.

Cialdini, R. B. (2001). *Influence: Science and practice* (4th ed.). Boston, MA: Allyn & Bacon.

Cohen, A. B., Hall, D. E., Koenig, H. G., & Meador, K. G. (2005). Social versus individual motivation: Implications for normative definitions of religious orientation. *Personality and Social Psychology Review, 9,* 48–61. doi:10.1207/s15327957pspr0901_4

de Tocqueville, A. (1864). Etudes economiques, politiques et litteraires. In *Oeuvres complètes d'Alexis de Tocqueville, publiees par Madame de Tocqueville* [Complete works of Alexis de Tocqueville, published by Madame de Tocqueville]. Paris, France: M. Lévy Frères

de Tocqueville, A. (1969). *Democracy in America* (13th ed.; J. P. Mayer, Ed., & G. Lawrence, Trans.). New York, NY: Doubleday. (Original work published 1862)

Edgerton, R. B. (1965). "Cultural" vs. "ecological." Factors in the expression of values, attitudes, and personality characteristics. *American Anthropologist, 67,* 442–447. doi:10.1525/aa.1965.67.2.02a00130

Falk, C. F., Heine, S. J., Yuki, M., & Takemura, K. (2009). Why do Westerners self-enhance more than East Asians? *European Journal of Personality, 23,* 183–203. doi:10.1002/per.715

Festinger, L. (1957). *A theory of cognitive dissonance.* Stanford, CA: Stanford University Press.

Fincher, C. L., & Thornhill, R. (2012). Parasite-stress promotes in-group assortative sociality: The cases of strong family ties and heightened religiosity. *Behavioral and Brain Sciences, 35,* 61–79.

Fincher, C. L., Thornhill, R., Murray, D. R., & Schaller, M. (2008). Pathogen prevalence predicts human cross-cultural variability in individualism/collectivism. *Proceedings of the Royal Society B: Biological Sciences, 275,* 1279–1285. doi:10.1098/rspb.2008.0094

Florida, R. (2002). *The rise of the creative class.* New York, NY: Basic Books.

Förster, J., Friedman, R., Butterbach, E. M., & Sassenberg, K. (2005). Automatic effects of deviancy cues on creative cognition. *European Journal of Social Psychology, 35,* 345–359. doi:10.1002/ejsp.253

Grossmann, I., Na, J., Varnum, M. E. W., Park, D. C., Kitayama, S., & Nisbett, R. E. (2010). Reasoning about social conflicts improves into old age. *Proceedings of the National Academy of Sciences of the United States of America.* Advance online publication. doi:10.1073/pnas.1001715107

Hamamura, T. (2011). Are cultures becoming individualistic? A cross-temporal comparison of individualism–collectivism in the United States and Japan. *Personality and Social Psychology Review, 16,* 3–24.

Heine, S. J., Lehman, D. R., Peng, K., & Greenholtz, J. (2002). What's wrong with cross-cultural comparisons of subjective Likert scales? The reference-group effect. *Journal of Personality and Social Psychology, 82,* 903–918. doi:10.1037/0022-3514.82.6.903

Hitokoto, H., Murabe, T., Narita, K., & Tanaka-Matsumi, J. (2010, July). *Regional and temporal variations of individualism-collectivism in Japan: A multi-level analysis of Japanese adults across prefectures.* Paper presented at the 20th International Congress of the International Association for Cross-Cultural Psychology, Melbourne, Victoria, Australia.

Hitokoto, H., & Uchida, Y. (2012). *Interdependent happiness: Cross-cultural and regional comparisons.* Unpublished manuscript, Kwansai Gakuin University.

Hofstede, G., Hofstede, J. H., & Minkov, M. (2010). *Cultures and organizations: Software of the mind* (3rd ed.). New York, NY: McGraw-Hill.

Imada, T. (2012). Cultural narratives of individualism and collectivism: A content analysis of textbook stories in the United States and Japan. *Journal of Cross-Cultural Psychology, 43,* 576–591.

Inglehart, R. F., & Baker, W. E. (2000). Modernization, cultural change, and the persistence of traditional values. *American Sociological Review, 65,* 19–51. doi:10.2307/2657288

Jokela, M. (2009). Personality predicts migration within and between U.S. states. *Journal of Research in Personality, 43,* 79–83. doi:10.1016/j.jrp.2008.09.005

Jokela, M., Elovainio, M., Kivimäki, M., & Keltikangas-Järvinen, L. (2008). Temperament and migration patterns in Finland. *Psychological Science, 19,* 831–837. doi:10.1111/j.1467-9280.2008.02164.x

Kashima, Y., Kokubo, T., Kashima, E. S., Boxall, D., Yamaguchi, S., & Macrae, K. (2004). Culture and self: Are there within-culture differences in self between metropolitan areas and regional cities? *Personality and Social Psychology Bulletin, 30,* 816–823.

Kashima, Y., Yamaguchi, S., Kim, U., Choi, S. C., Gelfand, J. M., & Yuki, M. (1995). Culture, gender, and self: A perspective from individualism–collectivism research. *Journal of Personality and Social Psychology, 69,* 925–937. doi:10.1037/0022-3514.69.5.925

Kim, H., & Markus, H. R. (1999). Deviance or uniqueness, harmony or conformity? A cultural analysis. *Journal of Personality and Social Psychology, 77,* 785–800. doi:10.1037/0022-3514.77.4.785

Kitayama, S., Conway, J. G., Pietromonaco, P. B., Park, H., & Plaut, V. C. (2010). Ethos of independence across regions of the United States: The production-adoption model of cultural change. *American Psychologist, 65,* 559–574. doi:10.1037/a0020277

Kitayama, S., Duffy, S., Kawamura, T., & Larsen, J. T. (2003). Perceiving an object and its context in different cultures: A cultural look at new look. *Psychological Science, 14,* 201–206. doi:10.1111/1467-9280.02432

Kitayama, S., Ishii, K., Imada, T., Takemura, K., & Ramaswamy, J. (2006). Voluntary settlement and the spirit of independence: Evidence from Japan's "Northern Frontier." *Journal of Personality and Social Psychology, 91,* 369–384. doi:10.1037/0022-3514.91.3.369

Kitayama, S., Karasawa, M., Matsubara, M., Grossman, I., Na, J., Varnum, M. E. W., & Nisbett, R. E. (2012). *East-West differences in cognitive style and social orientation: Are they real?* Unpublished manuscript, University of Michigan.

Kitayama, S., Markus, H. R., & Kurokawa, M. (2000). Culture, emotion, and well-being: Good feelings in Japan and the United States. *Cognition and Emotion, 14,* 93–124. doi:10.1080/026999300379003

Kitayama, S., Mesquita, B., & Karasawa, M. (2006). Cultural affordance and emotional experience: Socially engaging and disengaging emotions in Japan and the United States. *Journal of Personality and Social Psychology, 91,* 890–903. doi:10.1037/0022-3514.91.5.890

Kitayama, S., Park, H., Sevincer, A. T., Karasawa, M., & Uskul, A. K. (2009). A cultural task analysis of implicit independence: Comparing North America, Western Europe, and East Asia. *Journal of Personality and Social Psychology, 97,* 236–255. doi:10.1037/a0015999

Kitayama, S., Snibbe, A. C., Markus, H. R., & Suzuki, T. (2004). Is there any "free" choice? Self and dissonance in two cultures. *Psychological Science, 15,* 527–533. doi:10.1111/j.0956-7976.2004.00714.x

Kitayama, S., & Uskul, A. K. (2011). Culture, mind, and the brain: Current evidence and future directions. *Annual Review of Psychology, 62,* 419–449. doi:10.1146/annurev-psych-120709-145357

Knafo, A., & Schwartz, S. H. (2009). Accounting for parent-child value congruence: Theoretical considerations and empirical evidence. In U. Schönpflug (Ed.), *Cultural transmission: Psychological, developmental, social and methodological aspects* (pp. 240–268). New York, NY: Cambridge University Press. doi:10.1017/CBO9780511804670.012

Lakin, J. L., Chartrand, T. L., & Arkin, R. M. (2008). I am too just like you: Nonconscious mimicry as an automatic behavioral response to social exclusion. *Psychological Science, 19,* 816–822. doi:10.1111/j.1467-9280.2008.02162.x

Li, Y. J., Johnson, K. A., Cohen, A. B., Williams, M. J., Knowles, E. D., & Chen, Z. (2012). Fundamental(ist) attribution error: Protestants are dispositionally focused. *Journal of Personality and Social Psychology, 102,* 281–290. doi:10.1037/a0026294

Lieberson, S., & Bell, E. O. (1992). Children's first names: An empirical study of social taste. *American Journal of Sociology, 98,* 511–554. doi:10.1086/230048

Masuda, T., & Nisbett, R. E. (2001). Attending holistically versus analytically: Comparing the context sensitivity of Japanese and Americans. *Journal of Personality and Social Psychology, 81,* 922–934. doi:10.1037/0022-3514.81.5.922

Matsumoto, D., Willingham, B., & Olide, A. (2009). Sequential dynamics of culturally moderated facial expressions of emotion. *Psychological Science, 20,* 1269–1275. doi:10.1111/j.1467-9280.2009.02438.x

Matthews, L. J., & Butler, P. M. (2011). Novelty-seeking DRD4 polymorphisms are associated with human migration distance out-of-Africa after controlling for neutral population gene structure. *American Journal of Physical Anthropology, 145,* 382–389. doi:10.1002/ajpa.21507

McAdams, D. P. (2006). *The redemptive self: Stories Americans live by.* New York, NY: Oxford University Press. doi:10.1093/acprof:oso/9780195176933.001.0001

Miller, J. G. (1984). Culture and development of everyday social explanation. *Journal of Personality and Social Psychology, 46,* 961–978. doi:10.1037/0022-3514.46.5.961

Morling, B., & Lamoreaux, M. (2008). Measuring culture outside the head: A meta-analysis of individualism-collectivism in cultural products. *Personality and Social Psychology Review, 12,* 199–221. doi:10.1177/1088868308318260

Munafò, M. R., Yalcin, B., Willis-Owen, S. A., & Flint, J. (2008). Association of the dopamine D4 receptor (DRD4) gene and approach-related personality traits: Meta-analysis and new data. *Biological Psychiatry, 63,* 197–206. doi:10.1016/j.biopsych.2007.04.006

Murray, D. R., Trudeau, R., & Schaller, M. (2011). On the origins of cultural differences in conformity: Four tests of the pathogen prevalence hypothesis. *Personality and Social Psychology Bulletin, 37,* 318–329. doi:10.1177/0146167210394451

Niedenthal, P. M., Cantor, N., & Kihlstrom, J. F. (1985). Prototype matching: A strategy for social decision making. *Journal of Personality and Social Psychology, 48,* 575–584. doi:10.1037/0022-3514.48.3.575

Oishi, S. (2010). The psychology of residential mobility: Implications for the self, social relationships, and well-being. *Perspectives on Psychological Science, 5,* 5–21. doi:10.1177/1745691609356781

Oishi, S., & Diener, E. (2001). Goals, culture, and subjective well-being. *Personality and Social Psychology Bulletin, 27,* 1674–1682. doi:10.1177/01461672012712010

Oishi, S., Ishii, K., & Lun, J. (2009). Residential mobility and conditionality of group identification. *Journal of Experimental Social Psychology, 45,* 913–919. doi:10.1016/j.jesp.2009.04.028

Oishi, S., & Kisling, J. (2009). The mutual constitution of residential mobility and individualism. In R. S. Wyer, C. Chiu, & Y. Hong (Eds.), *Understanding culture: Theory, research, and application* (pp. 223–237). New York, NY: Psychology Press.

Oishi, S., Lun, J., & Sherman, G. D. (2007). Residential mobility, self-concept, and positive affect in social interactions. *Journal of Personality and Social Psychology, 93,* 131–141. doi:10.1037/0022-3514.93.1.131

Oishi, S., Rothman, A. J., Snyder, M., Su, J., Zehm, K., Hertel, A. W., . . . Sherman, G. D. (2007). The socioecological model of procommunity action: The benefits of residential stability. *Journal of Personality and Social Psychology, 93,* 831–844. doi:10.1037/0022-3514.93.5.831

Oyserman, D., Coon, H. M., & Kemmelmeier, M. (2002). Rethinking individualism and collectivism: Evaluation of theoretical assumptions and meta-analyses. *Psychological Bulletin, 128,* 3–72. doi:10.1037/0033-2909.128.1.3

Park, H., Conway, L. G., Pietromonaco, P. R., Plaut, V. C., & Kitayama, S. (2009). *A paradox of American individualism: Regions vary in explicit, but not in implicit, independence.* Unpublished manuscript, Hokkaido University, Sapporo, Japan.

Rentfrow, P. J., Mellander, C., & Florida, R. (2009). Happy states of America: A state-level analysis of psychological, economic, and social well-being. *Journal of Research in Personality, 43,* 1073–1082. doi:10.1016/j.jrp.2009.08.005

Sassen, S. (2001). *The global city: New York, London, Tokyo* (2nd ed.). Princeton, NJ: Princeton University Press.

Schaller, M., & Murray, D. R. (2011). Infectious disease and the creation of culture. *Advances in Culture and Psychology*, *1*, 99–151.

Schimmack, U., Oishi, S., & Diener, E. (2005). Individualism: A valid and important dimension of cultural differences between nations. *Personality and Social Psychology Review*, *9*, 17–31. doi:10.1207/s15327957pspr0901_2

Schönpflug, U. (2009). *Cultural transmission: Psychological, developmental, social, and methodological aspects*. New York, NY: Cambridge University Press. doi:10.1017/CBO9780511804670

Schooler, C., Mulatu, M. S., & Oates, G. (2004). Occupational self-direction, intellectual functioning, and self-directed orientation in older workers: Findings and implications for individuals and societies. *American Journal of Sociology*, *110*, 161–197. doi:10.1086/385430

Sevincer, A. T., & Kitayama, S. (2013). *Social orientation and residential preferences: Independent people are attracted to cosmopolitan cities*. Manuscript submitted for publication.

Sevincer, A. T., Kitayama, S., Pradel, S., & Singmann, H. (2012). *Cosmopolitan cities activate independent mindsets*. Unpublished manuscript, University of Hamburg, Hamburg, Germany.

Simmel, G. (1903). *Die Großstädte und das Geistesleben* [The metropolis and mental life]. Dresden, Germany: Petermann.

Singelis, T. M. (1994). The measurement of independent and interdependent self-construals. *Personality and Social Psychology Bulletin*, *20*, 580–591. doi:10.1177/0146167294205014

Smith, P. B., & Fischer, R. (2008). Acquiescence, extreme response bias, and culture: A multilevel analysis. In F. J. R. van de Vijver, D. A. van Hemert, & Y. E. Poortinga (Eds.), *Multilevel analysis of individuals and cultures* (pp. 285–314). New York, NY: Erlbaum.

Takemura, K., & Arimoto, H. (2008). Independent self in Japan's "northern frontier": An experiment of cognitive dissonance in Hokkaido. *Japanese Journal of Experimental Social Psychology*, *48*, 40–49. doi:10.2130/jjesp.48.40

Thelen, M. H., & Kirkland, K. D. (1976). On status and being imitated: Effects on reciprocal imitation and attraction. *Journal of Personality and Social Psychology*, *33*, 691–697.

Triandis, H. C., & Gelfand, M. J. (1998). Converging measurement of horizontal and vertical individualism and collectivism. *Journal of Personality and Social Psychology*, *74*, 118–128. doi:10.1037/0022-3514.74.1.118

Tsai, J. L., Miao, F., & Seppala, E. (2007). Good feelings in Christianity and Buddhism: Religious differences in ideal affect. *Personality and Social Psychology Bulletin*, *33*, 409–421. doi:10.1177/0146167206296107

Twenge, J. M., Abebe, E. M., & Campbell, W. K. (2010). Fitting in or standing out: Trends in American parents' choices for children's names, 1880-2007. *Social Psychological and Personality Science*, *1*, 19–25. doi:10.1177/1948550609349515

Uchida, Y., & Kitayama, S. (2009). Happiness and unhappiness in East and West: Themes and variations. *Emotion, 9*, 441–456. doi:10.1037/a0015634

Uskul, A. K., Kitayama, S., & Nisbett, R. E. (2008). Eco-cultural basis of cognition: Farmers and fishermen are more holistic than herders. *Proceedings of the National Academy of Sciences of the United States of America, 105*, 8552–8556. doi:10.1073/pnas.0803874105

Vandello, J., & Cohen, D. (1999). Patterns of individualism and collectivism across the United States. *Journal of Personality and Social Psychology, 77*, 279–292. doi:10.1037/0022-3514.77.2.279

Varnum, M. E. W. (2011). *Culture within: An exploration of the effects of social class and region on the self and cognitive habits*. Unpublished doctoral dissertation, University of Michigan.

Varnum, M. E. W. (2012). Conformity effect sizes are smaller on the frontier. *Journal of Cognition and Culture, 12*, 359–364.

Varnum, M. E. W., & Kitayama, S. (2011). What's in a name? Popular names are less common in frontiers. *Psychological Science, 22*, 176–183. doi:10.1177/0956797610395396

Yamagishi, T., Hashimoto, H., Li, Y., & Schug, J. (2012). Stadtluft macht frei (City air brings freedom). *Journal of Cross-Cultural Psychology, 43*, 38–45. doi:10.1177/0022022111415407

6

POLITICAL CULTURE
AND DEMOCRACY

ARIEL MALKA

In April 2008, during his primary campaign, then-Senator Barack Obama made a remark that stirred controversy. Characterizing the mind-set of economically strained small-town Americans, he stated that "they cling to guns or religion or antipathy toward people who aren't like them or anti-immigrant sentiment or anti-trade sentiment as a way to explain their frustrations" (Fowler, 2008, para. 6). Although he combined these characteristics with the disjunctive conjunction *or,* Mr. Obama listed attributes of a cultural stereotype that is familiar to many followers of U.S. politics. There is a type of person, in this framework, who is religious, rural, parochial, antihomosexual, nationalistic, xenophobic, and gun loving. This type of person is involved in a bitter political conflict with the type of person who is secular, urbane, elitist, unfavorable toward guns, prohomosexual, globally minded, and pro-immigration (see Fiorina, Abrams, & Pope, 2006, Chapter 1).

http://dx.doi.org/10.1037/14274-006
Culture Reexamined: Broadening Our Understanding of Social and Evolutionary Influences,
A. B. Cohen (Editor)

These contrasting bundles of attributes are evocative of what is called a *cultural difference*, and they are at the center of what commentators, journalists, and opportunistic political actors sometimes call the *culture war*. This culture war framework may be a good one for describing contemporary U.S. political elites (e.g., Poole & Rosenthal, 2007), but it is inadequate for describing the contemporary U.S. general public (e.g., Fiorina et al., 2006). Some researchers have noted that whatever degree of political cultural conflict does exist in the public occurs in the context of a powerful cultural mind-set that is favorable to democratic governance. In this mind-set, Americans whom one might consider misguided, naive, stupid, elitist, out of touch, or even repugnant still deserve political and civil rights, as long as they obey the law. Americans who would deny such rights to their opponents are generally constrained by strong norms against even expressing such a wish, much less acting on it. Others have noted that this conflict is one in which most Americans possess some of the attributes of each side and are, therefore, either uninvolved or involved in an inconsistent way depending on what happens to be psychologically salient for them. This situation of largely nonoverlapping identities and preferences may temper the political conflict in a way that has favorable implications for democracy.

This chapter has two goals. The first is to briefly review post–World War II empirical scholarship on the concept of political culture and its implications for democratic functioning. The second is to briefly review evidence bearing on the nature of the so-called culture war in the United States, which is sometimes described as a threat to American democracy. Comprehensive overviews of these two topics are impossible in a book chapter. Rather, I describe some of the major scholarly ideas about these topics and the empirical evidence associated with these ideas. In so doing, I use as an organizing framework the classic notion that democratic governance requires a mass cultural orientation favorable to sustaining a balance of "consensus and cleavage" (Almond & Verba, 1963, p. 489; Berelson, Lazarsfeld, & McPhee, 1954, p. 318).

I draw two conclusions from these reviews. The first is that successful democratic functioning does indeed appear to be facilitated by a mass cultural orientation that balances competitive political activity with a general trust in, and tolerance of, one's social surroundings. The second conclusion is that what exists of the American cultural conflict described earlier has taken form gradually since the 1970s and has been brought about by a downward dissemination of elite political discourse that has only reached (and has therefore only affected) Americans who pay relatively close attention to politics. Most Americans, therefore, have not aligned their various identities and preferences into conformity with one of the two culture war prototypes.

NATIONAL POLITICAL CULTURES AND DEMOCRACY

Psychologists who study *culture* often define it along the following lines: (a) It refers to a system of behaviors, values, and norms, along with the physical and institutional environmental characteristics that both derive from and reinforce these psychological elements; (b) it is constructed through interactions among individuals; and (c) it is intergenerationally transmitted (e.g., A. B. Cohen, 2009; Fiske, 2002; Triandis, 2007). This is an expansive definition that captures a wide range of psychological elements and their reciprocal impacts with the social and physical environment. It is therefore quite useful for describing social variation across groups of people. However, if one's goal is to gauge whether a group's culture explains some other group attribute, this definition leaves little that is "not-culture" for culture to explain (e.g., Elkins & Simeon, 1979). For example, if a nation's culture includes the practices, institutions, and physical concomitants of democracy (e.g., men and women casting ballots that are legitimately counted, journalists criticizing the leadership without getting arrested and tortured), then how can a nation's culture be said to cause democracy? The nation's culture, defined this way, must be said to *include* democracy.

Whether such an expansive definition is problematic depends on the theoretical goals of the scholarship. The primary goal of much political culture research has been to evaluate whether national political culture has an impact on democratic institutional functioning. If one were to adopt the expansive definition of culture, then this question really asks whether some elements of culture (belief systems or attitude clusters) have an impact on other elements of culture (democratic institutions). Many scholars of political culture have, in part for this reason, defined political culture more narrowly—as a "syndrome of attitudes" that is rooted in a group's historical circumstances but that is still malleable (Inglehart, 1988, p. 1214; see also McClosky & Zaller, 1984, pp. 16–17). *Attitudes* here refers broadly to mass belief systems, encompassing attitudes in the narrower social psychological sense (e.g., Eagly & Chaiken, 1998), values, and beliefs. Conceptualized as something distinct from actual democratic structures and practices, a society's political culture may be said to influence (or not influence) these structures and practices. I therefore use this definition.

Finally, the question of which social groups should be regarded as the "bearers of the culture" (Elkins & Simeon, 1979, p. 130) also depends on the goals of one's analysis. Some social units that are commonly studied as the bearers of political culture are political or regional subunits within nations (e.g., Erikson, McIver, & Wright, 1987), nations (e.g., Almond & Verba, 1963), and larger cultural zones consisting of multiple nations (e.g., Huntington, 1996). I limit the current discussion to the survey-based empirical inquiry into the mass (i.e., nonelite) political cultures of nations (but see Pye, 1991).

The Civic Culture

An early and influential survey study of national political cultures and democracy was reported in Almond and Verba's (1963) *The Civic Culture*. Almond and Verba proposed that there is a specific type of mass belief system that is conducive to democratic institutional functioning. Measuring mass beliefs in the United States, Britain, Germany, Italy, and Mexico, they found that citizens of the two English-speaking countries were more likely to possess a configuration of attitudes that these authors argued were favorable to democracy, including pride in their political systems, expectation of equal and consistent treatment by their governments, and a sense of subjective competence in their ability to influence government.

Weaknesses of this conceptual framework have been discussed by various authors (e.g., Elkins & Simeon, 1979; Jackman & Miller, 1996; Muller & Seligson, 1994; Reisinger, 1995). For example, some attitudinal differences between the societies with strong versus weak civic cultures were accounted for by structural differences (e.g., average education) between these societies (Elkins & Simeon, 1979). Also, causal direction between culture and institutions is uncertain (Muller & Seligson, 1994). A key example here is that some of the putatively causal cultural attributes (e.g., expectation of fair treatment by government) are perhaps more appropriately considered informant reports of actual political institutions, supposedly the dependent variable in the conceptual framework.

Notwithstanding these limitations, scholars of democracy have continued to explore the idea that "the evolution and persistence of mass based democracy requires the emergence of certain supportive habits and attitudes among the general public" (Inglehart, 1988, p. 1204). Such habits and attitudes, in this view, are not mere epiphenomena of economically deterministic processes (Marx, 1859/1977); rather, they independently influence institutional functioning (e.g., Banfield, 1958; Fukuyama, 1996; Harrison & Huntington, 2000; Inglehart, 1988; Putnam, 1993; Weber, 1905/2002). In this section, I argue that evidence has been consistent with the notion that democratic institutions are most likely to be maintained (and to emerge in the first place) when the population possesses a mass cultural orientation that balances political competition with a social mind-set that includes interpersonal trust and tolerance.

Limited-Intensity Political Conflict

That democratic governments must strike a balance between forceful leadership and responsiveness to citizens is an old idea. So is the classic civics textbook view of what type of citizen democratic governments require to function effectively: one who is politically aware, involved, and active. Textbook democracy requires that citizens hold their governments accountable, and citizens cannot do this if they do not know or care about what is going on politically.

So it came as a troubling surprise when modern survey methods revealed that citizens, on average, are not that interested in or knowledgeable about politics (e.g., Campbell, Converse, Miller, & Stokes, 1960; Converse, 1964; McClosky, 1964). Various explanations of how, and if, democracies still function well despite this fact have been debated. Some have focused on citizens' effective use of heuristics that do not require a lot of information or effort (e.g., Lupia & McCubbins, 1998; Popkin, 1991; Sniderman, Brody, & Tetlock, 1991). Others have noted methodological limitations of using free-report political descriptions (e.g., Marcus, Tabb, & Sullivan, 1974) and failing to account for random error in self-reported political attitudes (e.g., Achen, 1975; Ansolabehere, Rodden, & Snyder, 2008) when trying to infer levels of political interest, engagement, and sophistication among citizens. Others have argued that error in individual opinion is often random, rendering aggregate opinion and its fluctuation meaningful (e.g., Page & Shapiro, 1992). Still others have argued that democracy primarily works for attentive and knowledgeable (and usually wealthy) citizens (e.g., Delli Carpini & Keeter, 1996; see also Abramowitz, 2010; Bartels, 2010; Berinsky, 2002). An extreme extension of this reasoning is that contemporary democracy really serves to maintain and enhance the privileges of a lucky and well-organized minority.

Almond and Verba (1963), however, argued that although citizen engagement is crucial to democracy, the very limits to such engagement that are so often decried may also be crucial to democracy. For example, the combination of perceived political competence and sporadic actual political activity among citizens may allow elites to exercise decisive leadership, but to do so with the constraining fear that acting out of line will awaken segments of the public to exercise their "reserve of influence" (p. 481). Elite awareness of the innumerable "sleeping dogs" in the population may constrain their activity in a beneficial way (see also Stimson, 2004).

Almond and Verba (1963) also noted that the commitment to political preferences that does exist in democracies is "tempered in intensity by its subordination to a more general, overarching set of social values" (p. 490), including social trust and tolerance. A culture that is conducive to democracy, they argued, is one in which political conflict occurs in a context of general support for the democratic system, general trust in one's social surroundings, and general tolerance of different kinds of people. McClosky (1964) echoed this sentiment, noting that the "principles and practices of an 'open society' strongly reinforce tolerance for variety, contingency and ambiguity in matters of belief and conscience," often leading citizens to "ignore, tolerate, or play down differences" (p. 378). To McClosky, such a cultural mind-set makes up for the lack of universal endorsement of certain elements of democracy (e.g., due process and freedom of speech in certain situations). Several other scholars have stressed the importance for democracy of balancing political activity with tolerance and trust (e.g., Gibson, 1998; Lipset, 1960; Putnam, 1993; Warren, 1999). It may be helpful, in this regard, when the dimensions of conflict within a society are somewhat independent of one another, that is, when much of the political competition does not occur between two highly differentiated opponents who differ with each other on everything (e.g., Berelson et al., 1954; Coser, 1956; Dahl, 1961; Lipset, 1963). Relatively independent dimensions of conflict may facilitate trust and tolerance of those with whom one disagrees on a particular issue; these very individuals may be one's allies on a different political matter or one's friends because of other, politically irrelevant common interests.

Evidence Consistent With the Limited-Intensity Conflict View

Indeed, evidence has been consistent with the view that the cultural characteristics of limited-intensity political conflict are conducive to democratic functioning. Inglehart (2003) measured, using international surveys from the mid-1990s through the early 2000s, nations' mean levels of tolerance, interpersonal trust, political activism, life satisfaction, and "postmaterialist" values (i.e., concerns about freedom and participation exceeding concerns about survival and order; see Inglehart & Abramson, 1999). At the national level, these components of a self-expressive value syndrome were highly correlated with one another. Certain nations appear to have political cultures that balance political activism and participatory orientation, on the one hand, with a tolerance of those one opposes (or even hates), a trust that people in general are not going to harm one even if they have political power, and a sense that life is pretty good overall, on the other (cf. Jackman & Miller, 1996; Muller & Seligson, 1994). This self-expressive value syndrome possessed a staggering .83 correlation with quality of democratic functioning between 1981 and 2000, as measured by Freedom House (http://www.freedomhouse. org). Needless to say, one sees very few correlations of this magnitude in the social sciences, especially between measures as distinct as an aggregated mass belief cluster and an institutional characteristic of nations.

But does this cultural syndrome cause democracy, does democracy cause this cultural syndrome, or do other national characteristics—most notably level of socioeconomic development—cause both? The nature of the relation between socioeconomic development and democratic functioning has long been the subject of scholarly analysis, much of it guided by modernization theory (e.g., Boix & Stokes, 2003; Bollen & Jackman, 1985; Burkhart & Lewis-Beck,

1994; Dahl, 1973; Gibson, 2001; Huntington, 1991; Inglehart, 1997; Lerner, 1958; Lipset, 1960; North, Wallis, & Weingast, 2009; Przeworski, Alvarez, Cheibub, & Limongi, 2000; Przeworski & Limongi, 1997). The evidence suggests that countries with higher levels of socioeconomic development are more likely to be democracies and that high socioeconomic development has been associated with transition from authoritarian governance to democratic governance as well as sustenance of democratic governance (see Diamond, 2008, pp. 94–105).

In line with this evidence, Welzel, Inglehart, and Klingemann (2003) argued that socioeconomic development causes greater democracy at the national level. Moreover, they argued that this relation is mediated by a cultural orientation that is favorable to balancing political activity and liberty aspirations with trust and tolerance. They labeled this cultural orientation *mass emancipative values* and measured it as a composite of tolerance of diversity, inclination to civic protest, liberty aspirations, interpersonal trust, life satisfaction, and low religiosity.

Welzel et al. (2003) characterized the two main causal influences in their model as follows. Scarcity of material and social resources leads people to downward-adjust their higher order emancipative strivings, and improvement in resources leads such higher order strivings to become operative (Maslow, 1988). Then, when a nation has a high mass cultural level of emancipative values, this provides an incentive for *elite integrity*, referring to relatively low levels of corruption and relatively strong adherence to the rule of law (cf. O'Donnell & Schmitter, 1986). In this view, a mass belief system centering on the balance of trust and tolerance with activity and self-expression makes "authoritarian rule increasingly ineffective and costly" (p. 348) for elites. Moreover, it provides an incentive for opportunistic politicians to become supporters of democracy. Thus, via elite integrity, the mass emancipative values of nations cause those nations to become or to remain democratic.

Analyzing data from 73 nations representing 80% of the world's population, Welzel et al. (2003) found that, controlling for democratic tradition up until 1995, socioeconomic resources in the early 1990s had a strong effect on emancipative values measured in the mid-1990s. In this same model, with pre-1995 democratic tradition and early-1990s socioeconomic resources held constant, mid-1990s emancipative values had a strong impact on effective democracy in the late 1990s that was mediated by elite integrity. Thus, countries with relatively strong levels of a cultural orientation favorable to balancing cleavage and consensus in the mid-1990s were relatively likely to become more democratic (and relatively unlikely to become less democratic) from the mid to the late 1990s, for reasons extending beyond their material resources.

To be sure, socioeconomic development seems to affect democracy through various structural mechanisms that do not require culture as part of the explanation (e.g., Diamond, 2008; Muller, 1988; Muller & Seligson, 1994). Among these structural characteristics is economic inequality, whose complex role in democratization is the subject of debate (e.g., Freeman & Quinn, 2012; Houle, 2009). Moreover, other cultural characteristics—for example, degree of ethnic fractiousness, aspects of prior colonial experience, and degree of Protestantism—may affect democratization at certain historical junctures (Bollen & Jackman, 1985; Muller & Seligson, 1994). Also, regardless of these national characteristics, the timing and nature of democratic change are influenced by a wide range of factors, including foreign interference and aid, global economic structures, and a great variety of unpredictable events (Diamond, 2008, Chapters 4–7). However, mass value change would appear to in part account for why gains in resources tend to make countries more democratic. This observation led Inglehart and Welzel (2005) to predict that China's rapid development will produce democracy, via mass emancipative values, within 2 decades of 2005 (see also Diamond, 2008, Chapter 10).

From Individual Responses to Mass Cultural Characteristics

It is worth highlighting that political culture researchers such as Welzel and Inglehart refer to an aggregation of individuals' attitudes as a *mass cultural orientation*. Indeed, empirical evidence seems to provide strong justification for doing so. National mean levels of such attitudes, though influenced by socioeconomic development, are also predicted by historical societal attributes (e.g., Inglehart & Baker, 2000; Putnam, Leonardi, Nanetti, & Pavoncello, 1983), suggesting that there is "a durable cultural component underlying these responses" (Inglehart, 1988, p. 1207). Furthermore, these national mean levels of attitudes (an "aggregated mass characteristic") have enormous correlations with "genuine system characteristics" such as level of democracy and socioeconomic development (Welzel et al., 2003, p. 353; see also Inglehart & Baker, 2000). In one analysis, for example, national income–education correlated .91 with mass emancipative values, which dwarfed the average within-nation (between-person) correlation of .29 (Welzel et al., 2003). It is quite clear that "nations tend to create distinguished 'central tendencies' among their citizens' prevailing values" (Welzel et al., 2003, p. 351), mass tendencies that should be viewed as meaningful, socially transmitted cultural attributes of nations.

There is, of course, meaningful within-nation variability in these belief systems (e.g., Napier & Jost, 2008). Individuals within nations have great varieties of experiences for a great variety of reasons, including differential social treatment and differential genetic makeup. A nation's mean level of various mass characteristics is, however, an indicator of an important national cultural characteristic with which citizens are faced and within which they act. As Welzel et al. (2003) noted, each individual in a nation has an infinitesimal and essentially meaningless influence on the nation's mean level of a cultural attribute. However, the national mean level of a cultural attribute provides a part of the context in which the individual acts, and one that is strongly linked to the way the nation is governed and how much wealth it generates.

Generalizability Across Historical Contexts

One should not, however, take for granted that the influence of culture on democracy generalizes across cultural–historical contexts. It might be the case that certain cultural values only influence democratization under some cultural–historical circumstances but not under others. To put it another way, a Cultural–Historical Context × Mass Values interaction may exist in the prediction of change in democracy. One might interpret evidence reported by Muller and Seligson (1994) along these lines.

Muller and Seligson (1994) challenged the thesis that cultural attitudes cause democracy, using a sample of 27 predominantly European, North American, and Latin American nations. They reported findings that nations' civic cultural attitudes between 1981 and 1986 did not predict democracy level between 1981 and 1990 when controlling for democracy level between 1972 and 1980 and other nation-level covariates. Muller and Seligson's index of civic culture consisted of life satisfaction, trust, and opposition to revolutionary change. Notably, this index did not include indicators of valuing political activity or indicators of tolerance, and it may therefore have fallen short of capturing the cultural balance between consensus and cleavage emphasized here (indeed, Muller and Seligson did not intend to measure a construct based on the present conceptualization). Interestingly, when these scholars added national support for gradual reform (1981–1986), this mass attitude had a significant positive effect on change in democracy. Such a mass attitude would seem to reflect a valuing of political activity (reform) being performed in a tempered, socially sensitive way (gradualism). Nonetheless, that certain types of cultural variables did not predict change in democracy from the 1970s to the 1980s (Muller & Seligson, 1994) but did predict change in democracy from pre-1995 to post-1995 (Welzel et al., 2003) suggests that particular mass beliefs may have a greater influence on democratization under some circumstances than under other circumstances (see also Bollen & Jackman, 1985, for a study examining predictors of democratic change in the 1960s).

Overt Support for Democracy

It is also interesting to note that the value syndrome favoring the combination of political competition and trust and tolerance appears to be a stronger predictor of democratic institutional functioning than is overt support for democracy itself (Inglehart, 2003; see also McClosky, 1964). There now exists globally widespread overt support for democracy that both transcends cultural zones (e.g., Diamond, 2008) and appears to be rooted in a fairly accurate understanding of what democracy entails (e.g., Dalton, Shin, & Jou, 2007). However, such overt support is not enough for democratizing and for sustaining democracy, and if one wants to predict a country's democratization path, it seems that one would be better served by knowledge of the nation's tolerance, trust, and political activity than by knowledge of the nation's overt support for democracy. An interesting exception in this regard is Latin America, whose countries, with some exceptions, combine democratic institutions and overt support for democracy with low levels of trust (e.g., Lagos, 1997).

Finally, it is important to consider the distinction between overt support for democracy and the type of cultural orientation described earlier when reflecting on the political upheavals in Muslim Middle Eastern and North African countries that took form in early 2011 (referred to as the *Arab Spring*). Some have argued that Islam is not conducive to various aspects of progress, including democratization (Huntington, 1996). More convincing, however, is the view expressed by Diamond (2008) that any cultural inclination against democracy that Middle Eastern and North African Muslim societies now possess is the product of recent cultural circumstances rather than an enduring incompatibility of their religion with democracy. After all, one would not have to look hard in the Old Testament, the New Testament, the Koran, or any other piece of scripture to find prescriptions that are decidedly contrary to democratic values. Moreover, Muslim societies were far more progressive than were Christian societies through much of Islam's history. Muslim societies possess about the same level of overt democratic support as do non-Muslim societies (Diamond, 2008; Inglehart, 2003). The findings described earlier, however, would seem to suggest that the likelihood of democracy taking hold in these societies will in part depend on the adoption of a cultural orientation favoring the balance of consensus and cleavage. In particular, a cultural shift toward greater tolerance of disliked groups (e.g., minorities, homosexuals) may be necessary to provide an incentive for elite behavior conducive to democratization (see Inglehart, 2003, p. 54). Of course, though, economic factors, foreign influence, and ethnic fractiousness may be at least as important for determining democratic progress.

AN ANALYSIS OF THE AMERICAN CULTURE WAR

I have reviewed arguments and evidence that political cultures are favorable to democratic functioning when they are conducive to limited-intensity political conflict. The ultimate causal root of this cultural orientation is often (though certainly not always) socioeconomic development, which seems to bring about a mass value system that combines political expression with a broad social orientation encompassing tolerance and trust. Democracy appears to be more likely to come about, and more likely to be sustained, when the society's members possess this mass value configuration.

Various scholars of democracy have argued that nonoverlapping social and political cleavages play a strong role in producing limited-intensity conflict (e.g., Berelson et al., 1954; Coser, 1956; Dahl, 1961; Lipset & Rokkan, 1967; Lowi, 1979; Truman, 1951), which essentially means that political and social conflicts will not be dangerous to the extent that (a) the conflicts occur along many different lines (e.g., abortion stance, social welfare spending stance, religiosity, religious affiliation, region, social class, race, views of military action) and (b) these dimensions of conflict are not so highly correlated that most citizens find themselves aligned with one or the other camp on every dimension. Baldassarri and Gelman (2008) summarized these perspectives in the following way: "Intrasocial conflict is sustainable as long as there are multiple and nonoverlapping lines of disagreement" (p. 409).

The discourse of the culture war in the United States often implies that the dimensions of political and social variation are strongly overlapping and possess an essential conceptual connection (Fiorina et al., 2006; Seyle & Newman, 2006). This notion of strong overlap does appear to characterize contemporary U.S. political elites (e.g., Layman, Carsey, & Horowitz, 2006; Poole & Rosenthal, 2007), who have indeed become more polarized since the 1970s. However, the claim that the U.S. general public is polarized is a more controversial one (Abramowitz, 2010; Fiorina et al., 2006). Whether or not one finds evidence of polarization in U.S. public opinion depends, not surprisingly, on what indicators of polarization one considers (e.g., Hetherington, 2009; Levendusky, 2009).

Evidence Against Polarization

The most straightforward way to conceptualize polarization is as increased extremity of issue stances. Polarization occurs when the distributions of issue stances change over time such that more of the population moves from the middle to one of the extreme positions. On the basis of this standard, the U.S. public has generally not become more polarized (DiMaggio, Evans, & Bryson, 1996; Evans, 2003; Fiorina et al., 2006).

However, the type of polarization of interest here does not require increased issue extremity; rather, it involves multiple dimensions of conflict—including issue stances, political identities, social identities, and so forth—becoming aligned so that the population increasingly comes to resemble one of two highly differentiated political cultural groups. When one examines the intercorrelations of issue stances over time (e.g., conservative vs. liberal view on abortion correlating with conservative vs. liberal view on government health insurance), one finds only slight increases in interissue polarization (Baldassarri & Gelman, 2008). Moreover, various demographic characteristics have not become more strongly correlated with political attitudes (DiMaggio et al., 1996; Evans, 2003). Catholics and mainline Protestants have become more evenly balanced in their partisan allegiances over the past few decades (Putnam & Campbell, 2010). In many respects, then, the view of Americans as having come to possess one of two stereotypical bundles of cultural attributes is inaccurate.

Evidence for Polarization

Is it conservative to oppose the legality of abortion? It may surprise some followers of U.S. politics to learn that the answer to this question would depend on the point in time at which it was asked (Stimson, 2004). Both partisan identification (as Republican vs. Democratic) and ideological identification (as conservative vs. liberal) have become increasingly correlated with issue attitudes since the 1970s (Abramowitz & Saunders, 2006; Bafumi & Shapiro, 2009; Levendusky, 2009; Stoker & Jennings, 2008), especially cultural attitudes about issues such as abortion and gay rights (Baldassarri & Gelman, 2008). Cultural attitudes, in fact, possessed little to no relation with party identification and ideological identification in the early 1970s.

In this respect, Americans have, on average, moved more toward one of two opposing cultural prototypes during the past 4 decades—for example, conservative–Republican identifiers who oppose abortion or liberal–Democratic identifiers who support it. Some have referred to this process as *sorting* (Fiorina et al., 2006; Levendusky, 2009); because the parties have taken more distinct stands on various issues, people now have a better sense of which partisan and ideological group their preferences place them in. However, note that longitudinal findings have been consistent with both partisan identification (Layman & Carsey, 2002) and ideological identification (Malka & Lelkes, 2010, Study 1) causally influencing issue attitudes. Moreover, experimental evidence has suggested that both partisan cues (Bullock, 2011; G. L. Cohen, 2003; Goren, Federico, & Kittilson, 2009) and ideological cues (Malka & Lelkes, 2010, Study 2) can influence the political positions adopted by partisan and ideological identifiers. Regarding the changing link between partisan and ideological identification, Levendusky (2009) found that Americans have been more likely to adjust their ideological identifications and substantive political attitudes to match their partisan identifications than vice versa. Thus, the increased associations between political identities (partisan and ideological) and issue stances may not simply reflect people having a better idea of what party or ideological group their fixed issue stances place them in. Rather, these identities may actually have an impact on people's substantive stances when issues are discursively framed in partisan or ideological terms.

Not only have Americans become more inclined to organize their issue attitudes in partisan and ideological terms, but they have also become more inclined to base their political alignments on certain demographic characteristics, particularly in the religious realm. Since World War II, White evangelical Protestants have become lopsidedly Republican, whereas Black Protestants have become almost uniformly Democratic (e.g., Putnam & Campbell, 2010). Religiosity—defined as level of religious commitment, regardless of one's religious affiliation—appears to have become increasingly correlated with voting Republican (Fiorina et al., 2006; Putnam & Campbell, 2010) and conservative self-identification (Malka, Lelkes, Srivastava, Cohen, & Miller, 2012) in the early 1990s. Whether the U.S. electorate has become more polarized along class lines is a subject of debate (Abramowitz, 2010; McCarty, Poole, & Rosenthal, 2006). In some respects, then, the view of increased mass U.S. polarization in recent decades is a reasonable, though often exaggerated, one.

Whose Culture War

With respect to some political and social dimensions, Americans appear to have become more likely to resemble one of the two culture war prototypes; with respect to other dimensions, they have not. Even though Americans have become more likely to bundle certain attributes together (e.g., liberal identification and cultural progressivism), the degree to which the population is split into two opposing camps is, however, not close to that suggested in much of the culture war discourse (Fiorina et al., 2006). For example, estimates from 2004 national data suggested that only about 12% of the population identify as conservative, identify as Republican, and oppose abortion (Baldassarri & Gelman, 2008). Close to 90% of Democrats in this survey either did not self-identify as liberal or had a nonliberal view on abortion, affirmative action, or health care (Baldassarri & Gelman, 2008). In a combined set of representative U.S. samples from 1996 to 2008, religiosity (a composite of religious attendance and importance) had only very small correlations with conservative positions on social welfare, the environment, and defense, and religiosity had correlations indistinguishable from zero with conservative positions on racial policy, immigration, and gun control (Malka et al., 2012). Religiosity has been shown to correlate with liberal positions on both the death penalty (Carroll, 2004; Malka et al., 2012) and torture of terrorism suspects (Malka & Soto, 2011). The stereotypical ideologically aligned teams described early in this chapter would appear to have small memberships, even if they have become a bit larger during the past few decades.

Although across-the-board ideological alignment is not widespread in the U.S. general public, it does characterize a subset of the U.S. general public. As political scientists have long known, being aligned across multiple political dimensions is something that occurs only among people who are high in a family of indicators converging on the construct of political engagement. Typically, the only people who are aligned with one of the two ideological prototypes are those who are high in objective political knowledge, subjective political interest, political activism, inclination to vote, and related constructs (e.g., Abramowitz, 2010; Converse, 1964; Baldassarri & Gelman, 2008; Jacoby, 1995; Judd & Krosnick, 1989; Sniderman et al., 1991; Stimson, 1975; Zaller, 1992). A dispositional tendency to be opinionated may enhance the effects of political engagement on ideological alignment (Federico & Schneider, 2007). Being politically engaged is also associated with a greater likelihood of translating one's personality characteristics into political leanings (Federico & Goren, 2009; Federico, Hunt, & Ergun, 2009) and greater likelihood of translating one's religiosity into political conservatism (Malka et al., 2012).

That only those who are most politically engaged possess multiple characteristics of one of the culture war prototypes suggests that there are limits to the naturality of these group memberships (cf. Jost, Nosek, & Gosling, 2008). Instead, these groups exist as they do largely because of political discourse—the way in which politics, including the prevailing alignments, are discussed in the news media and, consequently, informal political communication.

Elite-Driven Dissemination of Culture War Rhetoric

As discussed earlier, political elites have become more polarized since the 1970s (Layman et al., 2006; Levendusky, 2009; Poole & Rosenthal, 2007; Rohde, 1991). The necessity of assembling a broad political coalition has led Republican elites to emphasize the *conservatism* of traditional moral stances, a term whose previous political implication had to do primarily with social welfare and scope of government stance (Adams, 1997; Stimson, 2004). Culturally traditional Democratic officeholders have seen their numbers dwindle, and liberal Republicans are no longer in office. The strategic statements made by political actors, conveyed and commented on by the news media, have increasingly emphasized linkages between cultural traditionalism and free market ideology and between cultural progressivism and an economically interventionist federal government (e.g., Hunter, 1991). The term *liberal* has become associated with a rejection of traditional American values and lax morality (Ellis & Stimson, 2009; Stimson, 2004). Also, since the 1960s, the parties have taken distinct stands on civil rights and have superimposed these positions over their social welfare divide (Carmines & Stimson, 1989). I contend that exposure to these messages that disparate political characteristics go together, and motivation to act consistently with these messages, is what makes people who are politically engaged more likely to resemble one of the culture war prototypes.

What evidence suggests that discursive messages are what drive the enhanced ideological alignment of those who are politically engaged? In a comprehensive analysis, Baldassarri and Gelman (2008) examined patterns of change in interissue correlations, partisan identity-issue correlations, and ideological identity-issue correlations among representative samples of Americans between 1972 and 2004. In one part of their analysis, these scholars gauged differences in the temporal changes across different subgroups of Americans. Their results indicated that increases in mass ideological alignment over this time period of elite-generated polarizing discourse were primarily confined to those Americans with relatively strong political engagement (see also Abramowitz, 2010). Americans who were interested in politics displayed greater increases in all three types of ideological alignment described earlier than did Americans who were uninterested in politics. Moreover, wealthy Americans displayed greater increases in all three types of ideological alignment than did low-income Americans. These findings dovetail with those demonstrating that political engagement is associated with greater application of motivated reasoning to support one's partisan–ideological group (Taber & Lodge, 2006).

The findings presented in this section suggest that Americans, on average, do not resemble one of the two culture war prototypes. During the past 4 decades, as discourse has conveyed the message of a more polarized political elite, Americans have, on average, become more likely to align some (but not other) social and political characteristics in accordance with the culture war framework. Finally, the politically engaged Americans, those with the motivation and the resources to devote time to following politics, are those who have shown the greatest increases in ideological alignment. Thus, it appears that messages from discourse since the 1970s have made the attentive public more ideologically aligned with one of the two culture war prototypes, but this enhanced conflict is balanced by the presence of a large number of Americans who possess a set of identities and beliefs that do not conform to one of these prototypes.

CONCLUSION

For only a limited segment of human history have people within societies regularly settled their political conflicts and transferred power without violence or direct threats thereof. Although it falls short of its ideals in a variety of ways, contemporary liberal democracy provides the best mechanism for doing so. The inner workings of governance in democracies are largely an elite phenomenon. However, evidence has suggested that the mass belief systems of general publics may not just be an incidental by-product of historical, institutional, and economic circumstances; rather, they may causally influence the degree to which a society is governed through democratic institutions. In both democratic and nondemocratic governments, elites are concerned about and attentive to mass opinion. Mass opinion is a key part of the context in which elites act, making some actions more rewarding and others more costly. A cultural orientation that balances trust and tolerance with political competition seems to be conducive to democratic institutional functioning because of the system of incentives that it places on elites.

For democracy to work, people must tolerate and support the rights of their opponents. They must trust that their opponents will tolerate them and support their rights. Such a situation is one of political competition, to be sure, but a competition that is tempered in intensity by other social considerations. According to various scholars, such limited-intensity political conflict is more likely, or only possible, when a sufficient degree of independence exists between the various lines of conflict in society. Few Americans display the entire pattern of opinions listed by Mr. Obama in the quotation in the opening paragraph of this chapter, and few Americans match the opposite ideological prototype. Americans can expect that if they disagree with their compatriots (even heatedly) on one issue, they will not necessarily disagree with these fellow citizens on any of a number of other matters, and they are hardly less likely to share other important characteristics with these people that can be a basis for friendship and mutual respect (cf. Jost et al., 2008). This state of affairs is better characterized by Mr. Obama's oft-quoted speech at the 2004 Democratic National Convention, in which he noted that characteristics such as being religious and having gay friends do not uniquely characterize red and blue states, respectively.

I conclude this chapter with a few points that may be worthy of consideration in research on political culture and the U.S. culture war. First, regarding the study of the mass beliefs that may be conducive to democracy, it may prove important to treat as separate constructs the various components of such a mass belief system. Tolerance is not the same thing as trust, and both of these are quite conceptually distinct from political activity. In fact, the combination of these two categories of attributes may be what can influence democratic functioning. To be sure, the various components of the mass cultural orientation described here are correlated with one another at the national level. Nonetheless, it would be worthwhile in some analyses to treat these different responses as indicators of separate nation-level constructs (e.g., Elkins & Simeon, 1979; Muller & Seligson, 1994) and to parse each of the bivariate relations among them (e.g., the trust–tolerance relation, the life satisfaction–political expression relation). Some of these relations may be accounted for by common origins in socioeconomic development, inequality, or some other nation-level structural or institutional variable. Also, these nation-level cultural attributes may have causal influences on one another. Treating these national culture dimensions as separate constructs is necessary for uncovering the processes that link them. For example, national life satisfaction may be an outcome of national cultural factors pertaining to autonomous self-expression (e.g., Fischer & Boer, 2011), and some cultural dimensions may be outcomes, rather than causes, of democracy (Muller & Seligson, 1994). Treating the cultural beliefs as separate constructs is also necessary for exploring the interesting possibility that some mass beliefs are conducive to democratization at some times but not at other times.

Next, the relation between the two types of societal characteristics discussed here, nonoverlapping identities and the balance of cleavage and consensus, would seem to be a worthy topic of investigation. Both of these national characteristics should, theoretically, be conducive to democracy, but their relation with one another may be quite complex. Nonoverlapping identities might be expected to produce a trusting and tolerant national culture. For example, ethnic fractiousness of nations seems to negatively influence democratic functioning (Muller & Seligson, 1994), perhaps because a relatively weak association between political position and ethnicity is favorable for democracy. But what influence does a democratic culture have on overlap between identities? It is likely that valuing of political self-expression may cause people to align with a political cultural prototype presented in discourse. Indeed, it is indisputable that politically engaged Americans, who are the most likely to vote and influence public affairs, are relatively likely to match one of the two opposing culture war prototypes. It is crucial to note in this regard, however, that although political engagement is associated with this form of polarization, it is also associated with relatively strong endorsement of fundamental democratic values, such as free speech and due process (e.g., McClosky, 1964; McClosky & Zaller, 1984). As Abramowitz (2010) pointed out, it is the polarized segment of the U.S. public "whose beliefs and behaviors most closely reflect the ideals of responsible democratic citizenship" (pp. 4–5).

Regardless, when examining cross-nationally the interplay between mass value characteristics of nations and overlapping versus nonoverlapping lines of conflict, it is clearly necessary to gauge the latter with respect to social identities and political positions that are salient in specific societies. For example, the associations between evangelical Protestantism and attitude toward abortion and between partisan identity and attitudes about guns are salient in the United States, but not in most other countries. The link between nonoverlapping identities and values conducive to democracy is one that should be addressed directly, in a manner that takes into account the identities that are especially salient to political conflict in each nation studied.

Finally, research should explore the possibility that the values of limited-intensity political conflict have a potential dark side. The mass beliefs that appear favorable to democracy involve trust and tolerance of one's opponents. Societies, however, are characterized by inequality in opportunity and material conditions, much of it the result of entrenched structural conditions. Also, all societies contain ideas and values that justify these aspects of the system as fair, natural, inevitable, and appropriate. It would seem natural for people who are economically disadvantaged to support urgent and radical change and to reject such system-justifying ideas, given the desperate circumstances in which they often find themselves, but research conducted within the framework of system justification theory has documented reasons why they might not (e.g., Jost, Banaji, & Nosek, 2004; Jost & Hunyady, 2005). Viewing all political opponents as respectable and worthy of trust and tolerance may reflect a Pollyannaish but comforting mind-set that ultimately perpetuates unequal social arrangements. Thus, the mass beliefs that promote democracy may, at the same time, serve to justify the unequal distribution of wealth and life chances within nations. This may not be the case, and indeed the mass beliefs conducive to democracy may have a positive influence, or no influence at all, on material equality. The unsettling possibility that some mass beliefs both promote democratic stability and justify systemically inequitable arrangements is, however, one that should be evaluated empirically.

REFERENCES

Abramowitz, A. I. (2010). *The disappearing center: Engaged citizens, polarization, and American democracy.* New Haven, CT: Yale University Press.

Abramowitz, A. I., & Saunders, K. L. (2006). Exploring the bases of partisanship in the American electorate: Social identity vs. ideology. *Political Research Quarterly, 59,* 175–187. doi:10.1177/106591290605900201

Achen, C. H. (1975). Mass political attitudes and the survey response. *American Political Science Review, 69,* 1218–1231. doi:10.2307/1955282

Adams, G. D. (1997). Abortion: Evidence of an issue evolution. *American Journal of Political Science, 41,* 718–737. doi:10.2307/2111673

Almond, G. A., & Verba, S. (1963). *The civic culture: Political attitudes and democracy in five nations*. Princeton, NJ: Princeton University Press.

Ansolabehere, S., Rodden, J., & Snyder, J. M. (2008). The strength of issues: Using multiple measures to gauge preference stability, ideological constraint, and issue voting. *American Political Science Review, 102,* 215–232. doi:10.1017/S0003055408080210

Bafumi, J., & Shapiro, R. Y. (2009). A new partisan voter. *Journal of Politics, 71,* 1–24. doi:10.1017/S0022381608090014

Baldassarri, D., & Gelman, A. (2008). Partisans without constraint: Political polarization and trends in American public opinion. *American Journal of Sociology, 114,* 408–446. doi:10.1086/590649

Banfield, E. C. (1958). *The moral basis of a backward society*. Glencoe, IL: Free Press.

Bartels, L. M. (2010). *Unequal democracy: The political economy of the new gilded age*. Princeton, NJ: Princeton University Press.

Berelson, B. R., Lazarsfeld, P. F., & McPhee, W. N. (1954). *Voting: A study of opinion formation in a presidential campaign*. Chicago, IL: University of Chicago Press.

Berinsky, A. J. (2002). Silent voices: Social welfare policy opinions and political equality in America. *American Journal of Political Science, 46,* 276–287. doi:10.2307/3088376

Boix, C., & Stokes, S. C. (2003). Endogenous democratization. *World Politics, 55,* 517–549. doi:10.1353/wp.2003.0019

Bollen, K. A., & Jackman, R. W. (1985). Economic and noneconomic determinants of political democracy in the 1960s. *Research in Political Sociology, 1,* 27–48.

Bullock, J. G. (2011). Elite influence on public opinion in an informed electorate. *American Political Science Review, 105,* 496–515. doi:10.1017/S0003055411000165

Burkhart, R. E., & Lewis-Beck, M. S. (1994). Comparative democracy: The economic development thesis. *American Political Science Review, 88,* 903–910.

Campbell, A., Converse, P. E., Miller, W. E., & Stokes, D. E. (1960). *The American voter*. New York, NY: Wiley.

Carmines, E. G., & Stimson, J. A. (1989). *Issue evolution: Race and the transformation of American politics*. Princeton, NJ: Princeton University Press.

Carroll, J. (2004, November 16). *Who supports the death penalty?* Retrieved from http://www.gallup.com/poll/14050/who-supports-death-penalty.aspx

Cohen, A. B. (2009). Many forms of culture. *American Psychologist, 64,* 194–204. doi:10.1037/a0015308

Cohen, G. L. (2003). Party over policy: The dominating impact of group influence on political beliefs. *Journal of Personality and Social Psychology, 85,* 808–822. doi:10.1037/0022-3514.85.5.808

Converse, P. E. (1964). The nature of belief systems in mass publics. In D. E. Apter (Ed.), *Ideology and discontent* (pp. 206–261). New York, NY: Free Press of Glencoe.

Coser, L. A. (1956). *The functions of social conflict*. New York, NY: Free Press.

Dahl, R. A. (1961). *Who governs? Democracy and power in an American city*. New Haven, CT: Yale University Press.

Dahl, R. A. (1973). *Regimes and oppositions*. New Haven, CT: Yale University Press.

Dalton, R. J., Shin, D. C., & Jou, W. (2007). Understanding democracy: Data from unlikely places. *Journal of Democracy, 18*, 142–156.

Delli Carpini, M. X., & Keeter, S. (1996). *What Americans know about politics and why it matters*. New Haven, CT: Yale University Press.

Diamond, L. (2008). *The spirit of democracy: The struggle to build free societies throughout the world*. New York, NY: Times Books.

DiMaggio, P., Evans, J., & Bryson, B. (1996). Have Americans' social attitudes become more polarized? *American Journal of Sociology, 102*, 690–755. doi:10.1086/230995

Eagly, A. H., & Chaiken, S. (1998). Attitude structure and function. In D. T. Gilbert, S. T. Fiske, & G. Lindzey (Eds.), *The handbook of social psychology* (4th ed., Vol. 1, pp. 269–322). New York, NY: McGraw-Hill.

Elkins, D. J., & Simeon, R. E. B. (1979). A cause in search of its effect, or what does political culture explain? *Comparative Politics, 11*, 127–145. doi:10.2307/421752

Ellis, C., & Stimson, J. A. (2009). Symbolic ideology in the American electorate. *Electoral Studies, 28*, 388–402. doi:10.1016/j.electstud.2009.05.010

Erikson, R. S., McIver, J. P., & Wright, G. C. (1987). State political culture and public opinion. *American Political Science Review, 81*, 797–814. doi:10.2307/1962677

Evans, J. H. (2003). Have Americans' attitudes become more polarized: An update. *Social Science Quarterly, 84*, 71–90. doi:10.1111/1540-6237.8401005

Federico, C. M., & Goren, P. (2009). Motivated social cognition and ideology: Is attention to elite discourse a prerequisite for epistemically motivated political affinities? In J. T. Jost, A. C. Kay, & H. Thorisdottir (Eds.), *Social and psychological bases of ideology and system justification* (pp. 267–291). New York, NY: Oxford University Press. doi:10.1093/acprof:oso/9780195320916.003.011

Federico, C. M., Hunt, C. V., & Ergun, D. (2009). Political expertise, social worldviews, and ideology: Translating "competitive jungles" and "dangerous worlds" into ideological reality. *Social Justice Research, 22*, 259–279. doi:10.1007/s11211-009-0097-0

Federico, C. M., & Schneider, M. C. (2007). Political expertise and the use of ideology: Moderating effects of evaluative motivation. *Public Opinion Quarterly, 71*, 221–252. doi:10.1093/poq/nfm010

Fiorina, M. P., Abrams, S. J., & Pope, J. C. (2006). *Culture war? The myth of a polarized America* (2nd ed.). New York, NY: Longman.

Fischer, R., & Boer, D. (2011). What is more important for national well-being: Money or autonomy? A meta-analysis of well-being, burnout, and anxiety across 63 societies. *Journal of Personality and Social Psychology, 101*, 164–184. doi:10.1037/a0023663

Fiske, A. P. (2002). Using individualism and collectivism to compare cultures—A critique of the validity and measurement of the constructs: Comment on Oyserman et al. (2002). *Psychological Bulletin, 128*, 78–88. doi:10.1037/0033-2909.128.1.78

Fowler, M. (2008, April 6). Obama: No surprise that hard-pressed Pennsylvanians turn bitter. *Huffington Post.* Retrieved from http://www.huffingtonpost.com/mayhill-fowler/obama-no-surprise-that-ha_b_96188.html

Freeman, J. R., & Quinn, D. P. (2012). The economic origins of democracy reconsidered. *American Political Science Review, 106*, 58–80. doi:10.1017/S0003055411000505

Fukuyama, F. (1996). *Trust: The social virtues and the creation of prosperity.* New York, NY: Free Press.

Gibson, J. L. (1998). A sober second thought: An experiment in persuading Russians to tolerate. *American Journal of Political Science, 42*, 819–850. doi:10.2307/2991731

Gibson, J. L. (2001). Social networks, civil society, and the prospects for consolidating Russia's democratic transition. *American Journal of Political Science, 45*, 51–68. doi:10.2307/2669359

Goren, P. B., Federico, G. P., & Kittilson, M. C. (2009). Source cues, partisan identities, and political value expression. *American Journal of Political Science, 53*, 805–820. doi:10.1111/j.1540-5907.2009.00402.x

Harrison, L. E., & Huntington, S. P. (2000). *Culture matters: How values shape human progress.* New York, NY: Basic Books.

Hetherington, M. J. (2009). Putting polarization into perspective. *British Journal of Political Science, 39*, 413–438. doi:10.1017/S0007123408000501

Houle, C. (2009). Inequality and democracy: Why inequality harms consolidation but does not affect democratization. *World Politics, 61*, 589–622. doi:10.1017/S0043887109990074

Hunter, J. D. (1991). *Culture wars: The struggle to define America.* New York, NY: Basic Books.

Huntington, S. P. (1991). *The third wave: Democratization in the late twentieth century.* Norman: University of Oklahoma Press.

Huntington, S. P. (1996). *The clash of civilizations and the remaking of the world order.* New York, NY: Simon & Schuster.

Inglehart, R. (1988). The renaissance of political culture. *American Political Science Review, 82*, 1203–1230. doi:10.2307/1961756

Inglehart, R. (1997). *Modernization and postmodernization: Cultural, economic, and political change in 43 societies.* Princeton, NJ: Princeton University Press.

Inglehart, R. (2003). How solid is mass support for democracy: And how can we measure it? *Political Science & Politics, 36*, 51–57.

Inglehart, R., & Abramson, P. (1999). Measuring postmaterialism. *American Political Science Review, 93*, 665–677. doi:10.2307/2585581

Inglehart, R., & Baker, W. E. (2000). Modernization, cultural change, and the persistence of traditional values. *American Sociological Review, 65*, 19–51. doi:10.2307/2657288

Inglehart, R., & Welzel, C. (2005). *Modernization, cultural change, and democracy.* New York, NY: Cambridge University Press.

Jackman, R. W., & Miller, R. A. (1996). The poverty of political culture. *American Journal of Political Science, 40*, 697–716. doi:10.2307/2111790

Jacoby, W. G. (1995). The structure of ideological thinking in the American electorate. *American Journal of Political Science, 39*, 314–335. doi:10.2307/2111615

Jost, J. T., Banaji, M. R., & Nosek, B. A. (2004). A decade of system justification theory: Accumulated evidence of conscious and unconscious bolstering of the status quo. *Political Psychology, 25*, 881–919. doi:10.1111/j.1467-9221.2004.00402.x

Jost, J. T., & Hunyady, O. (2005). Antecedents and consequences of system-justifying ideologies. *Current Directions in Psychological Science, 14*, 260–265. doi:10.1111/j.0963-7214.2005.00377.x

Jost, J. T., Nosek, B. A., & Gosling, S. D. (2008). Ideology: Its resurgence in social, personality, and political psychology. *Perspectives on Psychological Science, 3*, 126–136. doi:10.1111/j.1745-6916.2008.00070.x

Judd, C. M., & Krosnick, J. A. (1989). The structural basis of consistency among political attitudes: Effects of political expertise and attitude importance. In A. R. Pratkanis, S. J. Breckler, & A. G. Greenwald (Eds.), *Attitude structure and function* (pp. 99–128). Mahwah, NJ: Erlbaum.

Lagos, M. (1997). Latin America's smiling mask. *Journal of Democracy, 8*, 125–138. doi:10.1353/jod.1997.0042

Layman, G. C., & Carsey, T. M. (2002). Party polarization and conflict extension in the American electorate. *American Journal of Political Science, 46*, 786–802. doi:10.2307/3088434

Layman, G. C., Carsey, T. M., & Horowitz, J. M. (2006). Party polarization in American politics: Characteristics, causes, and consequences. *Annual Review of Political Science, 9*, 83–110. doi:10.1146/annurev.polisci.9.070204.105138

Lerner, D. (1958). *The passing of traditional society: Modernizing the Middle East.* New York, NY: Free Press.

Levendusky, M. (2009). *The partisan sort: How liberals became Democrats and conservatives became Republicans.* Chicago, IL: University of Chicago Press. doi:10.7208/chicago/9780226473673.001.0001

Lipset, S. M. (1960). *Political man: The social basis of politics.* New York, NY: Doubleday.

Lipset, S. M. (1963). *The first new nation.* New York, NY: Basic Books.

Lipset, S. M., & Rokkan, S. (1967). Cleavage structures, party systems, and voter alignments: An introduction. In S. M. Lipset & S. Rokkan (Eds.), *Party systems and voter alignments: Cross-national perspectives* (pp. 1–64). New York, NY: Free Press.

Lowi, T. J. (1979). *The end of liberalism*. New York, NY: W. W. Norton.

Lupia, A., & McCubbins, M. D. (1998). *The democratic dilemma: Can citizens learn what they need to know?* Cambridge, England: Cambridge University Press.

Malka, A., & Lelkes, Y. (2010). More than ideology: Conservative–liberal identity and receptivity to political cues. *Social Justice Research, 23,* 156–188. doi:10.1007/s11211-010-0114-3

Malka, A., Lelkes, Y., Srivastava, S., Cohen, A. B., & Miller, D. T. (2012). The association of religiosity and political conservatism: The role of political engagement. *Political Psychology, 33,* 275–299. doi:10.1111/j.1467-9221.2012.00875.x

Malka, A., & Soto, C. J. (2011). The conflicting influences of religiosity on attitude toward torture. *Personality and Social Psychology Bulletin, 37,* 1091–1103. doi:10.1177/0146167211406508

Marcus, G. E., Tabb, D., & Sullivan, J. L. (1974). The application of individual differences scaling to the measurement of political ideologies. *American Journal of Political Science, 18,* 405–420. doi:10.2307/2110710

Marx, K. (1977). *A contribution to the critique of political economy*. Moscow, USSR: Progress. (Original work published 1859)

Maslow, A. (1988). *Motivation and personality* (3rd ed.). New York, NY: Harper & Row.

McCarty, N., Poole, K. T., & Rosenthal, H. (2006). *Polarized America: The dance of ideology and unequal riches*. Cambridge, MA: MIT Press.

McClosky, H. (1964). Consensus and ideology in American politics. *American Political Science Review, 58,* 361–382. doi:10.2307/1952868

McClosky, H., & Zaller, J. (1984). *The American ethos: Public attitudes toward capitalism and democracy*. Cambridge, MA: Harvard University Press.

Muller, E. N. (1988). Democracy, economic development, and income inequality. *American Sociological Review, 53,* 50–68. doi:10.2307/2095732

Muller, E. N., & Seligson, M. A. (1994). Civic culture and democracy: The question of causal relationships. *American Political Science Review, 88,* 635–652. doi:10.2307/2944800

Napier, J. L., & Jost, J. T. (2008). The "antidemocratic personality" revisited: A cross-national investigation of working-class authoritarianism. *Journal of Social Issues, 64,* 595–617. doi:10.1111/j.1540-4560.2008.00579.x

North, D. C., Wallis, J. J., & Weingast, B. R. (2009). *Violence and social orders: A conceptual framework for interpreting recorded human history*. New York, NY: Cambridge University Press. doi:10.1017/CBO9780511575839

O'Donnell, G. A., & Schmitter, P. C. (1986). *Transitions from authoritarian rule: Tentative conclusions about uncertain democracies*. Baltimore, MD: Johns Hopkins University Press.

Page, B. I., & Shapiro, R. Y. (1992). *The rational public: Fifty years of trends in Americans' policy preferences*. Chicago, IL: University of Chicago, Press. doi:10.7208/chicago/9780226644806.001.0001

Poole, K. T., & Rosenthal, H. (2007). *Ideology and congress*. New Brunswick, NJ: Transaction.

Popkin, S. L. (1991). *The reasoning voter: Communication and persuasion in presidential campaigns*. Chicago, IL: University of Chicago Press.

Przeworski, A., Alvarez, M. E., Cheibub, J. A., & Limongi, F. (2000). *Democracy and development*. Cambridge, England: Cambridge University Press.

Przeworski, A., & Limongi, F. (1997). Modernization: Theories and facts. *World Politics, 49*, 155–183. doi:10.1353/wp.1997.0004

Putnam, R. D. (1993). The prosperous community: Social capital and public life. *American Prospect, 13*, 35–42.

Putnam, R. D., & Campbell, D. E. (2010). *American grace: How religion divides and unites us*. New York, NY: Simon & Schuster.

Putnam, R. D., Leonardi, R., Nanetti, R. Y., & Pavoncello, F. (1983). Explaining institutional success: The case of the Italian regional government. *American Political Science Review, 77*, 55–74. doi:10.2307/1956011

Pye, L. (1991). Political culture revisited. *Political Psychology, 12*, 487–508. doi:10.2307/3791758

Reisinger, W. M. (1995). The renaissance of a rubric: Political culture as concept and theory. *International Journal of Public Opinion Research, 7*, 328–352. doi:10.1093/ijpor/7.4.328

Rohde, D. W. (1991). *Parties and leaders in the postreform house*. Chicago, IL: University of Chicago Press. doi:10.7208/chicago/9780226724058.001.0001

Seyle, D. C., & Newman, M. L. (2006). A house divided? The psychology of red and blue America. *American Psychologist, 61*, 571–580. doi:10.1037/0003-066X.61.6.571

Sniderman, P. M., Brody, R. A., & Tetlock, P. E. (1991). *Reasoning and choice: Explorations in political psychology*. Cambridge, England: Cambridge University Press. doi:10.1017/CBO9780511720468

Stimson, J. A. (1975). Belief systems: Constraint, complexity, and the 1972 election. *American Journal of Political Science, 19*, 393–417. doi:10.2307/2110536

Stimson, J. A. (2004). *Tides of consent: How public opinion shapes American politics*. New York, NY: Cambridge University Press. doi:10.1017/CBO9780511791024

Stoker, L., & Jennings, M. K. (2008). Of time and the development of partisan polarization. *American Journal of Political Science, 52*, 619–635. doi:10.1111/j.1540-5907.2008.00333.x

Taber, C. S., & Lodge, M. (2006). Motivated skepticism in the evaluation of political beliefs. *American Journal of Political Science, 50*, 755–769. doi:10.1111/j.1540-5907.2006.00214.x

Triandis, H. C. (2007). Culture and psychology: A history of the study of their relationships. In S. Kitayama & D. Cohen (Eds.), *Handbook of cultural psychology* (pp. 59–76). New York, NY: Guilford Press.

Truman, D. (1951). *The governmental process*. New York, NY: Knopf.

Warren, M. (Ed.). (1999). *Democracy and trust*. Cambridge, England: Cambridge University Press. doi:10.1017/CBO9780511659959

Weber, M. (2002). *The Protestant ethic and the spirit of capitalism*. New York, NY: Penguin. (Original work published 1905) doi:10.1522/cla.wem.sec

Welzel, C., Inglehart, R., & Klingemann, H. D. (2003). The theory of human development: A cross-cultural analysis. *European Journal of Political Research, 42,* 341–379. doi:10.1111/1475-6765.00086

Zaller, J. (1992). *The nature and origins of mass opinion*. New York, NY: Cambridge University Press. doi:10.1017/CBO9780511818691

7

FOOD AND CULTURE

BENOÎT MONIN AND LAUREN M. SZCZUREK

The need to include cultural factors to explain behavior seems particularly obvious when it comes to food, given an easily observed cultural diversity: People around the world eat very different things. Children are often first exposed to the diversity of cultures by the description of their stereotypical foods (e.g., "French people eat frogs and snails") and manners of eating (e.g., "Chinese people eat with chopsticks"). Yet this diversity in food preferences and customs has been dismissed by cultural psychologists as superficial and trivial, as though it misses the point of meaningful psychological differences by focusing on distracting variations in tastes and practices. Acknowledging cultural differences in traditional food preferences and habits is sometimes discounted as "cultural tourism" (Aldridge, Calhoun, & Aman, 2000), and cultural psychologists warn against the fallacy that "multicultural understanding can be achieved through lessons about the food and festivals of minority

We are grateful to Hazel R. Markus for her extremely helpful comments and suggestions on a previous version of this chapter.

http://dx.doi.org/10.1037/14274-009
Culture Reexamined: Broadening Our Understanding of Social and Evolutionary Influences,
A. B. Cohen (Editor)

groups" (Pattnaik, 2003, p. 205), resulting in a superficial and stereotypical understanding of cultural differences.

So should cultural psychologists avoid the study of food as trivial? In this chapter, we try to show that doing so would be a shame. Given the paramount importance of food in daily life, it can provide a valuable window through which to explore and understand cultural contexts. We propose that food is an important but understudied aspect of culture and is deserving of thoughtful analysis that goes beyond deriding fairs and festivals as a parody of multiculturalism (Rozin, 1996, 2007). Food is unique in that it ties the intimate, domestic, and familial to society at large and to institutional and corporate forces that shape and are shaped by individual-level processes. It is also a great illustration of the fact that individuals in the modern world find themselves at the confluence of many cultures, pushed and pulled in a force field of cultural influences. When it comes to food, everyone is multicultural.

This chapter consists of three parts. In the first part, we elaborate on our claim that food is a worthy object of analysis for cultural psychologists, likely to provide insights beyond those offered by more traditional objects of study in cultural psychology, and we sketch out how traditional models in cultural psychology can cast light on observed differences in the food domain. After this appetizer, in the next two parts we sink our teeth into the meat of the subject and explore two ways in which we argue that food provides novel insights about cultural processes. In the second part, we discuss the fact that, when it comes to food, individuals exist at the confluence of multiple cultural influences and reflect on the consequences of this fact for conceptions of culture and universal multiculturalism. In the third part, we reflect on the role of institutions (e.g., corporations, government, media) in shaping the food culture of the global industrialized world and what it means in the context of culinary multiculturalism.

APPETIZER: WHY STUDY FOOD AND CULTURE

Social scientists have long lamented that culture escapes any easy definition, and even cultural anthropologists, for whom cultures are the main object of study, are reluctant to pin it down except in very general terms. Markus and Kitayama, two of the pioneers of cultural psychology, good naturedly remarked that in their 1991 seminal review they managed to "write an entire lengthy article about culture and not define culture" (Markus & Kitayama, 2003, p. 281). Social psychologists, when they tackle culture, seem to fear being reductionist and worry that if they "psychologize" culture and make it merely a component of individuals' mental life, they will miss the important fact that culture is necessarily shared and transmitted or the fact that it is captured in institutions and artifacts that go well beyond individuals. This is why Kim and Markus (1999) emphasized the "dynamic process of the mutual constitution of culture and the psyche" (p. 797). Indeed, one first stab at the study of food and culture would be to start an inventory of the many cultural components that involve food: knowledge and methods (which, in the food context, takes the form of knowing which foods are edible, which ones are tasty or not, scripts such as recipes, and cleaning and cooking methods; the reification of these practices into texts; spaces—kitchens, restaurants, stores, slaughterhouses, creameries, bakeries, etc.—and tools for growing, cooking, and consuming the food), preferences and tastes (in actual foods and ingredients, in table manners, in prized dishes vs. taboo foods, etc., all well documented in Paul Rozin's reviews, e.g., Rozin, 2007), and social practices (rituals and scripts about the proper production, preparation, ingestion, and excretion of food, again involving manners and taboos but also embodying and expressing values and concepts about purity; community; the proper place of men and women, adults and children; the public and private sphere, etc.; these practices include holidays, religious practices such as saying grace, taking communion, keeping kosher, observing Ramadan [Johnson, White, Boyd, & Cohen, 2011], and social scripts such as a first date). Although necessarily incomplete, such a quick flyover of the diverse landscape is a reminder of the difficulty of the task at hand, because of the vast breadth of components that make up a culture.

Food Cultures or Food-Related Cultural Practices

Because, as we have just outlined, food permeates so many dimensions of the cultural experience, we refer in this chapter to *food cultures,* as in the *Chinese food culture.* A food culture is, however, really only one aspect of a broader culture, so the Chinese food culture, for example, is a part of Chinese culture at large. Yet we believe it would be reductionist to refer instead to *food-related cultural practices* because we believe that food relates to cultural elements other than practices (e.g., attitudes, beliefs, artifacts). As Saroglou and Cohen (2011) wrote about religion, food, depending on context, is part of culture, constitutes culture, includes and transcends culture, is influenced by culture, shapes culture, and interacts with culture in influencing cognitions, emotions, and actions. So we use *food culture* as shorthand for those aspects of a culture that pertain to food, keeping in mind that those aspects are not neatly quartered in one aspect of culture but rather are wide ranging and that a food culture and culture at large are mutually constitutive. Even the extent to which food is central to and constitutive of a culture is an interesting cultural difference that would deserve its own study. We think that carving out the food dimension of culture specifically (and labeling it a food culture) has analytical value because of our emphasis later in this chapter on everyday multiculturalism. Food is perhaps the most accessible point of entry into a culture for outgroup members, and individuals in diverse societies routinely engage other cultures via food (i.e., engage in a foreign food culture even if they remain more oblivious to the larger culture in which it is nested), be it through sampling dishes, learning recipes, buying ingredients, role-playing eating practices and rituals, using cooking tools, and even shaping their palates to enjoy initially unpleasant novel tastes (e.g., hot chili, raw fish, smelly cheese). Delineating food cultures as an object of study gives us insight into these processes of cultural sampling, which are less frequent in other cultural domains, simply because, as we discuss next, food is ubiquitous and exploring food options is encouraged among omnivores.

What's So Special About Food

When compared with other objects of cultural construction, eating, as a worldwide behavior, and food, as a universal object of daily concern and attention throughout human history, both have some interesting unique properties. First, food is ubiquitous. Humans are constant eaters, and satisfy this need several times a day at every age, which differs from the satisfaction of other needs, such as sex, which is not necessary for the survival of the individual and is engaged in much less frequently and not throughout the life span. Also, people eat publicly and often in social settings, which differs from the satisfaction of other needs such as sex, excretion (another food-related need), sleeping, or grooming. Compared with other animals that eat less frequently because they save energy with frequent sleep between highly specialized food-gathering attempts (felines) or even cease eating for whole seasons and curtail their metabolic needs via hibernation (rodents), humans require a constant intake of caloric input to sustain their uniform level of activity. Throughout history and in all parts of the world, food production, preparation, and intake have been central to all cultures, and they have both defined and been shaped by other cultural elements. Food production has shaped cultures as surely as it has shaped landscapes and bodies.

Second, food highlights the interplay between culture and nature, in this case human biology. Foodstuffs physically interact with the bodies of individuals in a given culture to affect modal body shape, sexual ideals, health, longevity, and so forth. Different cultural groups look different in part because they are shaped by the foods they eat, which are in turn determined by an interaction between cultural elements and the availability of ingredients in the environment of that culture's historical evolution. Paul Rozin (e.g., 1996, 2007) has shown that the study of food casts light on important questions about cultural processes; for example, by documenting food universals and connecting them to the specific biological needs of an omnivore, he showed how such motives were transformed and integrated into cultural systems and formed the substrates of cultural habits. Through case studies of specific foods such as sugar, milk, chili powder, chocolate, and meat, Rozin provided new insights into the cultural formation and transmission of food preferences. He eloquently used the study of food as a way to reconcile and clarify the relationship between biological–evolutionary and cultural processes and to explore the familiar nature–nurture question in novel and fascinating ways. We do not attempt to recapitulate Rozin's invaluable contributions to the field of food and culture in this chapter, and refer interested readers to his many excellent articles (e.g., Rozin, 1996, 2007). Instead, our hope is to shed light on aspects of the study of food and culture that have traditionally received less attention, such as how individuals negotiate the interplay of multiple cultural influences in the food domain and how macro actors battle to shape food culture in ways that serve their institutional interests.

Third, the study of food casts light on the reciprocal influences between cultures and the geographical and ecological contexts in which they developed and evolved (Diamond, 1997). Food production processes shape physical landscapes (e.g., fields, irrigation, wells, mills, pastures, cattle) as much as they shape cultures. The foods historically available in an ecological environment have shaped and been shaped by the knowledge, preferences, attitudes, and social practices of the individuals within a cultural context. Indeed, even the process by which food is produced has an impact on culture at a deep level. D. Cohen, Nisbett, Bowdle, and Schwarz (1996) argued that populations that have historically relied on livestock and herding for food are more likely to have developed a culture of honor that prescribes violent retaliation against provocation (a cultural trait that would be functional in an economy in which the main source of food and marker of wealth is so easily stolen), whereas populations that have historically relied on growing crops for food (as made possible by better soil or irrigation, as a result of geological history) are much less so inclined because the needs of agrarian production instead reward compromise and cooperation. Thus, the means of procuring the food that is available in one's ecological environment, determined in part by geological (accidental) history, can affect the psychological make-up of a population because such cultural modules provide solutions to the specific challenges of food production in this ecological–geological niche: Geological accidents may make rich soils scarce and herding a good option, and herding may in turn favor the development of a culture of honor, so that food effectively serves as the mediator between geology and psychology (see Uskul, Kitayama, & Nisbett, 2008).

Fourth, humans are omnivores, and exploration and variety seeking are encouraged and rewarded. Children in many cultures are discouraged from being fussy about unfamiliar foods and encouraged to try novel tastes. As with other omnivore species, curiosity about novel foodstuffs (coupled with safety mechanisms such as the ability to empty one's stomach even after ingestion [i.e., vomiting]) enabled humans to quickly adapt to new environments with unfamiliar sources of nourishment. It is one reason why we argue that humans are multicultural when it comes to food—because although plenty of food norms exist in one culture about which familiar foods are good and which are bad, there has always been a functional advantage in the food domain to openness and exploration and to learning vicariously from what other (cultural) groups are eating. Because of the frequency of eating and the fact that humans' omnivorous nature encourages variety seeking and exploration in their diet, one individual's diet typically reflects multiple cultural influences in the course of the same week or even day, especially in a modern cosmopolitan society such as the United States.

Fifth, food cultures are characterized by strong parental involvement for many years. Whereas other cultural influences are quickly abdicated to agents of socialization outside of the home, and in particular to peer groups (Harris, 1998), food remains in many societies a mode of direct transmission of cultural tastes and practices within the familial sphere. Parents prepare or at least choose (or, increasingly in modern society, order, as we discuss in the third section) the foods eaten by children and adolescents for many years, so parents have a more direct influence on these preferences and tastes (than, say, on entertainment or even clothing, which parents have little involvement in manufacturing). Foods are communally shared at the dinner table, parents prepare lunches for children to take with them when they are apart, children learn to cook by imitating parents in the family kitchen, and many of the traditions and holidays that celebrate and reaffirm a family's identity and hybrid cultural inheritance center on food (e.g., Thanksgiving, Christmas, Passover, Ramadan, birthdays). Thus, food culture is both intimately transmitted in the familial and domestic sphere and is also the medium through which much of a family's culture and traditions are transmitted. Food is thus an interesting area in which to study culture because it brings to the fore the importance of families as groups that have their own subcultures and traditions, a unit that rarely receives much attention in cultural psychology.

In short, although it is easy to dismiss food as a trivial matter of sustenance and of superficial cultural significance, eating is such a frequent and omnipresent activity, and food shapes physical reality in such tangible ways, that they cannot be ignored. Physical correlates can be observed both upstream and downstream of the focal act of ingestion: Upstream, food shapes the economy, the organization of labor, and prototypical occupations (see the cowboy culture in the Western United States); markers of wealth and status (e.g., silverware on a wedding registry); and the physical landscape in which cultures evolved, from pastures to open-field crop growing. Downstream, specific foods shape the lives and even the bodies of individuals who frequently ingest them, and even affect when people will die. Finally, we also note that food is unique in that it is a domain in which variety seeking and a form of multiculturalism are encouraged, and we end by noting the role of parental involvement and the central place of food as the repository of familial cultures.

Food Culture Reflects Well-Documented Cultural Differences

The relationship between eating and culture is bidirectional. On the one hand, a culture is shaped by nutritional constraints such as the foods that were available in a population's historical environment, the caloric needs associated with its climate and lifestyle (e.g., the need for hearty diets in cold weather) and the food conservation challenges associated with prevalent temperatures (leading to the development of cultural practices such as the curing of meat with salt, and taboos against foods [e.g. pork] most likely to spoil in the dominant climate). On the other hand, culture shapes food practices, preferences, and beliefs, as aspects of a culture initially unrelated to food are expressed and enacted in the preparation and consumption of food, and in the social rituals associated with its consumption. So food culture both shapes and is shaped by culture as a whole. Humans typically eat food in social settings, and so common eating becomes the locus of much cultural transmission and reenactment. If social eating is one way to transmit and reenact culture, then researchers should expect to find the cultural models already documented in other domains (e.g., independence vs. interdependence; see Markus & Kitayama, 1991) expressed in the food domain. Indeed, one version of this chapter could simply document how well-known patterns in cultural psychology can be observed in the food domain, as they have been documented elsewhere. Although we chose another route for most of the chapter, we need to start out by acknowledging the ways in which the food domain does reflect well-known cultural differences just like other contexts.

Models of the Self and Table Manners

Cultural models of the self are expressed, for example, in the realm of table manners: How food should be served, shared, and ingested is deeply rooted in the kind of cultural differences well documented by others, such as the distinction made between cultures in which the self is construed independently of others and cultures in which the self is construed interdependently (Markus & Kitayama, 1991). In the interdependent cultural context of Japan, for example, the host chooses food for guests and serves them as a way of making sure guests feel welcome and accommodated. Contrast this with the independent model prominent in Western contexts, such as the United States, in which hosts commonly tell guests to "make themselves at home" and choose whatever they would like to eat for themselves, and where the perfect host empowers every guest to express his or her idiosyncratic preferences (Markus & Kitayama, 2003). One of the authors, brought up in a French cultural context, grew up regaled with shocking stories of American exchange students helping themselves to the fridge whenever they felt hungry and, conversely, of French exchange students staying with American families starving while they anxiously awaited formal family meals that never came—without ever thinking it appropriate to make themselves a sandwich in someone else's home. It is important to stress once more that, beyond just noting trivial cultural differences, such an example is a reflection of deeper conceptions of what it means to be a self and that these conceptions both shape these manners and are reinforced every time these manners are enacted.

Food also plays an important role in establishing and maintaining social bonds. The sharing of food is a major expression of solidarity and an indicator of close relationships (Rozin, 1996). The sharing of food can also signify shared values, as in the case of traditional meals that accompany celebrations or holidays. When sharing food, people may enact culturally specific rituals that center around the values or beliefs of the group. These food practices play a functional role by helping people address fundamental social motives, such as identifying and creating a bond among group members, signaling within-group status, and preserving ingroup–outgroup boundaries (e.g., by keeping kosher; see Johnson et al., 2011).

Food Taboos and Cultural Conceptions of Morality

Another domain in which food echoes cultural differences already well documented elsewhere is in the domain of food taboos (Rozin, 1996). In Orthodox Jewish communities, the act of eating nonkosher foods, which is prohibited by Jewish law, is considered a serious sin, as is the mixing of some kosher foods, such as dairy and meat (Grunfeld, 1982). In India, certain foods are prohibited for members of some social castes, and it is considered immoral and impolite for members of these castes to eat these foods (Appadurai, 1981). Although secular contemporary Americans may initially think of their culinary world as relatively free of food taboos other than extreme ones (e.g., human flesh, excrement), plenty of things are in fact taboo for many American eaters that would not be taboo in other parts of the world: certain parts of the body (e.g., offal, bone marrow, brains) and some animals. For example, horse meat is still commonly eaten in many parts of continental Europe, as is rabbit, both dishes that would be taboo to large segments of the U.S. population who would give those animals the status of pet or service animal. Animals whose flesh is deemed appropriate to eat in some cultures is taboo in others. These taboos are powerful and can influence opinions of a person who has violated them even when the act occurred in a context in which it was not taboo, as is apparent from the 2012 controversy over President Obama's eating dog meat, a taboo act in the United States, when he was a boy in Indonesia, where it was not taboo at the time (Delaney, 2012).

Apart from national norms and practices, other cultural identities also influence what is perceived as taboo. Haidt, Koller, and Dias (1993) asked respondents from various social backgrounds in Brazil and the United States whether it was wrong to eat a family dog after the dog was accidentally killed. In both cultures, individuals of high socioeconomic status (SES) were less likely to deem the behavior immoral.[1] Thus, food taboos may be enforced less by educated members of Western societies, who strive for tolerance of cultural differences and who may thus be reluctant to rely on culture-shaped disgust as the arbiter of morality—apparently especially when no one is getting hurt. Later work (Graham, Haidt, & Nosek, 2009) has suggested that whereas conservative members of U.S. society include things such as purity and respect for tradition when determining right from wrong and are thus likely to focus their taboos on foods that they consider disgusting (e.g., offal) or violating religious edicts (e.g., pork for Jews), more liberal members of U.S. society focus more exclusively on fairness and harm as criteria for morality and are therefore likely to focus their taboos on foods that require animal suffering (e.g., foie gras), involve prototypical victims (e.g., veal) or victims who blur the boundary between animal and human intelligence (e.g., tuna when dolphins get hurt or palm oil because of its impact on the habitat of great apes), or exploit poor farmers in other countries (e.g., the popularity of fair-trade products). Thus, in the same way that table manners illustrate the well-documented differences between independent and interdependent models of the self, we propose that food taboos are likely to similarly recapitulate documented dimensions of morality.

As demonstrated by taboos, food takes on a moral dimension in many different cultures. Beyond these taboos, food choices can also interact with more broadly held cultural values to result in moral judgment. For example, in U.S. cultural contexts, people view individuals who eat unhealthy foods more negatively than individuals who eat healthy foods on both moral (e.g., virtuous, ethical) and nonmoral (e.g., attractive, likable) traits (Steim & Nemeroff, 1995). Two cultural beliefs seem to underlie these negative moral judgments of individuals eating unhealthy foods. One, the "you are what you eat" belief, is commonly found across cultural contexts (Frazer, 1890/1959; Nemeroff & Rozin, 1989) and stipulates that people take on the properties of the foods they consume—thus, people eating bad food must be bad. The other belief

---

[1] In a food-related twist, lower SES American adults surveyed by Haidt et al. (1993) were identified as such by approaching individuals as they left a McDonald's fast-food restaurant in West Philadelphia.

underlying negative moral judgments is the Puritan ethic, an idea prominent in U.S. cultural contexts. The Puritan ethic stipulates that people will ultimately be rewarded for self-discipline and thus should be industrious, deny themselves pleasure, and avoid immediate gratification (Steim & Nemeroff, 1995). Conversely, individuals whose food choices are based on a moral principle (e.g., vegetarians) are sometimes disliked by the mainstream when mainstream members perceive such elective dietary restrictions to be an implicit indictment of their own eating habits and resent that restricted eaters seem to think that they are morally superior to others (Minson & Monin, 2012).

Cultural Beliefs About the Relation Between Food and Affect

In addition to the "right" way to eat and food taboos, people also learn from others in their cultural context about what foods should be offered on what occasion (e.g., in Italy, rice is a traditional gift for couples moving into their first home because it represents fertility). Interestingly, these gestures of goodwill are often accompanied and supported by beliefs about the healing or mood-regulating power of foods for those who are ill (e.g., chicken soup in Judaism; Rennard, Ertl, Gossman, Robbins, & Rennard, 2000) or feeling emotionally distressed (e.g., chocolate; Macht & Mueller, 2007). These beliefs then shape preferences and behavior: A woman who reaches for a carton of ice cream when heartbroken may feel that her impulse is completely natural and self-generated, but these gender-stereotypic behaviors have been modeled in cultural contexts and enshrined in cultural products such as television (e.g., *Friends* [Junge & Zuckerman, 1996]; *How I Met Your Mother* [Kang & Greenberg, 2007]) and film (e.g., *Bridget Jones's Diary* [Bevan, Fellner, Cavendish, & Maguire, 2001]; *Legally Blonde* [Kidney, Platt, & Luketic, 2001]) so that when, on his talk show, TV host Jon Stewart served a pint of ice cream to actor Robert Pattinson after Pattinson's highly publicized 2012 breakup, the connection was immediately clear—and comedic because it played against cultural gender stereotypes. Beliefs about the mood-altering nature of food go well beyond the animistic beliefs of traditional societies. Witness the enduring U.S. cultural myth, puzzling to foreigners, that sugar makes children hyperactive. Multiple medical studies have shown this myth to be false (see Wolraich, Wilson, & White, 1995), and yet it endures, in part because the cultural expectations that American parents bring to sugar leads to self-fulfilling prophecies and confirmation biases.

Beliefs about the relationship between food and affect have deep significance for the cultural construal of its meaning and function and lead to important consequences in terms of public health. What is the meaning of food? What is it for? Is it a source of relaxation, enjoyment, and nourishment, or is it a source of stress, negativity, and fear? The answers to these questions vary greatly by cultural context, and the resulting attitudes toward food can powerfully shape people's approach toward eating and subsequently affect their health. Rozin, Fischler, Imada, Sarubin, and Wrzesniewski (1999) explored attitudes toward food and the role of food in four broad cultural contexts: the United States, Japan, Flemish Belgium, and France. They noted that in the United States food was seen as a source of worry and concern and contrasted this with the French view of food as a source of pleasure and relaxation. This attitudinal difference was accompanied by higher consumption of fatty foods by the French: Of a sample of French adults (Drewnowski et al., 1996), 96% obtained more than 10% of their daily calories from saturated fat, in stark violation of U.S. dietary guidelines. However, this diet did not manifest itself in worse physical health. In fact, cardiovascular disease occurs at a much lower rate in France than in the United States, a fact that has been referred to as the *French paradox* (Renaud & de Lorgeril, 1992; Richard, Cambien, & Ducimetière, 1981). Although research on the French paradox had previously focused on searching for protective elements in the French diet (e.g., red wine), Rozin et al. set out to explore differences in stress in relation to eating. To do so, each group was given a survey in their native language regarding the kinds of foods they ate, as well as their general attitudes toward and associations with food. In all areas of interest, American women were more worried about and dissatisfied with food, whereas French and Belgian men tended to view food most positively. Despite being more concerned about weight and diet, Americans tended to view themselves as less healthy eaters than did members of other groups. Of a range of factors that were asked about, the only one that predicted body mass index was the Worry factor, a measure of how much participants worried about food. This research suggested that too much concern over food may be counterproductive, negatively affecting quality of life and having no or even negative effects on health. When people learn to view food as a source of stress and worry, they may focus too much on quantity and not enough on quality, freshness, and balance (Pollan, 2008; Rozin et al., 1999).

Identifying New Directions in the Study of Food and Culture

Until now, we have discussed how differences between cultures when it comes to food reflect differences in models of the self, in conceptions of morality, and in beliefs about affect and self-regulation. Although these differences were a natural place to start, we want to take this opportunity to add to the reflection on culture by going beyond pointing out how well-known cross-national differences (e.g., whether the self is defined more in independent or interdependent ways; Markus & Kitayama, 1991) are reflected in the food domain. Such an application of well-supported theories would no doubt expand their reach but teach relatively little that is new to the student of culture. Instead, we want to use the domain of food and eating to explore two relatively (to our knowledge) little-discussed dimensions of culture that are brought into sharp relief in this context. Both arise from recent developments in the study of culture that go beyond simple bipolar, unilinear dimensions in psychological make-up to emphasize many forms of culture (A. B. Cohen, 2009) and the mutual constitution of culture and the psyche through the reciprocal processes of cultural maintenance and transformation and of the formation of the psychological (Kim & Markus, 1999).

The two questions that we propose to explore in the remainder of this chapter are the following:

1. As cultural psychologists increasingly stress the importance of multiple forms of culture, what are the processes of everyday multiculturalism? Food and eating are ideal domains in which to study these processes because individuals' cooking and eating habits reflect on a daily basis a hodgepodge of influences, from the cultural mix of their ancestral lineage (e.g., Polish and Italian American parents), to regional influences (e.g., growing up in New Jersey), familial practices (e.g., a partner from the United Kingdom), as well as the multiplicity of cultural culinary influences and experiences available in contemporary U.S. society (e.g., patronizing a Japanese restaurant, following a recipe in a French cookbook, watching a TV show on Mexican cuisine). How do these various cultural idioms contribute to a repertoire that individuals then draw on in their daily food experience, and how do individuals draw on and contribute to cultural frameworks that are not their own but with which they are familiar?

2. The second question that we propose to explore comes from taking the institutional aspects of cultures seriously and pointing to the macro actors (e.g., government agencies, corporations, media, activist groups) who struggle to influence the discourse about food and to define the cultural meanings of food as well as the legitimacy of cultural practices and understandings. This dimension of the cultural experience is rarely explored. Even though cultural psychologists have, of course, included media products in their empirical analyses (e.g., Kim & Markus, 1999), authors have not stressed much the struggles for cultural influence driven by often conflicting interests and the tremendous power wielded by some institutional actors, in particular corporations, through the medium of advertising, in shaping the food culture that suffuses modern society.

Although we treat these two questions in turn in the next two sections, they are not completely independent, and we can also gain insights by looking at their intersection. Indeed, the cultural elements that broader institutional actors attempt to introduce in society become part of the sometimes contradictory cultural repertoire that individuals grapple with in their everyday multiculturalism. Because of the quotidian and personal nature of eating, its study reveals the interplay of micro cultural components ranging from family traditions (holiday rituals and the transmission of tastes and know-how, as well as actual physical culinary tools) all the way to macro cultural components such as large institutions (government agencies, the food industry) and cultural products (media and advertising) contributing to and being shaped by food culture. It is also a particularly fruitful place to study how people juggle the multiplicity of culinary cultures in which they engage.

In contrast to other models in social psychology, the great strength of the cultural approach is that it acknowledges the dynamic process of the mutual constitution of culture and the psyche (Kim & Markus, 1999). Individual selves participate in and influence everyday practices, which in turn shape individuals. Messages from and changes within institutions also directly influence individuals, just as individuals influence institutions. In the rest of this chapter, we examine different levels of the culture cycle from the unique vantage point of food, a universally important commodity for which people's interactions and preferences are fundamentally shaped by cultural practices, beliefs, and ideas.

MAIN COURSE: WHEN IT COMES TO FOOD, WE ARE ALL MULTICULTURAL

Although we have spent some time illustrating how the food domain recapitulates the dimensions already documented by cultural psychologists, we now turn to something that we believe is more unique about food and eating. We propose that food provides a unique entryway into the multiplicity of cultural influences that any given individual shapes—and is shaped by—on a daily basis. Recent scholarship in cultural psychology (e.g., this book; A. B. Cohen, 2009; Markus & Connor, 2013; Snibbe & Markus, 2005; Stephens, Markus, & Fryberg, 2012) has stressed the importance of going beyond broad national differences to identify the multiplicity of cultural influences within a given culture. As we see it, at least two important components of this critique are as follows:

1. First, going beyond the collectivist–individualist, independent–interdependent, or even East–West coarse-grained distinctions

that have driven initial progress in cultural psychology (e.g., Triandis, 1990; Markus & Kitayama, 1991), cultural psychologists now increasingly stress the need to use more fine-grained distinctions within a given culture, such as religion (e.g., A. B. Cohen & Rozin, 2001), social class (e.g., Snibbe & Markus, 2005; Stephens et al., 2012), or region (e.g., Nisbett & Cohen, 1996; Kitayama, Ishii, Imada, Takemura, & Ramaswamy, 2006).

2. Second, and following from the first point, multiple forms of culture are represented not only within a country but also within an individual. Individuals participate in, are shaped by, and shape multiple cultures. A Kenyan physician will shape and be shaped by nationality but also by tribal ancestry, religion, profession, social class, and so forth. To understand the role of culture in shaping cognition and behavior, researchers must understand the interplay of these various cultural influences within any given individual.

A Complex Multiculturalism

Indeed, previous authors have acknowledged the multiplicity of cultural influences. Snibbe and Markus (2005), for example, wrote that "individuals are never monocultural, as they are always interacting with multiple cultural contexts (e.g., contexts of gender, ethnicity, SES, region, religion, and sexual orientation). Cultural contexts are therefore not monolithic: Unique combinations of cultural models intersect within individuals" (p. 704). Similarly, A. B. Cohen (2009) wrote that "all people are in fact multicultural" (p. 200).

When cultural psychologists talk about multiculturalism, or multiple identities of the same kind (most commonly national or ethnic identities), two cases seem to predominate. First, they often look at individuals in transition between two cultures (e.g., immigrants), a case that has received extensive attention by sociologists under the heading of acculturation. This example of multiculturalism is what A. B. Cohen (2009) had in mind when he lamented that "the focus is almost always cultural transition between countries" (p. 200) and argued that authors should start studying transitions between SES categories, regions, or religions. The emphasis, though, is still on transitions—and therefore on extraordinary and temporary situations—and on demographic exceptions. The second case of multiculturalism often studied in ethnic studies results from individuals with mixed heritages, such as children of biracial couples or second-generation immigrants who are not strictly speaking in transition, having been born where they live, but who nonetheless struggle between the cultural influences they receive at home and the mainstream cultural influences of their home country (Guendelman, Cheryan, & Monin, 2011).

Yet we suggest that there is more to multiculturalism than immigrants and biracial couples. The food domain vividly illustrates that individuals in a modern society are the repository of a great number of cultural models and that they fluidly engage with and enact them on a daily basis. It both provides a wonderful setting to show the value added by the new multiple-cultures approach and also provides a challenge for this approach. It seems so natural to apply the multiple-cultures approach to the food domain that this logic can be pushed further than in other domains, and in doing so, it may provide some insights into its limits. In particular, two big questions arise: (a) How far can researchers push the balkanization of cultural identities while not stripping the concept of its pragmatic utility altogether and (b) presented with a whole repertoire of cultural identities, practices, norms, preferences, and ways of being, how do individuals pick and choose which culture to enact at any given moment?

The Limits of Cultural Fragmentation

Although there is a clear appeal to using a more fine-grained analysis to study culture, it also raises some interesting conceptual questions about the limits of the fragmentation of culture, again of two kinds: First, what is the difference between a culture and an identity? Can every social identity be thought of as being based on cultural elements? Is there a male culture, a youth culture, a disabled culture, and so forth? Although it has been argued that a group can be thought of as having a culture to the extent that it shares values, roles, practices, norms, and self-definitions (A. B. Cohen, 2010), it is unclear what degree of shared cultural elements is necessary to claim a group has or makes up a culture, which risks reducing the concept's usefulness. Second (which in a way is merely a rephrasing of the first question), how few people are sufficient to constitute a culture? What are the necessary components of a culture? This question may seem too abstract when one looks at other cultural components such as models of the self, or even language, but food and eating brings it to the fore because so many culinary practices, tastes, and artifacts are developed and transmitted within families or even within couples given the domestic and quotidian nature of the domain. Although they may echo the practices of the broader culture as a whole, family cultures pertaining to holiday traditions, table manners, preparation or layout of foods, and so forth all have specificities idiosyncratic to a given familial context—and will also be central to that family's identity, so much so that they will be reenacted by children once they are adults themselves, in memory of those who passed away and in celebration of the commonality of the kinship group (i.e., Dad's chicken soup recipe, served in Grandma's tureen). They are not just family variants, or simply quirky idiosyncrasies, they are also variants that are central to people's self-definitions, affective memories, nostalgia, and definition of *home* and that grown children are highly motivated to pass on to their own offspring as having special value and significance. These features give family traditions (e.g., holiday menus), norms (e.g., table manners), rehearsed practices (e.g., recipes), and physical artifacts (e.g., handed-down serving dishes) the weight of cultural components. Using the language and concepts of cultural psychology seems in our mind fruitful to understand people's relationship with their complex family heritage—but at the same time it could read like a *reductio ad absurdum,* and does the balkanization of cultural groups into ever-smaller units for analytical purposes strip culture of any useful content (besides making it much harder to study with the usual tools used by psychologists)? With this in mind, and to the extent that our challenge has some value, it makes it relevant to all kinds of other groupings and social identities. Is there not a cultural aspect to a weekly departmental happy hour that celebrates and perpetuates the department's traditions around drinks and snacks? To the yearly barbecue block party at which gossip is exchanged and neighbors reminisce about shared fond memories? To the daily snack time in a middle school section during which group values are instilled and enacted?

We spent some time on families in this section because they seem to be the focal locus of food cultures, and food and eating provide a wonderful entryway to the question of what to make of cultures emerging at various levels of group size. We used the context of families to illustrate a broader point and as a challenge to proponents of the multiple-culture approach, a challenge that becomes apparent when one starts analyzing the food domain. The first challenge for students of culture is to identify the definitional boundaries that would preserve the usefulness of the concept of culture as it is applied to smaller and smaller groupings.

Ubiquitous Multiculturalism

If one grants cultural status to familial traditions, practices, know-hows, norms, and so forth, then as families recombine by bringing together the recipients of two different familial cultural traditions, they create a new "pooling" or unique combination, and a unique familial culture develops and will be further passed on, mixed with others as the children marry, and so forth. Some elements will overlap (homophily after all guaranteeing that children are likely to wed spouses who share some cultural similarities), some will be blended in the new familial unit, and yet others will survive side by side. When it comes to food, individuals are thus the recipients of multiple familial and cultural heritages. This multiplicity is most apparent when these family traditions reflect different ethnic heritages (e.g., as with the child of an Irish–Italian couple), but it is also true to a degree even when obvious ethnic differences are absent because of the familial cultural variations that are cherished and transmitted with care even within one given ethnic or ancestral tradition. Even though such idiosyncratic familial cultural traditions may seem outside the reach of conventional psychological methods, it seems fruitful to recognize their importance in the cultural make-up of individuals, and one value in studying food and eating is that it brings these components to the fore. Thus, the second challenge raised is what to make of the multiplicity of coexisting and sometimes conflicting cultural influences that affect and are affected by a given individual.

A Uniquely American Experience?

All scholars presuming to make cultural claims need to question whether they are merely commenting on their own culture, and we are no exception. The cultural mosaic we have described is very much inspired by the reality of the 2013 United States, and the tensions and personal struggles revealed have the greatest relevance in this culture. Indeed, the examples in this chapter predominantly come from our host culture. The push in the literature to recognize the internal nuances of cultures is likely to legitimize such tendencies, because an informant from within any culture is best able to make such distinctions (and still retain the credibility of an outside observer in regard to the subgroup he or she identified), and investigators are likely to increasingly look inward to document cultural processes within their own culture. Although we recognize this possible shortcoming, we submit two comments. First, precisely because the processes we talk about are exacerbated in U.S. culture, it makes it a wonderful place to start documenting them. Second, the forces we discuss (e.g., cultural mixing through migrational fluxes, top–down cultural impositions by powerful corporations and their media minions, familial vs. regional traditions) are increasingly present around the globe with the progress of globalization through international trade, the Internet, migration, and so forth. In parts of the world still outside the reach of globalization, our analysis may have less purchase, but we propose that these parts are becoming increasingly rare.

Practicing Multiculturalism

Acknowledging that individuals walk around as the recipients and enactors of multiple cultural traditions raises novel questions. The most obvious one is what will determine which cultural component comes online at any given moment to guide cognition and behavior. A second and related question is whether individuals who have been exposed to multiple food cultures can be influenced by the cultural repertoires, practices, know-hows, and so forth of cultures that they do not recognize as their own. We discuss these issues, which once again we feel are revealed by the study of food but go well beyond the food domain to inform all of culture, in this section.

Cultural Role-Playing

Why do European Americans request chopsticks at Chinese restaurants? Beyond tasting different foods, the local culinary tourism that individuals engage in when dining at an establishment of another culture has a component of cultural role-playing. Individuals want to sample the foods of different cultures and consume them in a way that models and reproduces the means (e.g., using chopsticks) and style (e.g., sitting on the floor) of eating prominent in that culture. It is unlikely that this act is motivated by the belief that it will improve the gustatory experience; it instead seems to reflect a hankering for the "authentic" cultural experience, not unlike tourists' hankering to sample the genuine everyday life of the country they are visiting. Besides the dated Orientalism caricatured in our example, such cultural role-playing occurs in more subtle ways throughout the food domain, whether individuals are trying to capture the Southern soul food experience at a barbecue, an Italian dinner on pasta night, or a French menu and table layout for a fancy dinner. Any practice that does not directly improve the gustatory experience can be chalked up to such role-playing and is intriguing from the point of view of the multiculturalism that we are discussing.

The intriguing question is how individuals relate to a food culture that they know well (even in stereotypic terms) but do not, properly speaking, belong to. A likely answer is that the repertoire of food cultures that individuals know enables them to enact the qualities that they stereotypically associate with each ethnic tradition, such as warmth and communality for Italian food, simplicity and elegance for Japanese food, and so forth. When the Italian-themed Olive Garden restaurant chain advertised "When you're here, you're family," it capitalized on the fact that most Americans recognize the stereotypical Italian family meal, drawn out, loud, and copious, as familiar and appealing. It bet on the fact that even Americans with no Italian heritage recognize this cultural model (depicted in countless movies) and are enough drawn to this fantasy of Tuscan *dolce vita* to drive to their local strip mall and dine under plastic replicas of grape-laden trellises. Along the same lines, the Italian-American chain Buca di Beppo proclaims on its website, "In the spirit of Italian culture, our dishes are served family style and are meant to be shared"; thus, it not only offers a sample of Italian tastes, it also lets American diners engage in a foreign cultural practice that embodies and reaffirms communality, even when dining with acquaintances who are not family members.

Influence of Cultures Other Than One's Own

When individuals are not deliberately role playing a different culture for the duration of a meal, they can still be influenced by the models of cultures other than their own or by models offered by one of the multiple cultures of which they are the recipients. So what are we to make of our analysis of cultural models that may affect individuals who do not belong to that culture? Bargh, Chen, and Burrows (1996) showed that priming social categories can affect the behavior of individuals, even if they do not belong to this category: White participants primed with faces of African Americans acted more rude and hostile, suggesting that the stereotypes they held about members of that group were activated and affected their behavior. To what extent can cultures function in a similar way? How does knowing about Italian cuisine and culinary tradition affect the preferences and habits of a contemporary African American individual? Conversely, the mainstream food preferences of White Americans affect the eating habits of recent Asian immigrants in multiple ways. What is the difference between these external cultural influences and the influence of cultures that one embraces as one's own?

A case that makes this issue salient pertains to the food preferences of ethnic minorities in the United States. For example, Oyserman, Fryberg, and Yoder (2007) investigated identity-based motivations and documented how racial minority students (depending on the study, a mix of Hispanic, Black, Asian, and Native Americans), compared with White students, were more likely to see health-promoting behaviors such as eating healthy foods as incompatible with their social identities and instead as being typically White and middle class. Making social class and ethnic identity salient resulted in low-SES minority students reporting more health fatalism and less engagement with health promotion. These minority students are obviously well aware of the mainstream middle-class White cultural model and relationship to food, so this example reveals the already interesting tensions between the cultural models that people know about and the ones that influence their behavior. Here, the rejection of the majority cultural model can lead minority members to suboptimal health habits, even though they are recipients of the mainstream cultural model too.

Viewing unhealthy behaviors as consistent with a valued group identity may have contributed to recent trends in life expectancy (Olshansky et al., 2012). Between 1990 and 2008, despite well-documented improvements in longevity for most Americans, alarming disparities persisted for Black Americans as well as less educated White Americans, whose life expectancies were actually reduced in this time span. As researchers struggle to understand what factors are contributing to these trends, such as decreased access to health care and increased suicide rates, cultural factors that promote unhealthy food choices should also be included.

Distancing From One's Own Culture

Food and eating provide many of the visible markers of a culture and may therefore be easy triggers to capture cultural differences. Indeed, eating habits are a strong and automatic way to prime cultural stereotypes about others. Macrae, Bodenhausen, and Milne (1995) showed participants a video of a Chinese woman either eating noodles with chopsticks or putting on makeup and then presented them with a lexical decision task. Participants who saw the chopstick version were faster than unprimed control participants at identifying words related to the Chinese stereotype (e.g., calm) but slower at identifying female-relevant words. Such primed stereotypes can also affect the self. In Ambady, Shih, Kim, and Pittinsky (2001), the math performance of Asian girls improved after they colored a picture of Asian children eating with chopsticks. The simple cultural practice of eating with chopsticks thus encapsulated for both outsiders and participants in the culture much more than its significance in the food domain and instead summoned a whole cultural stereotype with real consequences in terms of perception and performance.

Because of the significance of food preferences and eating habits in identifying someone as coming from a minority culture, individuals who, contrary to Oyserman et al.'s (2007) participants, long to be accepted by the mainstream but fear rejection because of their cultural heritage may downplay their food culture to fit in. Cheryan and Monin (2005) showed that many Asian Americans reported feeling such "identity denial" through, for example, often-asked benign-sounding questions such as "Where are you really from?" It follows that a group that wants to affirm its belongingness to an overarching common identity would do so by espousing mainstream food preferences and downplaying ethnic cultural preferences and habits. Guendelman et al. (2011) found that a majority of a sample of Asian Americans (68%, vs. 27% for White Americans) reported that they would have been embarrassed if White Americans had seen some of the ethnic foods they ate at home while growing up. Next, Asian Americans whose belongingness was threatened (e.g., by being asked whether they spoke English) were 3 times more likely to report American staple dishes as their favorite (instead of Asian dishes) than when it was not threatened—and they were also more likely to order and actually eat American food than ethnic food in the laboratory. The foods ordered to affirm an American identity also had more fat and calories, explaining a possible mechanism for why the obesity rates of second-generation immigrants are similar to those of White Americans. If second-generation immigrants feel compelled to demonstrate their American identity, ordering less healthy dishes that seem American seems to be one means of doing so.

Others' Food Choices Can Be Threatening to the Self

In Western culture, the food-related judgments of others extend beyond the general healthiness or unhealthiness of one's diet. Vegetarians report being pestered by others about their dietary choices, saying that their diet seems to bother meat eaters (Adams, 2003). Resentment toward vegetarians can be seen on cultural products such as T-shirts (e.g., "Nobody likes a vegetarian") and bumper stickers (e.g., "Vegetarian: Sioux word for lousy hunter"). Indeed, Western meat-eating participants put down vegetarians relative to nonvegetarians on potency (Monin & Norton, 2003), a measure relating to a person's perceived strength or agency. As discussed previously, further research has demonstrated that negative attitudes toward vegetarians are related to how much people expect vegetarians to see themselves as morally superior to nonvegetarians; supporting this interpretation, when people imagine being morally reproached by vegetarians, they rate vegetarians more negatively than when moral judgment is not anticipated (Minson & Monin, 2012). In the context of our discussion of multiple cultures, and following our description of tensions between minority and mainstream food cultures, it is noteworthy that the vegetarian culture is resented by a portion of the mainstream who see it as a reproach of mainstream practices.

When it comes to food, individuals in modern societies are effectively multicultural. Migrationary movements and greater tolerance for outgroups results in individuals with mixed cultural heritages even within the mainstream (e.g., upper-middle-class Whites in the United States), whereas the experience of culinary exploration of ethnic foods and cultural role-play when it comes to food is common enough for modern individuals to raise questions about the place of a dominant culture and how it relates to this multiplicity of influences, tastes, and practices. We next isolate the influence specifically imposed on individuals by large-scale actors such as governments, corporations, and the media.

A RICH DESSERT: INSTITUTIONAL ACTORS AND FOOD CULTURE

Much of our analysis so far has focused on individual or small-group cultural processes, such as the ways people prepare and serve food and the sharing of food among family and friends. However, as industrialization and globalization increase, a tension between these everyday experiences with food and the institutional processes that influence them emerges. Although people identify, claim, and feel familiar with the individual and small-group processes, the cultural cycle also includes the institutionalization of these practices (Markus & Kitayama, 2010).

Acknowledging the multiple food cultures that individuals juggle in modern society would be naive if one did not recognize that not all cultural messages and frameworks are created equal. In particular, everyday lives in media-soaked, digitally hyperconnected industrialized societies are shaped not just by existing cultural elements but also by actors who joust at the macro level to dominate the representational space, define meanings, constrain behavior, and legitimize ways of being that serve their agenda. Without subscribing to conspiracy theories or even Marxist sociology, it is useful to recognize the increasing role of centralized government and corporations in crafting and molding culture, as facilitated by mass media. Although such cultural criticism may sound as though it harkens back to the leftist critical analysis of the 1960s, it is given new relevance at a time at which TV commercials follow people everywhere, whether they are pumping gas, sitting in an airplane, waiting at the doctor's, or just paying for groceries. The ubiquity of cheap LCD TVs ushered in a world of constant representational bombardment that cannot be ignored as a major cultural input for individuals in industrialized societies. And this is not even mentioning the encroachment of commercials in the home via constant TV viewing or in every private moment via smartphone advertising. Individuals typically underestimate the influence of such ubiquitous background messages, which directly contributes to their pernicious effectiveness because individuals do not put up adequate cognitive barriers or reduce exposure (Wilson & Brekke, 1994).

The food domain is a particularly interesting arena in which to study this struggle for the representational space because the financial interests at stake are so transparent at the very top, yet they can shape choices at the most individual, domestic, intimate level. When a woman alone in her apartment indulges in a square of Dove chocolate, this seemingly personal decision is at the confluence of decades of institutional messages (e.g., television advertisements) about how women can regulate their mood with chocolate, images associating female sensual pleasure with Dove candy, as well as countervailing narratives about idealized body shapes and the guilt associated with indulging in a sugary and rich food such as chocolate. These messages, which constitute the culture this woman is reacting to just as much as the prescriptions transmitted by her parents and peers, often come from less benevolent sources with their own agendas. We think it is useful to acknowledge the role of these forces in shaping culture and that this role is particularly apparent in the food domain. Here we depart somewhat from the cultural psychologist's mantra to consider the mutual constitution of various cultural levels to focus more on top–down processes, mainly for analytical purposes— although it would be interesting to consider that acknowledging reciprocal processes does not necessarily mean that both sides are on an equal footing: It is possible that institutional actors affect individual cultural representations more than individuals are able to affect what values and representations are embraced by institutional actors.[2]

Much of our analysis in this section relies on examples in the media because social psychology has not traditionally spent much time analyzing the role of institutional actors, in part because it is poorly equipped to do so both conceptually and methodologically. Cultural psychologists have already connected media representations with individual-level cultural representations (as in Kim & Markus, 1999, or Moscovici, 1961), but they have more often described these processes as a self-reinforcing echo chamber than as resulting from a deliberate agenda serving the interest of a group, agency, or corporation. We think the food domain illustrates that taking a less benign look at this processes is sobering. We illustrate the importance of institutional actors in shaping cultural representations by focusing on government agencies and corporations.

Government Agencies: Promoting a Healthy Culture?

One first institutional actor is the government. Agencies strive to comply with their mandate by shaping the discourse on food and changing behaviors in a way that serves their constituents. In a multiagency context as large as the U.S. government, the fact that various agencies serve different needs can lead to countervailing influences that are then reflected as contradictory components of the food culture. The most salient contribution of the U.S. government to the discourse on food is perhaps through the Surgeon General, the National Institutes of Health, and the U.S. Department of Agriculture. Such bodies have regularly raised the alarm in recent years about the rise in the number of individuals classified as overweight or obese (about 69% of the adult U.S. population in 2010 according to the National Center for Health Statistics, 2011) and have pledged a "war on obesity" manifest in many government initiatives. One cultural artifact that resulted from these efforts was the food pyramid published by the U.S. Department of Agriculture in 1992 and 2005, attempting to guide individuals toward the proper amount of food groups to ensure a balanced diet, which was recently replaced by the nutrition plate diagram called MyPlate (http://www.choosemyplate.gov; see also Neuman 2011).

At the same time, government agencies pursuing goals other than public health have also had an impact on food culture that can defeat the goal

---

[2]Food meanings are imposed by those in power. A good reminder of this is captured in the English language. After the Norman conquest of England, the Anglo-Saxon words used to refer to farm animals (*ox/bull, sheep, pig/swine, chicken*) by the herders who raised them were replaced once the meat was served at the dinner table of the farmers' masters with words of Norman origin (*beef, mutton, pork, poultry*) much closer to present-day French (*boeuf, mouton, porc, poulet*). To this day, this reflection of the military domination of one cultural group by another remains enshrined in the English words used to refer to meat.

of promoting healthy diets. For years, the food pyramid was the source of controversies suggesting that it resulted from a confluence of institutional interests and in particular that lobbyists for food and agricultural producers' professional associations carried undue influence over the place given to foods that might serve their interests better than the average eater's health (Reyes, 2008). When the Obama administration released the new MyPlate scheme under the First Lady's patronage, the Harvard School of Public Health unveiled an alternative prescription, with the chair of its Department of Nutrition going on record lamenting that MyPlate "mixes science with the influence of powerful agricultural interests, which is not a recipe for healthy eating" ("Harvard Researchers Launch Healthy Eating Plate," 2011, para. 2).

Such conflicts of interest abound in the federal food policies that trickle down with very real consequences on the landscape that makes up the American food culture. Controversy arose around the idea that food stamps could be used to buy junk foods, such that the federal government was in effect subsidizing the health-damaging diet of its poorest population (Ludwig, Blumenthal, & Willett, 2012). Another example of unanticipated negative shaping of a food culture is when the federal government started handing out wheat flour to some Native American populations on reservations to supplement their diet (Miller, 2008). Because wheat flour is not a staple in Native American cooking, this led to the creation of frybread, a type of flat dough that is fried in oil or lard and is particularly unhealthy, contributing in some small part to the poor diet in this population, and possibly to its high rates of obesity (Story et al., 1999).

Yet another setting in which special interests and conflicting government goals clash is school lunches. The behind-the-scenes struggle between federal agencies striving to fund the program, food and beverage industry giants such as Tyson or Archer Daniels Midland, parents and activist pressure groups, and local school administrators determines what lands on the 187 billion plates served every year to U.S. schoolchildren (Haskins, 2005), with obvious cultural repercussions for the imprinting of these children when it comes to what constitutes "normal" food. The U.S. public got a glimpse of this representational struggle in 1981 when the U.S. Department of Agriculture suggested cutting costs by counting pickle relish and ketchup as the vegetable portion of the five required school-lunch food items. The backlash against this suggestion led to its quick retraction (and the reinstatement of $1 billion in funding that the Reagan administration was trying to cut out of the program), but it is just an extreme case of the kind of high-stakes skirmish that affects what schoolchildren will encounter as normal fare every day and will come to embrace as normative of their culture.

Institutions are influenced by culture, as in the case of setting up government subsidies to support the growing of foods that are needed and well-liked.

For example, the establishment of corn subsidies in the United States pre-dates the Great Depression and initially helped to guarantee that farmers could make a living selling corn, thereby ensuring that corn would be available for sale, thus filling a public need. However, institutions also help shape culture by determining which foods are readily available and affordable. For example, returning to corn subsidies, on which the U.S. government spent approximately $7 billion each year (more than twice as much as for any other subsidized crop; U.S. Department of Agriculture 2006 fiscal year budget) until the federal subsidy expired in 2011. The artificially low cost of corn products compared with other forms of sugar (as a result of government subsidies) resulted in the replacement of sugar with high fructose corn syrup in many products and foods. Although the health effects of replacing glucose with fructose are still under investigation, many Americans are wary of high fructose corn syrup, so much so that in 2010 the Corn Refiners Association applied to rename high fructose corn syrup as "corn sugar" (another representational gambit) although this application was rejected by the Food and Drug Administration (Perlman, 2011). Even if high fructose corn syrup is identical to other forms of sugar, the massive subsidies to corn and the replacement of sugar with corn syrup allow corporations to offer sweet and unhealthy foods at a much cheaper price, starting a vicious circle that has contributed to the current obesity crisis.

One of the most striking misalignment of special interests came in the form of a particularly cheesy pizza pie served by Domino's in 2010. The Department of Agriculture, which releases the MyPlate guidelines and publically decries the rise in obesity, at the same time funded an organization called Dairy Management to promote the interests of the dairy industry by helping Domino's develop a new line of pizzas with 40% more cheese, chipping in for a $12 million marketing campaign; praising Taco Bell's quesadillas for using 8 times more cheese than other items on the menu; and supporting an advertising campaign touting the unfounded claim that people could lose weight by eating more dairy products (Moss, 2010). Although this effort undoubtedly resulted from a good-faith effort to protect the livelihood of the nation's dairy farmers, it is noteworthy because the tangible consequences of this deliberate decision to protect the interests of one group trickle down to determine the food landscape of millions of Americans, affecting what options are available, what flavors and portion sizes are deemed acceptable and attractive, and thus shaping cultural representations as surely as they shape the bodies and health outcomes of millions of Americans.

Corporations and the Media

Whereas the ambivalent influence of government agencies in defining the U.S. food culture may surprise some readers, the role of corporations, and in particular of large agribusinesses and food and beverage giants, is more commonly recognized. The Federal Trade Commission found that in 2004 American children saw an average of 15 TV ads for food products every day (Holt, Ippolito, Desrochers, & Kelley, 2007), which has surely increased in the 10 years since because of the ubiquity of TV and the media. As we argued earlier, TV ads make up a large part of the cultural fabric that these individuals grow up with, as well as the food meanings and culinary referents that they in turn transmit, in terms of desirable foods, modes of eating, portions, and styles of food. As an example, a series of 2013 Chef Boyardee TV ads featured children getting home from school to an empty house and heating up canned ravioli after performing a raucous dance routine in the kitchen, while a voiceover said, "It's your time"—and for those viewers who may be deterred by the fear that parents or peers may disapprove of eating a bowl of ravioli as an after-school snack, the power of such social pressures is played down with the grammatically shaky punch line, "Chef don't judge" (http://www.youtube.com/watch?v=XgLhtPQ11BY, http://www.youtube.com/watch?v=sEX_FVbocyg). Thus, the cultural message is that prescriptive norms may be of little importance and may in fact be overly judgmental. Interestingly, such a message of rebelliousness and youthful independence is completely at odds with the cultural message portrayed at the same time on the official Chef Boyardee website (http://www.chefboyardee.com/), most likely targeted at parents, that touts the communal message "Dinner tastes better when you cook it together" with clips of loving children helping their mothers cook dinner with ConAgra Foods products (and mum about the fact that they snuck a bowl of ravioli before their mom came home).

Just as the earlier ketchup-as-vegetable example was the tip of the iceberg of the fight over the construal of foods to satisfy multiple interests in the government context, extreme examples of attempts at manipulating representations by corporations have revealed a ubiquitous effort at manipulating cultural meanings to serve the interests of large corporations. When Ferrero advertised its Nutella spread as made with "simple quality ingredients like hazelnuts, skim milk, and a hint of cocoa" and presented it as part of a balanced breakfast, many parents embraced this representation of the child-pleasing spread as a healthy food. It was thus a surprise to some of them when they later realized that its main ingredients were palm oil and sugar, with 100 calories per tablespoon or, as one parent who started a class-action lawsuit against the company put it in court documents, that it was "the next best thing to a candy bar." Ferrero ended up agreeing to a $3 million settlement and changing its packaging and advertising to avoid the confusion, but it stands as an example of a company pushing the envelope of representation to increase sales of its product (Jaslow, 2012). Note that even if Ferrero were to protest that it never tried to mislead the public, from a cultural analysis standpoint it is worth noting that as a result of this marketing campaign, that is how the product was construed by many in the population.

Just as commercial messages attempt to shape the perception of foods, they also try to change the practices of eating, at times by pushing back against the conventions of the prevailing culture, either by suggesting new ways of acting or, more often, by attempting to license existing practices that individuals may engage in with some degree of guilt or fear of social censure. We already described the "Chef don't judge" campaign as an example of an encouragement to break cultural norms to serve immediate gratification (and the long-term interests of ConAgra Foods). Similarly, Mexican-themed food chain Taco Bell's 2007 "fourthmeal" campaign centered on late-night eating, implying that a fourth large caloric intake was appropriate by calling it a meal. When nutritionists criticized the chain for promoting eating a fourth meal late at night as normal or appropriate, Taco Bell insisted that this behavior was already popular among young people, and their campaign merely gave it a name (White, 2007). Although the existing eating habits of some may have inspired the campaign, Taco Bell's goal also seemed to be to encourage others who had never gone for a fourth meal to do so and to legitimize this behavior for those already engaging in it. In one commercial, a man commandeers a DJ's microphone in a crowded club to announce, "Everyone's a fourthmealer. Some just don't know it yet." Similar messages have since been taken up by other fast-food chains, such as McDonald's 2012 "nocturnivore" campaign, which offers breakfast beginning at midnight (Tuttle, 2012), and Jack-in-the-Box's "munchies meal" box, marketed for late-night binges. Although campaigns such as these may fulfill a need for those already looking for late-night food, they are also shaping the ideas of those who have never previously considered late-night food, sending a cultural message about appropriate eating times and practices.

All-night dining also reflects the overwhelming abundance of food in Western industrialized societies, and in the United States in particular. Campaigns promoting a fourth meal present a sharp and chilling contrast to similarly ubiquitous campaigns in North Korea promoting the idea of having only two meals a day because of dramatic food shortages (Demick, 2009). Yet, all-night dining should not be considered simply as a symbol of the opulence of the richest nation on earth, because such food services also cater to the many people forced to work multiple jobs at odd hours of the day to make ends meet in U.S. society and who thus cannot necessarily take their meals at traditional hours. Besides, it is only made possible by a restaurant industry that relies on poorly paid, low-skilled workers working long hours and on a cuisine built around prepackaged and frozen ingredients, easy-to-follow systematized preparation procedures, and heavy reliance on salt and fat for flavor.

The availability of certain foods is also worth mentioning because it strongly affects the food culture of social groups and is also to a large degree controlled by the business decisions of large corporations. Thus, nutrition and public health experts have lamented the appearance of "food deserts," or urban areas with little access to the fresh and affordable foods necessary for a healthy diet, which predominantly affects isolated individuals such as single mothers, children, or older adults in poor neighborhoods (Beaulac, Kristjansson, & Cummins, 2009; see also Stephens et al., 2012). Instead of relying on cultural staples for sustenance, individuals in such environments often have to rely on fast-food restaurants or convenience stores and consume a particularly unhealthy diet. Processed foods may come to replace produce as ingredients in recipes, as in the cultural oddity called a "Frito pie," in which cheese and canned chili are added to Fritos corn chips, sometimes right in the bag.

The fast-food industry influences not only what and how people eat but also how they think and behave more broadly, even in domains unrelated to food. For example, fast food has become a multimillion dollar industry and is present in varying degrees all over the world, as evidenced by the ranking of McDonald's golden arches as one of the most globally recognized cultural symbols (Schlosser, 2001). However, the pervasiveness of fast food shapes far more than people's waistlines and instead seems to be cognitively associated with a general quickening of the pace of daily life, so much so that simple exposure to symbols of fast food can lead to individuals becoming faster. Zhong and DeVoe (2010) found that even unconscious exposure to fast-food symbols (e.g., McDonald's arch) increases reading speed. Furthermore, thinking about fast food leads people to prefer other time-saving products (e.g., high-efficiency detergent, a three-in-one skincare solution; Zhong & DeVoe, 2010). Most strikingly, exposure to fast-food symbols reduced people's willingness to save and led them to prefer immediate gains over future returns, a strategy that ultimately puts their economic interests at risk (Zhong & DeVoe, 2010). Thus, the pervasiveness of fast food and its culture of time efficiency and immediate gratification have important implications for people's preferences and behaviors.

Broader Social Trends and Reciprocal Processes

Although we have focused on top–down effects to illustrate the secret war for consumers' and citizens' plates waged by large corporations and government agencies to serve their interests or those of their constituents, food culture also involves corporations and the media in less obviously top–down ways. One of the major trends in American food culture in the past decades is the outsourcing of food preparation and the increased reliance on precooked meals, processed dishes, and eating out (Kant & Graubard, 2004). As a result of busier lives and women working outside of the home more, dining out and bringing commercially prepared food home have become increasingly embraced as practical alternatives to actual grocery shopping and cooking. This creates a vicious circle because young adults starting their own homes now have sometimes had limited exposure to parents who cook and are thus less likely to have picked up rudimentary culinary skills themselves. Although the commercial outsourcing of food preparation certainly serves the interests of large restaurant chains and processed food producers, it is likely that this trend follows from broader sociological trends that are outside corporate control and that they have at best adapted to cash in on it.

A number of intriguing countercultural elements have emerged in reaction to this trend of increasingly outsourcing food preparation. First, several social movements reacting to the prevalence of unhealthy, chemically enhanced fast food have gained more prominence: the slow-food movement; vegetarians, vegans, and others who eschew animal products; new consumer appetite for organic or fair-trade agricultural products; and an increased mindfulness of the humane treatment of farm animals. As the population as a whole is slowly moving away from the actual preparation of food, a high proportion of the public is reacting by embracing increased purity of ingredients. As food distribution channels and production processes become increasingly distant and nebulous in large corporations, a large chunk of the population is turning to more proximal distribution channels to have a more intimate, direct experience with their food and retain a modicum of control over and knowledge about its origin. The success of community-supported agriculture, in which individuals buy a share or membership from a farmer and receive a box of seasonal produce each week delivered directly from the farmer is another example of individuals trying to bypass large institutional actors to reclaim a more intimate relationship with their food.

Another response to the recession of cooking as a daily chore has been to elevate it to the degree of entertainment. Cooking shows have multiplied on American television, and although a segment of the audience may be watching to pick up tips or recipes, these shows increasingly seem to be produced for entertainment value, with the epitome being the cooking competition, originally imported from Japan (*Iron Chef*) but now cloned repeatedly (*Top Chef*, *Chopped!*, *Cupcake Wars*). TV chefs have become celebrities in their own right, and cable channels devoted to displaying food preparation have enjoyed mushrooming viewership. In contrast to fashion, music, or visual art, cooking would seem a priori to make for bad television because onscreen food can be neither smelled nor tasted. So there is something particularly fascinating about millions of viewers eating takeout or microwaved dinners while watching the preparation of intricate dishes that they will never enjoy.

Some writers have discussed this apparent fetishization of the visual appearance of food and its preparation as "food porn," and the parallel seems appropriate. There is a decoupling in modern American culture between, on the one hand, the base act of food ingestion, which falls to new lows every time a munchie box is sold late at night by a teenager working at Jack-in-the-Box to someone who chews it mindlessly while sitting in the driver's seat, and, on the other hand, the most sublimated depictions of food preparation, idealized when a smiling chef is filmed on a terrace overlooking a Hawaiian bay discussing the proper way to whisk a mayonnaise. Again, this trend clearly involves corporations and the media industry in particular, but although we think it is worth discussing here, we did not want to imply that it is driven by top–down processes, although, of course, corporations benefit from this public love story with food porn because they can advertise their products to an already salivating audience.

In this third section, we have explored the role of large institutional actors in shaping food culture. We have argued that such an analysis is useful for cultural psychologists to consider more generally. Besides recognizing the mutually constitutive processes between various levels of the cultural matrix, it can be productive not to be naïve about the interests at stake in this mutual constitution and the fact that the actors with the power and resources (e.g., corporations, public agencies) have more than their share of influence in shaping the American food culture. We illustrated this with several examples and then discussed some reciprocal processes that involve these institutional actors but are not as clearly instigated by them, such as the reduction in home cooking and the countercultural movements that followed, as well as the more puzzling phenomenon of food porn, which elevates cooking as a spectacle and as an object of sublimated fascination.

We realize, of course, that much of the analysis in this section again applies predominantly to the U.S. context. Our claim, as before, is that the trends seen in the United States are likely to be observed in some version in other industrialized countries and that the spread of American cultural products, media, and restaurant chains throughout the global economy guarantees that many of the trends we discussed will be exported to other parts of the world.

SUMMARY AND CONCLUDING COMMENTS

In this chapter, we considered what cultural psychologists stand to gain by studying food and eating. In the first section, we acknowledged cultural differences in table manners, food taboos, and affective associations with food, which we connected to familiar models of differences between cultures. These models recognize that cultures differ in their treatment of food in systematic ways. The remaining two sections did not look at differences between national cultures but instead exposed and problematized the multiple cultural influences faced by any given individual in modern society. In the first section, we raised the issue of universal multiculturalism by proposing that familial cultures matter a great deal and by acknowledging that individuals in modern society are showered with various cultural representations, not all coming from their own home culture, and yet are somehow integrated. In our third section, we exposed the role of institutional actors, in particular how government agencies and food- and beverage-producing corporations struggle for influence in shaping the culture because of the very large financial interests at stake. Although not wanting to start conspiracy theories, we also think it can be productive to be realistic about the power of these actors in shaping the cultural landscape and thus the world. In closing, we reiterate our claim that cultural psychologists have much to gain by studying the food domain, and we more modestly propose that they consider incorporating in their analyses some of the questions and directions that we have sketched out here.

REFERENCES

Adams, C. J. (2003). *Living among meat eaters: The vegetarian's survival handbook*. New York, NY: Three Rivers Press.

Aldridge, J., Calhoun, C., & Aman, R. (2000). Misconceptions about multicultural education. *Focus on Elementary, 12*, 3.

Ambady, N., Shih, M., Kim, A., & Pittinsky, T. L. (2001). Stereotype susceptibility in children: Effects of identity activation on quantitative performance. *Psychological Science, 12*, 385–390. doi:10.1111/1467-9280.00371

Appadurai, A. (1981). Gastro-politics in Hindu South Asia. *American Ethnologist, 8*, 494–511.

Bargh, J. A., Chen, M., & Burrows, L. (1996). Automaticity of social behavior: Direct effects of trait construct and stereotype activation on action. *Journal of Personality and Social Psychology, 71*, 230–244. doi:10.1037/0022-3514.71.2.230

Beaulac, J., Kristjansson, E., & Cummins, S. (2009). A systematic review of food deserts, 1966-2007. *Preventing Chronic Disease, 6*(3).

Bevan, T., Fellner, E., Cavendish, J. (Producers), & Maguire, S. (Director). (2001). *Bridget Jones's diary* [Motion picture]. United Kingdom: Universal Pictures.

Cheryan, S., & Monin, B. (2005). Where are you *really* from? Asian Americans and identity denial. *Journal of Personality and Social Psychology, 89*, 717–730. doi:10.1037/0022-3514.89.5.717

Cohen, A. B. (2009). Many forms of culture. *American Psychologist, 64*, 194–204. doi:10.1037/a0015308

Cohen, A. B. (2010). Just how many different forms of culture are there? *American Psychologist, 65,* 59–61. doi:10.1037/a0017793

Cohen, A. B., & Rozin, P. (2001). Religion and the morality of mentality. *Journal of Personality and Social Psychology, 81,* 697–710.

Cohen, D., Nisbett, R. E., Bowdle, B. F., & Schwarz, N. (1996). Insult, aggression, and the Southern culture of honor: An experimental ethnography. *Journal of Personality and Social Psychology, 70,* 945–959. doi:10.1037/0022-3514.70.5.945

Delaney, A. (2012, April 17). Dog wars escalate: Barack Obama ate dog meat. *Huffington Post.* Retrieved from http://www.huffingtonpost.com/2012/04/17/dog-wars-obama-dog_n_1433223.html

Demick, B. (2009). *Nothing to envy: Ordinary lives in North Korea.* New York, NY: Spiegel & Grau.

Diamond, J. M. (1997). *Guns, germs and steel: The fate of human societies.* New York, NY: Norton.

Drewnowski, A., Henderson, S. A., Shore, A. B., Fischler, C., Preziosi, P., & Hercberg, S. (1996). Diet quality and diversity in France: Implications for the French paradox. *Journal of the American Dietetic Association, 96,* 663–669.

Frazer, J. G. (1959). *The new Golden Bough: A study in magic and religion* (abridged; T. H. Guster, Ed.). New York, NY: Macmillan. (Original work published 1890)

Graham, J., Haidt, J., & Nosek, B. A. (2009). Liberals and conservatives rely on different sets of moral foundations. *Journal of Personality and Social Psychology, 96,* 1029–1046.

Grunfeld, D. I. (1982). *The Jewish dietary laws: Vol. 1. Dietary laws regarding forbidden and permitted foods, with particular reference to meat and meat products* (3rd ed.). London, England: Soncinco Press.

Guendelman, M. D., Cheryan, S., & Monin, B. (2011). Fitting in but getting fat: Identity threat and dietary choices among U.S. immigrant groups. *Psychological Science, 22,* 959–967.

Haidt, J., Koller, S. H., & Dias, M. G. (1993). Affect, culture, and morality, or is it wrong to eat your dog? *Journal of Personality and Social Psychology, 65,* 613–628.

Harris, J. R. (1998). *The nurture assumption: Why children turn out the way they do.* New York, NY: Free Press.

Harvard researchers launch healthy eating plate. (2011, September 14). *HSPH News.* Retrieved from http://www.hsph.harvard.edu/news/press-releases/healthy-eating-plate/

Haskins, R. (2005). The school lunch lobby. *Education Next, 5*(3), 11–17.

Holt, D. J., Ippolito, P. M., Desrochers, D. M., & Kelley, C. R. (2007). *Children's exposure to TV advertising in 1977 and 2004: Information for the obesity debate* (Federal Trade Commission, Bureau of Economics Staff Report). Washington, DC: Federal Trade Commission, Bureau of Economics. Retrieved from http://www.ftc.gov/os/2007/06/cabecolor.pdf

Jaslow, R. (2012). Nutella health claims net $3.05 million settlement in class-action lawsuit. *CBS News*. Retrieved from http://www.cbsnews.com/8301-504763_162-57423319-10391704/nutella-health-claims-net-$3.05-million-settlement-in-class-action-lawsuit/

Johnson, K. A., White, A. E., Boyd, B. M., & Cohen, A. B. (2011). Matzah, meat, milk, and mana: Psychological influences on religio-cultural food practices. *Journal of Cross-Cultural Psychology, 42*, 1421–1436.

Junge, A. (Writer), & Zuckerman, S. (Director). (1996). The one with the metaphorical tunnel [Television series episode]. In K.S. Bright, M. Kauffman, & D. Crane (Producers), *Friends*. Burbank, CA: Warner Bros. Studios.

Kang, K. (Writer), & Greenberg, R. (Director). (2007). Little Boys. [Television series episode]. In C. Thomas & C. Bays (Producers), *How I met your mother*. Los Angeles, CA: 20th Century Fox Television.

Kant, A. K., & Graubard, B. I. (2004). Eating out in America, 1987-2000: Trends and nutritional correlates. *Preventive Medicine, 38*, 243–249.

Kidney, R., & Platt, M. E. (Producers), & Luketic, R. (Director). (2001). *Legally blonde* [Motion picture]. United States: Metro-Goldwyn-Mayer.

Kim, H., & Markus, H. R. (1999). Deviance or uniqueness, harmony or conformity? A cultural analysis. *Journal of Personality and Social Psychology, 77*, 785–800.

Kitayama, S., Ishii, K., Imada, T., Takemura, K., & Ramaswamy, J. (2006). Voluntary settlement and the spirit of independence: Evidence from Japan's "Northern frontier." *Journal of Personality and Social Psychology, 91*, 369–384.

Ludwig, D. S., Blumenthal, S. J., & Willett, W. C. (2012). Opportunities to reduce childhood hunger and obesity: Restructuring the Supplemental Nutrition Assistance Program (the food stamp program). *JAMA, 308*, 2567–2568.

Macht, M., & Mueller, J. (2007). Immediate effects of chocolate on experimentally induced mood states. *Appetite, 49*, 667–674.

Macrae, C. N., Bodenhausen, G. V., & Milne, A. B. (1995). The dissection of selection in person perception: Inhibitory processes in social stereotyping. *Journal of Personality and Social Psychology, 69*, 397–407.

Markus, H. R., & Connor, A. (2013). *Clash! 8 cultural conflicts that make us who we are*. New York, NY: Hudson Street Press.

Markus, H. R., & Kitayama, S. (1991). Culture and the self: Implications for cognition, emotion, and motivation. *Psychological Review, 98*, 224–253.

Markus, H. R., & Kitayama, S. (2003). Culture, self, and the reality of the social. *Psychological Inquiry, 14*, 277–283.

Markus, H. R., & Kitayama, S. (2010). Cultures and selves: A cycle of mutual constitution. *Perspectives on Psychological Science, 5*, 420–430.

Miller, J. (2008, July). Frybread. *Smithsonian Magazine*. Retrieved from http://www.smithsonianmag.com/people-places/frybread.html

Minson, J. A., & Monin, B. (2012). Do-gooder derogation: Putting down morally-motivated others to defuse implicit moral reproach. *Social Psychological and Personality Science, 3*, 200–207.

Monin, B., & Norton, M. I. (2003). Perceptions of a fluid consensus: Uniqueness bias, false consensus, false polarization and pluralistic ignorance in a water conservation crisis. *Personality and Social Psychology Bulletin, 29*, 559–567.

Moscovici, S. (1961). *La psychanalyse, son image et son public: Etude sur la représentation sociale de la psychanalyse* [Psychoanalysis, its image and its audience: A study of the social representation of psychoanalysis]. Paris, France: Presses Universitaires de France.

Moss, M. (2010, November 6). While warning about fat, U.S. pushes cheese sales. *New York Times*. Retrieved from http://www.nytimes.com/2010/11/07/us/07fat.html

National Center for Health Statistics. (2011). *Health, United States: With special feature on socioeconomic status and health*. Washington, DC: U.S. Department of Health and Human Services.

Nemeroff, C., & Rozin, P. (1989). "You are what you eat": Applying the demand-free "impressions" technique to an unacknowledged belief. *Ethos: The Journal of Psychological Anthropology, 20*, 96–115.

Neuman, W. (2011, June 2). Nutrition plate unveiled, replacing food pyramid. *New York Times*. Retrieved from http://www.nytimes.com/2011/06/03/business/03plate.html

Nisbett, R. E., & Cohen, D. (1996). *Culture of honor: The psychology of violence in the South*. Boulder, CO: Westview Press.

Olshansky, S. J., Antonucci, T., Berkman, L., Binstock, R. H., Boersch-Supan, A., Cacioppo, J. T., . . . Rowe, J. (2012). Differences in life expectancy due to race and educational differences are widening, and many may not catch up. *Health Affairs, 31*, 1803–1813.

Oyserman, D., Fryberg, S. A., & Yoder, N. (2007). Identity-based motivation and health. *Journal of Personality and Social Psychology, 93*, 1011–1027.

Pattnaik, J. (2003). Learning about the "other": Building a case for intercultural education among minority children. *Early Childhood Education, 74*, 204–211.

Perlman, S. (2011). FDA rejects industry bid to change name of high fructose corn syrup to "corn sugar." *CBS News*. Retrieved from http://www.cbsnews.com/8301-504763_162-57444586-10391704/fda-rejects-industry-bid-to-change-name-of-high-fructose-corn-syrup-to-corn-sugar/

Pollan, M. (2008). *In defense of food: An eater's manifesto*. New York, NY: Penguin Books.

Renaud, S., & de Lorgeril, M. (1992). Wine, alcohol, platelets, and the French paradox for coronary heart disease. *Lancet, 339*, 1523–1526.

Rennard, B. O., Ertl, R. F., Gossman, G. L., Robbins, R. A., & Rennard, S. I. (2000). Chicken soup inhibits neutrophil chemotaxis in vitro. *Chest, 188*, 1150–1157.

Reyes, R. (2008, July 15). Food pyramid frenzy: Lobbyists fight to defend sugar, potatoes and bread in recommended U.S. diet. *Wall Street Journal*. Retrieved from http://online.wsj.com/article/0,,SB109104875075676781,00.html

Richard, J., Cambien, F., & Ducimetière, P. (1981). Particularité épidémiologiques de la maladie coronarienne en France [Epidemiological peculiarities of coronary disease in France]. *Presse Médicale, 10*, 1111–1114.

Rozin, P. (1996). Towards a psychology of food and eating: From motivation to module to model to marker, morality, meaning, and metaphor. *Current Directions in Psychological Science, 5*, 18–24.

Rozin, P. (2007). Food and eating. In S. Kitayama & D. Cohen (Eds.), *Handbook of cultural psychology* (pp. 391–416). New York, NY: Guilford Press.

Rozin, P., Fischler, C., Imada, S., Sarubin, A., & Wrzesniewski, A. (1999). Attitudes to food and the role of food in life in the U.S.A., Japan, Flemish Belgium, and France: Possible implications for the diet–health debate. *Appetite, 23*, 163–180.

Saroglou, V., & Cohen, A. B. (2011). Psychology of culture and religion: Introduction to the JCCP special issue. *Journal of Cross-Cultural Psychology,42*, 1309–1319.

Schlosser, E. (2001). *Fast food nation: The dark side of the all-American meal*. New York, NY: Harper Perennial.

Snibbe, A. C., & Markus, H. R. (2005). You can't always get what you want: Educational attainment, agency, and choice. *Journal of Personality and Social Psychology, 88*, 703.

Steim, R. I., & Nemeroff, C. J. (1995). Moral overtones of food: Judgments of others based on what they eat. *Personality and Social Psychology Bulletin, 21*, 480–490.

Stephens, N. M., Markus, H. R., & Fryberg, S. A. (2012). Social class disparities in health and education: Reducing inequality by applying a sociocultural self model of behavior. *Psychological Review, 119*, 723–744.

Story, M., Evans, M., Fabsitz, R. R., Clay, T. E., Rock, B. H., & Broussard, B. (1999). The epidemic of obesity in American Indian communities and the need for childhood obesity-prevention programs. *American Journal of Clinical Nutrition, 69*(4, Suppl.), 747S–754S.

Triandis, H. C. (1990). Cross-cultural studies of individualism and collectivism. In J. Berman (Ed.), *Nebraska Symposium on Motivation, 1989* (pp. 41–133). Lincoln: University of Nebraska Press.

Tuttle, B. (2012, August 8). Fast-food chain wants you to eat more than the usual breakfast, lunch, and dinner. *Time Magazine*. Retrieved from http://moneyland.time.com/2012/08/08/fast-food-chains-want-you-to-eat-more-than-the-usual-breakfast-lunch-and-dinner/

U.S. Department of Agriculture. (2006). *Fiscal year 2006 budget summary and annual performance plan*. Retrieved from http://www.usda.gov/documents/FY06budsum.pdf

Uskul, A. K., Kitayama, S., & Nisbett, R. E. (2008). Ecocultural basis of cognition: Farmers and fishermen are more holistic than herders. *Proceedings of the National Academy of Sciences, USA, 105*, 8552–8556.

White, G. (2007, February 6). "Fourthmeal" hits the spot for many, but nutritionists cringe at habit. *The Ledger*. Retrieved from http://www.theledger.com/article/20070206/NEWS/702060313?p=1&tc=pg

Wilson, T. D., & Brekke, N. (1994). Mental contamination and mental correction: Unwanted influences on judgments and evaluations. *Psychological Bulletin, 116*, 117–142.

Wolraich, M. L., Wilson, D. B., & White, J. W. (1995). The effect of sugar on behavior or cognition in children. *JAMA, 274*, 1617–1621.

Zhong, C., & DeVoe, S. E. (2010). You are how you eat: Fast food and impatience. *Psychological Science, 21*, 619–622.

8

GENDERED SEXUAL CULTURES

ANGELA G. PIRLOTT AND DAVID P. SCHMITT

Social psychologists tend to define culture in terms of transmitted, shared, and enduring intergroup differences in cognition (e.g., beliefs, norms, values), affect (e.g., display rules, emotional syndromes, facial expressiveness), behavior (e.g., eating traditions, social scripts, sexual taboos), and knowledge (e.g., how to prepare food, build shelter, and care for children; see Triandis, 1994). So a particular way of thinking, feeling, or acting can be considered "cultural" to the extent that it is maintained across generations (Imada & Yussen, 2012), common among members of a group (or cultural subgroup; see D. E. Brown, 1991; Olson, 2011), and persists to some degree over time. In this chapter, we explore whether certain features of gender-linked sexuality may be properly considered cultural by social psychologists and suggest that considering them so adds to our basic understanding of gender, sexuality, and general cultural processes. In particular, we review evidence suggesting that sexual variation that differs across men and women may legitimately represent transmitted,

http://dx.doi.org/10.1037/14274-007
Culture Reexamined: Broadening Our Understanding of Social and Evolutionary Influences,
A. B. Cohen (Editor)

191

shared, and enduring gendered sexual culture. At the same time, we argue that certain features of gendered sexual culture are fundamentally caused by and often strategically interact with differences in men's and women's evolved sexual psychologies.

EVOLUTION AND THE GENERATION OF CULTURE

From an evolutionary perspective, classifying a gendered feature of human sexuality as either entirely natural (i.e., biological) or entirely cultural (i.e., socially influenced) is almost always a fallacious characterization. Indeed, a tremendous amount of what most psychologists consider cultural has deep-seated roots in human biology (Buss, 2001; Laland, Odling-Smee, & Myles, 2010). Rather than viewing culture as a simplistic first cause of almost all human behavior—a common assumption of the standard social science model (see Tooby & Cosmides, 1992)—evolutionary psychologists, human ethologists, and behavioral ecologists consider much of human culture as reflecting and deeply interacting with humans' innate biology (G. R. Brown, Dickens, Sear, & Laland, 2011; Gaulin, 1997; Kaplan & Lancaster, 2003; Mesoudi, 2009). Some features of sexual culture may serve as a potent phenotypic extension of people's most basic human tendencies (e.g., the existence of formal rules regarding pair bonding, marriage, and fidelity; Keller, 1990; Kenrick, Nieuweboer, & Buunk, 2010), whereas other aspects of sexual culture emerge as specially designed consequences of humanity's evolved psychological architecture—people's common human nature—facultatively interacting in adaptive ways with local environmental contexts (e.g., the level of local pathogens affects the form, content, and intensity of certain marital desires and behaviors; Gangestad, Haselton, & Buss, 2006; Low, 1990; Nettle, 2009; Schmitt, 2011).

Unlike advocates of the standard social science model, who argue that culture independently generates most of what it means to be human (e.g., Durkheim, 1895/1962; Eagly, 1987; Geertz, 1973; for a review, see Plotkin, 2004), modern evolutionists have argued that culture often flows from humans' biology, feeds back into their biology, and is a strategic partner with human nature in the ontogenetic generation of human behavior (Boyd & Richerson, 1985; Ridley, 2003; Rogers, 1988). Just as human language varies across cultures but also involves evolved psychological adaptations and key ontogenetic learning experiences to develop normally (Pinker, 1994), aspects of people's sexuality may simultaneously vary across cultures, involve evolved psychological adaptations, and depend on key gendered learning experiences (Cronk, 1999; Mealey, 2000). Some evolutionists have further argued that even human attributes entirely culturally transmitted via domain-general learning can be described at a deep, ultimate level as "evolved" attributes (Tinbergen, 1963). As seminally noted by Tooby and Cosmides (2005):

> To say a behavior is learned in no way undermines the claim that the behavior was organized by evolution. Behavior—if it was learned at all—was learned through the agency of evolved mechanisms. If natural selection had built a different set of learning mechanisms into an organism, that organism would learn a different set of behaviors in response to the very same environment. It is these evolved mechanisms that organize the relationship between the environmental input and behavioral output, and thereby pattern the behavior. For this reason, *learning is not an alternative explanation to the claim that natural selection shaped the behavior,* although many researchers assume that it is. The same goes for culture. Given that cultural ideas are absorbed via learning and inference—which is caused by evolved programs of some kind—a behavior can be, at one and the same time, *cultural, learned,* and *evolved.* (pp. 31–32)

In this chapter, we limit ourselves to discussing a particular aspect of sexuality that may be simultaneously cultural, learned, and evolved: patterns of sexual desires and mating behaviors that are, on average, differentially expressed by human males and females. We call this form of culture *gendered sexual culture.* Gendered sexual culture, in our view, is likely produced and maintained by several key forces, including evolved sex differences in sexual psychology, gender roles (aspects of which may reflect, reinforce, and be generated by evolved sex differences in sexuality), individual and cultural differences in the extent to which individuals adopt gender roles (again, aspects of which may depend on evolved sex differences in sexuality), and many other biological and sociohistorical factors (see Figure 8.1).

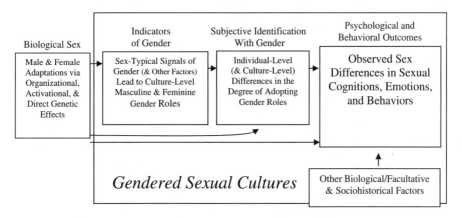

Figure 8.1. Multiple origins of sex differences in gendered sexual cultures.

Humans' evolved biology reliably generates sex-linked cultural expressions of sexuality in two fundamental ways. The first is through *pancultural universals* of gendered sexual culture—sex differences that pervade all, or nearly all, studied human cultures—such as sex differences in certain mate preferences (Buss, 1989), attachment styles (Schmitt et al., 2003), and sociosexual attitudes (Schmitt, 2005). We explore how sex differences across many psychological domains serve to facilitate gendered sexual cultures relating to men's and women's different reproductive and parenting challenges (Trivers, 1972). Our thesis is that whether as a result of organizational or activational effects of sex hormones on the human brain (Ellis, 2011), direct genetic effects on sexuality that differ between males and females (McCarthy & Arnold, 2011; Ngun, Ghahramani, Sánchez, Bocklandt, & Vilain, 2011), or indirect consequences of humans' evolved reproductive physiology leading to divided labors (Wood & Eagly, 2002, 2012), some evolved sex differences are robust enough to persistently generate gendered features of sexual culture all around the world.

The second way humans' evolved adaptations can reliably generate cultural expressions of gendered sexuality is via *facultative adaptations* (Gangestad, 2011; Nettle, 2011). That is, in the presence of particular ecological stressors or other adaptively relevant stimuli, specific cues in the environment can activate, via domain-specific mechanisms, a set of behavioral responses that reliably give rise to cultural differences, a phenomenon also known as *evoked cultures* (Tooby & Cosmides, 1992). Certain ecological elements appear to strategically elicit larger (or sometimes smaller) sex differences in gendered sexual culture, such as accentuating or attenuating sex differences in mate preferences (Gangestad et al., 2006), insecure attachment styles (Belsky, 1999; Del Giudice, 2011), and short-term mating tendencies (Schmitt, 2005). As noted in Table 8.1, many of these sex differences appear to functionally respond to pathogens and other ecological stressors as facultative adaptations or evoked sexual cultures (Schmitt, 2011).

PANCULTURAL SEX DIFFERENCES AND THE GENERATION OF GENDER AS CULTURE

To some degree, human males and females seem to produce and experience distinct forms of gendered sexual culture—each with their own beliefs and values reflected in sex-typical cognitions, emotions, and behaviors in the realm of sexuality (Aboim, 2010; Davies & Shackelford, 2008; Wood & Eagly, 2010). Compared with the "ethnographic hyperspace" of all possible sexual cultures one can imagine (Cronk, 1999), humans display rather limited cultural variation in sex-differentiated sexualities (D. E. Brown, 1991; Ellis,

TABLE 8.1

Examples of Pan-Cultural and Facultative Sex Differences in
Gendered Sexual Cultures

Pan-cultural sexuality	Facultative sexuality
Men more than women emphasize physical attractiveness in long-term mate choice, mate retention, and mate expulsion (Buss, 1989, 2001).	Both men and women emphasize physical attractiveness in long-term mates more greatly in high-pathogen environments, and because effects are greater among men, the size of sex differences in physical attractiveness preferences is larger in high-pathogen environments (Gangestad & Buss, 1993; Gangestad, Haselton, & Buss, 2006).
Men more than women possess dismissing romantic attachment styles linked to short-term mating (Schmitt et al., 2003).	Both men and women possess more dismissing romantic attachment styles in high-pathogen environments, and because effects are greater among women, the size of sex differences in dismissing attachment is smaller in high-pathogen environments (Schmitt, 2008).
Men more than women possess unrestricted sociosexual attitudes (Schmitt, 2005).	Humans become more restricted in high-pathogen environments (Schaller & Murray, 2008).
	Both men and women become more unrestricted in cultures with female-biased sex ratios, and because effects are greater among women, the size of sex differences in sociosexuality is smaller in female-biased sex ratio environments (Schmitt, 2005).

2011). Indeed, because some sex differences in beliefs and values appear to be universal or pan-cultural expressions of gendered sexuality, an essential question for social scientists to address is how it is even possible that all cultures come to express sex-differentiated sexuality in nearly the exact same way (Ellis, 2011).

Why Pan-Cultural Sex Differences in Sexual Attitudes and Behaviors

Evolutionary psychologists have suggested that within the domain of gendered sexual culture, some of the differences in men's and women's sexualities stem from an evolutionary history in which profound differences existed in obligatory parental investment burdens. According to parental investment theory (Trivers, 1972), the relative proportion of parental investment—the time and energy devoted to caring for individual offspring (at the expense of mating and creating additional offspring)—varies across males and females of different species. In some species, males tend to provide more parental investment than females (e.g., the Mormon cricket; Gwynne, 1984). In other species, females possess the weightier investment burdens (e.g., most mammals; Alcock, 2001; Clutton-Brock, 1991). Sex differences in parental investment burdens are systematically linked to processes of sexual selection such that the lesser investing sex is intrasexually more competitive, especially over gaining reproductive access to members of the opposite sex; is more aggressive with their own sex; tends to die earlier; tends to mature later; and generally competes for mates with more vigor than the heavier investing sex (R. D. Alexander & Noonan, 1979). Furthermore, the lesser investing sex of a species is intersexually less discriminating in mate choice than the heavier investing sex. The lesser investing sex is willing to mate more quickly, at lower cost, and with more partners than is the heavier investing sex (Bateson, 1983; Clutton-Brock & Parker, 1992).

Among humans, many men invest heavily as parents. Men teach social skills, emotionally nurture children, and invest resources and prestige in their children (Khaleque & Rohner, 2012). Nevertheless, men incur much lower levels of obligatory or "minimum necessary" parental investment in offspring than do women because women are obligated to incur the costs of internal fertilization, placentation, and gestation to reproduce. Furthermore, all female mammals, including ancestral women, carry obligatory investments associated with lactation, which can last several years in human foraging environments (Kelly, 1995), years during which it is harder for women than men to reproduce and invest in additional offspring (Blurton Jones, 1986). Finally, across all known cultures men typically invest less in active parenting effort than women (Low, 1989; Quinn, 1977). The evidence within humans, then, points to a sex difference in evolved mating and parenting pressures that should give rise to several persistent features of gendered sexual cultures.

Sex Differences in Mate Preferences

Men's and women's mate preferences tend to overlap in many domains—kindness, intelligence, good personality, sense of humor (Buss & Barnes, 1986; Feingold, 1992; Li, Bailey, Kenrick, & Linsenmeier, 2002; Sprecher, Sullivan, & Hatfield, 1994), yet evidence has also demonstrated significant differences between men's and women's mate preferences related to different minimal levels of parental investment. In the context of long-term mating (e.g., marriage), women more than men tend to prefer partners who display cues of commitment and resource provisioning (Buss & Barnes, 1986; Feingold, 1992; Li et al., 2002; Sprecher et al., 1994), whereas men more than women tend to desire cues of beauty and youth (Buss & Barnes, 1986; Feingold, 1992; Li et al., 2002; Sprecher et al., 1994). These sex-differentiated mate preferences have been documented as pervasive across cultures, in nationally representative samples, and among older adults; in studies of real-life personal ads, online dating choices, and actual marital choice; and in studies of the outcomes of these preferences, such as studies of marital satisfaction, retention, and divorce (for a review, see Schmitt et al., 2012).

In the context of short-term mating relationships, men conform to the typical mammalian male in their greater willingness to engage in casual sex outside of long-term relationships (Buss & Schmitt, 1993; Oliver & Hyde, 1993). Men's greater indiscriminate interest in multiple short-term partners has been documented as a pan-cultural universal in several studies (Lippa, 2009; Schmitt, 2005), and findings from diverse studies of extradyadic mating, short-term mate poaching, sexual fantasy content, and postcoital regret all support the view that men's short-term mate preferences are different from women's (for a review, see Buss & Schmitt, 2011).

Sex Differences in Mating Behaviors

This asymmetry in human parental investment should result in the lesser investing sex (i.e., men) displaying greater intrasexual competitiveness and lower intersexual choosiness in mate preferences. These different mate and relationship preferences translate into the sex-specific domains that men and women use to attract partners (Schmitt & Buss, 1996).

Consistent with predictions, as self-promotion strategists men, more so than women, use indicators of resource investment, such as status and resources, whereas women use indicators of fertility, such as attractiveness and youth (Schmitt & Buss, 1996); and as competitor derogation strategists, men, more so than women, engage in violence and physical aggression against other men as a way to achieve social status (e.g., Archer & Coyne, 2005; Eagly & Steffen, 1986). These reproductive strategies have also been demonstrated cross-culturally: Numerous studies have shown that men pan-culturally exhibit greater physical size and competitive aggression (Archer & Lloyd, 2002; Harvey & Reynolds, 1994; Hyde, 1986), riskier life history strategies (Daly & Wilson, 1988), relatively delayed maturation (Geary, 2010), and earlier death than do women across all known cultures (R. D. Alexander & Noonan, 1979). It is difficult to account for these pervasive features of gendered sexual culture without reference to evolved sex differences in basic reproductive strategies.

Indeed, dozens of psychological sex differences related to basic reproductive strategies have been shown to reliably replicate and appear to be universal. For instance, Ellis (2011) identified 65 apparent universal sex differences in cognition, emotion, and behavior. Each sex difference had been empirically replicated in at least 10 studies, most across multiple cultures, and if just one study failed to replicate the sex difference, it was eliminated from consideration as pancultural. Within the sexual domain, Ellis documented pan-cultural sex differences in strength of sex drive, desires for promiscuous sex, and various age- and status-related mate preferences (see also Baumeister, Catanese, & Vohs, 2001). Clearly, sex differences in parental investment obligations appear to have a pan-cultural influence on men's and women's fundamental sexual cultures.

Sex Differences in Attachment Styles

Del Giudice (2009a, 2009b) proposed that romantic attachment serves to facilitate long-term pair bonding and parental investment. In stable environments, men's and women's attachment styles should converge in secure attachment styles, but in unstable environments, men and women should adopt different attachment styles. To the extent that romantic attachment styles reflect mating strategies (Kirkpatrick, 1998) and that avoidant or dismissing attachment styles reflect decreased willingness to engage in long-term relationships (Jackson & Kirkpatrick, 2007), men are expected to report greater avoidant attachment and women greater anxious attachment, thus enabling men to engage in sexual activity under conditions of reduced commitment and parental investment and women to maximize closeness with kin and partner. Cross-culturally, many of these sex differences have robustly emerged (Schmitt, 2008; Schmitt et al., 2003).

Sex Differences in Attitudes, Personality, and Emotions

Sex differences in obligatory parental investment and sexual selection pressures have likely elicited sex differences in attitudes, personality characteristics, and emotions in ways that would facilitate effectively managing the different parenting and mating challenges faced by men and women. More so than women's, men's attitudes endorse worldviews that foster social hierarchies—social dominance orientation (Pratto, Sidanius, & Levin, 2006), agency over community (Gaeddert, 1985), and independence over interdependence (Cross & Madson, 1997; Gabriel & Gardner, 1999; Guimond, Chatard, Marinot, Crisp, & Redersdorff, 2006)—that enable men to compete with other men for status and access to resources—partner traits desired by women. Men's and women's personalities differ in ways predicted by their different parenting and reproductive challenges—women, more so than men, are warm, agreeable, and open to feelings, which enhances their ability to nurture kin, whereas men, more so than women, are assertive and open to ideas, again enabling them to achieve status (Costa, Terracciano, & McCrae, 2001). Finally, men and women differ in their experience of specific emotions: Men experience more sexual jealousy (Buss, Larsen, Westen, & Semmelroth, 1992;

Buunk, Angleitner, Oubaid, & Buss, 1996; DeSteno, Bartlett, Braverman, & Salovey, 2002; Harris, 2003; Hupka & Bank, 1996), thus alleviating problems of paternal uncertainty, whereas women experience more sexual regret (Roese et al., 2006), thereby enhancing women's selectivity in partner selection to minimize reproducing with an unstable long-term partner.

Many of these and other sex differences in sexuality have been empirically documented as prevalent across cultures (Broude & Greene, 1976; Frayser, 1985), including across foraging cultures that represent the psychological contexts within which humans evolved (Marlowe, 2003). Whether because of organizational or activational effects of sex hormones on the human brain or direct genetic effects that differ between men and women, some sex differences in sexuality are robust enough to transcend human populations and consistently emerge within sexual cultures (see Figure 8.1). In summary, men's and women's attitudes, personalities, emotions, and behaviors differ predictably in ways to better manage these challenges given their different reproductive and parenting challenges. Furthermore, the felt experience of these different attitudes, emotions, and behaviors mimics cultural differences such that the experience of gender for men and women is to some degree parallel across different cultures.

GENDER ROLES AS EXPRESSIONS OF GENDERED SEXUAL CULTURES

Biological sex may indirectly affect sex differences in sexual cultures by influencing the content of the cultural beliefs and values that are typically associated with biological sex, commonly referred to as gender roles of masculine and feminine forms of sociocultural expression (Eagly, 1987; Hoffman, 1977; Rose & Rudolph, 2006; Williams & Best, 1990). These gender roles may reflect sex-linked features of human physiology (e.g., facial traits, waist-to-hip ratios, degrees of muscularity; Frederick & Haselton, 2007; Mealey, 2000), cognitive capacities (e.g., mental abilities; Silverman, Choi, & Peters, 2007), emotional styles (e.g., empathizing and tending vs. befriending; Nettle, 2007), and basic personality traits (e.g., neuroticism; Schmitt, Realo, Voracek, & Allik, 2008) that are, empirically speaking, established pan-cultural universals. Gender roles also contain culturally variable content that is sometimes largely unrelated to evolved biology (e.g., hair length, clothing patterns; Wood & Eagly, 2010), and gender roles can vary in potency, extremity, and within-sex pervasiveness across cultures (Low, 2000; Wood & Eagly, 2012). In so doing, the potency of culture-level gender roles may serve to amplify or attenuate fundamental sex differences in evolved biology (Pasternak, Ember, & Ember, 1997; Mealey, 2000).

Individual Differences in Gendered Sexual Culture Adoption

An important note is that the process by which individuals adopt these gender roles and in essence succumb to the gendered sexual culture generated by evolved biology (and other factors) may, itself, depend on features directly related to biological sex. That is, the evolutionary biology of men and women that gives rise to psychological sex differences and affects the content of gender roles may also affect the degree to which individuals adopt gender roles (G. R. Brown, Laland, & Borgerhoff Mulder, 2009). One way this occurs is through human males and females possessing gender-specific learning biases, mechanisms designed to some degree to lead boys and girls to differentially learn their respective gender roles (Maccoby, 1998; Mealey, 2000). In addition, individual differences may exist within men and women—such as individual differences in personality, mate value, and age—that lead to differences in the adoption of gender roles and the expression of typical gendered sexual culture. For instance, emerging evidence has suggested that masculine, high-status, and promiscuous men (as do feminine, agreeable, and attractive women) display the most marked and stereotypical sex differences in mate preferences (Back, Penke, Schmukle, & Asendorpf, 2011; Buss & Shackelford, 2008; Cunningham & Russell, 2004; Eastwick et al., 2006; Kavanagh, Robins, & Ellis, 2010; Penke, Todd, Lenton, & Fasolo, 2007; Surbey & Brice, 2007).

Thus, the degree of gender role self-identification with the gendered sexual culture of one's biological sex is probably influenced by organizational, activational, and direct genetic effects related to biological sex combined with the gender roles of a particular gendered sexual culture (see Figure 8.1). The degree of gender role self-identification, in turn, influences the degree to which psychologists observe sex differences in gendered sexual cultures. Previous research has identified several factors that lead men and women to adopt gender roles more or less strongly (Hundhammer & Mussweiler, 2012; Wood & Eagly, 2010). Notably, we suggest that the degree of gendered self-identification may well vary across sexual cultures involving different ages, mate values, and local ecologies, making psychology's tendency to oversample Western, educated, industrialized, rich, and democratic ("WEIRD") college undergraduates (Henrich, Heine, & Norenzayan, 2010) a concern in the study of gendered sexual cultures.

Gendered Sexual Culture is Learned

A gendered view of sexual culture suggests that sex differences in attitudes, personality characteristics, and behaviors contain an evolved blueprint for some psychological sex differences, but much of the content of gender roles is also developed, taught, and learned. Cross-cultural studies have shown overwhelming consistency in finding that nurturing activities are fostered for girls more so than for boys (Barry, Bacon, & Child, 1957; B. B. Whiting & Edwards, 1988; J. W. M. Whiting & Whiting, 1975). Cross-culturally, parents encourage gender-stereotypic play and household chores for girls and boys, such as girls' playing with dolls to foster caregiving and boys' playing with action figures to foster aggressive rough-and-tumble or status-seeking behaviors (Lytton & Romney, 1991). Furthermore, children also seek out sex-segregated activities in childhood (Maccoby, 1998). The direct socialization of children and their selection of gender-typed activities signal the ability of gendered sexual culture to be learned and developed. Again, however, the suggestion that gendered sexual culture involves a large degree of learning does not undermine the basic evolutionary blueprint underlying these sex-specific roles, because studies of play have suggested that many features of young female caregiving play and young male rough-and-tumble play are moderated by sex hormones, are observed very early in human infancy, and are common among males and females of other primate species (G. M. Alexander & Hines, 2002; G. M. Alexander & Saenz, 2011; Hassett, Siebert, & Wallen, 2008).

Thus, although sex differences undoubtedly result from processes of learning and gender role socialization (Little, Jones, DeBruine, & Caldwell, 2011), facets of these processes—both the biased content of what is learned and the innate motivation to learn gender—may themselves be at least partially derived products of humans' evolved biology (see Kenrick, 1987; Maccoby, 1998; Mealey, 2000). Indeed, most theories of learning and gender role socialization alone only predict how people learn gender; they cannot alone explain why so many pan-cultural universals of sexuality exist (Ellis, 2011; Smuts, 1995; Vandermassen, 2005).

FACULTATIVELY EVOKED VARIATION OF GENDERED SEXUAL CULTURE

Just as all humans have callus-producing mechanisms within their skin, yet only some people (i.e., those experiencing repeated stress to the skin) have their calluses facultatively evoked, all humans may possess gendered sexual culture–producing mechanisms within their brains that emerge only when evoked by combinations of biological sex and local ecological environments (e.g., callous romantic attitudes and fast-paced sexual strategies; Gangestad, 2011; Lancaster, 1994). This facultative and highly plastic form of psychological adaptation may help to explain many of the cultural variations in the size of human sex differences and in the degrees to which men and women differ in their manifest sexual cultures (Cashdan, 2008; Gangestad et al., 2006; Kaplan & Lancaster, 2003; Smith, 2011).

In addition to pan-cultural universals, then, evolutionary psychologists consider many cultural variations in sexuality and mating strategies—variations to some extent culturally transmitted, shared, and enduring via gendered socialization—as naturally flowing from humans' evolved biology. This may seem counterintuitive because some researchers would regard any cultural variation as evidence against the causal importance of evolved biology (Eagly & Wood, 1999; Hoffman, 1977; Rose & Rudolph, 2006). However, an increasing trend in evolutionary psychology is to identify ways in which people's common human nature takes different adaptive forms depending on localized contexts (Belsky, Steinberg, & Draper, 1991; Gangestad & Simpson, 2000; Nettle, 2010). Just as the adaptive calluses of people's skin need environmental stimulation to arise, evolutionary psychologists expect that some of humans' adaptive sex differences in sexuality need environmental stimulation to arise (Schmitt, 2011). For example, ecological factors such as pathogen prevalence, sex ratio, and environmental harshness may affect the magnitude of sex differences in mate preferences, mating behaviors, and attachment styles.

Variation in Mate Preferences

Norms and values in the realm of mate preferences have been portrayed as varying across cultures because of the way that people's common human nature adaptively responds to local ecological and reproductive contingencies (Kenrick et al., 2010; Schmitt, 2005; Tybur & Gangestad, 2011). Gangestad et al. (2006) explained the mechanism of cultural variation in mate preferences as a function of if–then commands: If the environmental input is x, then the behavioral response is y; if environments have high pathogen prevalence, then people's mating desires especially emphasize physical attractiveness. To some degree, men already value attractiveness in female partners because many physical attributes of women are indicators of female fertility. For women, the selection of attractive male partners in high pathogen-load environments is heightened because certain physical attributes of men are indicators of men's ability to develop a healthy immune system, a trait that is more vital in high-pathogen ecologies and could be passed on to women's offspring (see also Hamilton & Zuk, 1982; Low, 1990). Gangestad et al. documented that the culture-level emphasis on physical attractiveness and intelligence in mate preferences intensifies across 29 societies (i.e., is a form of evoked culture) when local ecologies are high in pathogens, precisely when both physical attractiveness and intelligence would provide critical adaptive benefits via a prospective mate's genetic quality.

Variation in Mating Behaviors

Schmitt (2005) documented that men are universally more unrestricted in sociosexuality than are women (see also Lippa, 2009) and furthermore that culture-level desires for casual sex tend to intensify across 48 societies when the sex ratio (the number of men relative to women) is especially low, presumably because men are able to impose a more short-term–oriented mating strategy on women in male-scarce reproductive environments (see also Lancaster, 1994; Pedersen, 1991). Again, this reflects how behavioral adaptations respond to environmental inputs: If men are scarce, then sexual behaviors shift toward short-term mating; if women are scarce, then sexual behavior shifts toward long-term mating. These sorts of recurring patterns observed by evolutionary psychologists—functional patterns that strongly deviate from the random ethnographic hyperspace of all possible gendered sexual cultures (Cronk, 1999)—provide clues as to how culturally variable sexualities can adaptively result from the evolved biology of human males and females (Nettle, 2009).

Variation in Attachment Styles

Several combinations of life history and attachment theories have suggested that certain critical experiences during childhood play a role in the development of human mating strategies (Belsky, 1999; Chisholm, 1993). Perhaps most prominent among these theories is the psychosocial acceleration theory (Belsky et al., 1991). According to this model, early social experiences adaptively channel children down one of two reproductive pathways. Children who are socially exposed to high levels of stress—especially insensitive or inconsistent parenting, harsh physical environments, and economic hardship—tend to develop insecure attachment styles. These children also tend to physically mature earlier than those children who are exposed to less stress. According to Belsky et al. (1991), attachment insecurity and early physical maturity subsequently lead to the evolutionarily adaptive development of what is called an *opportunistic reproductive strategy* in adulthood (i.e., short-term mating). In cultures with unpredictable social environments, therefore, children adaptively respond to stressful cues by developing the more viable strategy of short-term mating.

Conversely, those children exposed to lower levels of stress and less environmental hardship tend to be more emotionally secure and to physically mature later (Belsky, 1999). These children are thought to develop a more "investing" reproductive strategy in adulthood (i.e., long-term mating) that pays evolutionary dividends in low-stress environments. Although the causal mechanisms that influence strategic mating are most prominently located within the family, this model also suggests that certain aspects of culture may be related to mating strategy variation (see also Schmitt, 2008).

Schmitt et al. (2003) speculated that because men are already more interested in unrestricted short-term mating than women, the shift in high-stress cultures to a more dismissing attachment style may be more conspicuous among women. Schmitt et al. measured the romantic attachment styles of more than 17,000 people from 56 nations. They related insecure attachment styles to various indexes of familial stress, economic resources, mortality, and fertility and found overwhelming support for psychosocial acceleration theory and the hypothesis that sex differences in dismissive attachment would be smaller in high-stress cultures.

Although both men and women shift toward dismissive attachment in high-stress cultures, the strength of this shift is more profound among women. For example, nations with higher fertility rates, higher mortality rates, higher levels of stress (e.g., poor health and education), and lower levels of resources tended to have higher levels of insecure romantic attachment. Because these associations were greater among women, the size of sex differences in dismissing attachment is facultatively smaller in high-pathogen environments (Schmitt, 2008). Again, the predictable variation in attachment style reflects if–then behavioral responses to environmental input: If the environment is harsh and unstable, then use attachment strategies maximizing opportunistic mating (i.e., dismissive or avoidant attachment styles).

In summary, variability in sex differences across cultures may result from adaptations that respond to environmental input to maximize successful responses to the mating and parenting challenges faced by men and women. This variation does not discredit an evolutionary perspective by failing to yield evidence of pan-cultural universals but instead demonstrates the specificity by which humans respond adaptively to ecological constraints, such as facultative responses to pathogen prevalence, imbalanced sex ratios, and environmental harshness.

CONCLUSION

Historically, culture has been viewed as a prospective explanatory force. Culture exists, and then human psychology results. Of course, not all people within a culture share the same features of human psychology. Variations within cultures along the dimensions of sex, age, and status can easily lead one toward skepticism about the legitimacy of culture as a primary causal force. In addition, all cultures change over time. Without a mechanism for explaining why cultures change, any theory of culture and its influence on human psychology is necessarily incomplete (Cavalli-Sforza & Feldman, 1981; Mace & Holden,

2005; Ross, 2004). Historically, these limitations have led some to consider culture an "essentializing force" and argue that it fails to acknowledge multi-cultures, cocultures, and cultural change. Evolutionary psychologists, behavioral ecologists, and human ethologists have revitalized the study of culture, offering the argument that culture is both a cause and a strongly expected consequence of evolved human nature (Olson, 2011; Way & Lieberman, 2010).

Evolutionary perspectives on culture provide two key improvements over classic cross-cultural psychology and cultural anthropology. First, evolutionary psychology perspectives offer mechanisms for why cultural variations exist. As previously discussed, Gangestad et al. (2006) explained the mechanism of cultural variation in mate preferences as a facultative if–then adaptation within humans' universal psychological repertoire: If environments have high pathogen prevalence, then mating desires adaptively emphasize physical attractiveness. If the local environment has low pathogen prevalence, then adaptive desires deemphasize physical attractiveness in potential mates. Second, evolutionary psychology perspectives offer explanations of cultural change (Mesoudi, Whiten, & Laland, 2006). When levels of pathogen prevalence shift within a culture, the corresponding emphasis on physical attractiveness should shift in that culture as well. Thus, evolutionary perspectives such as that of Gangestad et al. possess the ability to explain pan-cultural universals and facultative variations, something very much missing from standard accounts of culture and sexuality.

Certainly culture is a proximate cause of behavior, yet culture is also an intermediate and bidirectional mechanism between human psychology and behavior. As we portray in Figure 8.1, humans' evolved psychological architecture creates pan-cultural sex differences within the context of gendered sexual cultures, and the conditional or facultative nature of human psychological adaptation gives rise to predictable forms of cultural variability between the sexes. It is not the case that every evolutionary theory of cultural variation will turn out to be correct, nor is it the case that all aspects of culture are subject to evolutionary explanation, at least in terms of genetic evolution (although see G. R. Brown et al., 2011; Laland et al., 2010). Yet only by combining genetic and cultural levels of evolution in sophisticated ways will more complete and scientifically fruitful explanations of human sexual psychology and gendered sexual culture be possible.

REFERENCES

Aboim, S. (2010). Gender cultures and the division of labour in contemporary Europe: A cross-national perspective. *Sociological Review, 58*, 171–196. doi:10.1111/j.1467-954X.2010.01899.x

Alcock, J. (2001). *Animal behavior* (7th ed.). Sunderland, MA: Sinauer Associates.

Alexander, G. M., & Hines, M. (2002). Sex differences in response to children's toys in nonhuman primates (*Ceropithecus aethiops sabaeus*). *Evolution and Human Behavior, 23,* 467–479. doi:10.1016/S1090-5138(02)00107-1

Alexander, G. M., & Saenz, J. (2011). Postnatal testosterone levels and temperament in early infancy. *Archives of Sexual Behavior, 40,* 1287–1292. doi:10.1007/s10508-010-9701-5

Alexander, R. D., & Noonan, K. M. (1979). Concealment of ovulation, parental care, and human social interaction. In N. A. Chagnon & W. Irons (Eds.), *Evolutionary biology and human social behavior: An anthropological perspective* (pp. 436–453). North Scituate, MA: Duxbury.

Archer, J., & Coyne, S. M. (2005). An integrated review of indirect, relational, and social aggression. *Personality and Social Psychology Review, 9,* 212–230. doi:10.1207/s15327957pspr0903_2

Archer, J., & Lloyd, B. B. (2002). *Sex and gender* (2nd ed.). New York, NY: Cambridge University Press. doi:10.1017/CBO9781139051910

Back, M. D., Penke, L., Schmukle, S. C., & Asendorpf, J. B. (2011). Knowing your own mate value: Sex-specific personality effects on the accuracy of expected mate choices. *Psychological Science, 22,* 984–989. doi:10.1177/0956797611414725

Barry, H., III, Bacon, M. K., & Child, I. L. (1957). A cross-cultural survey of some sex differences in socialization. *Journal of Abnormal and Social Psychology, 55,* 327–332. doi:10.1037/h0041178

Bateson, P. (Ed.). (1983). *Mate choice*. Cambridge, England: Cambridge University Press.

Baumeister, R. F., Catanese, K. R., & Vohs, K. D. (2001). Are there gender differences in strength of sex drive? Theoretical views, conceptual distinctions, and a review of relevant evidence. *Personality and Social Psychology Review, 5,* 242–273. doi:10.1207/S15327957PSPR0503_5

Belsky, J. (1999). Modern evolutionary theory and patterns of attachment. In J. Cassidy & P. R. Shaver (Eds.), *Handbook of attachment* (pp. 141–161). New York, NY: Guilford Press.

Belsky, J., Steinberg, L., & Draper, P. (1991). Childhood experience, interpersonal development, and reproductive strategy: An evolutionary theory of socialization. *Child Development, 62,* 647–670. doi:10.2307/1131166

Blurton Jones, N. (1986). Bushman birth spacing: A test for optimal interbirth intervals. *Ethology and Sociobiology, 7,* 91–105. doi:10.1016/0162-3095(86)90002-6

Boyd, R., & Richerson, P. J. (1985). *Culture and the evolutionary process*. Chicago, IL: University of Chicago Press.

Broude, G. J., & Greene, S. J. (1976). Cross-cultural codes on twenty sexual attitudes and practices. *Ethnology, 15,* 409–429. doi:10.2307/3773308

Brown, D. E. (1991). *Human universals*. New York, NY: McGraw-Hill.

Brown, G. R., Dickens, T. E., Sear, R., & Laland, K. N. (2011). Evolutionary accounts of human behavioural diversity. *Philosophical Transactions of the Royal Society B: Biological Sciences, 366,* 313–324. doi:10.1098/rstb.2010.0267

Brown, G. R., Laland, K. N., & Borgerhoff Mulder, M. (2009). Bateman's principles and human sex roles. *Trends in Ecology & Evolution, 24,* 297–304. doi:10.1016/j.tree.2009.02.005

Buss, D. M. (1989). Sex differences in human mate preferences: Evolutionary hypotheses tested in 37 cultures. *Behavioral and Brain Sciences, 12,* 1–49. doi:10.1017/S0140525X00023992

Buss, D. M. (2001). Human nature and culture: An evolutionary psychological perspective. *Journal of Personality, 69,* 955–978. doi:10.1111/1467-6494.696171

Buss, D. M., & Barnes, M. (1986). Preferences in human mate selection. *Journal of Personality and Social Psychology, 50,* 559–570. doi:10.1037/0022-3514.50.3.559

Buss, D. M., Larsen, R. J., Westen, D., & Semmelroth, J. (1992). Sex differences in jealousy: Evolution, physiology, and psychology. *Psychological Science, 3,* 251–255. doi:10.1111/j.1467-9280.1992.tb00038.x

Buss, D. M., & Schmitt, D. P. (1993). Sexual strategies theory: An evolutionary perspective on human mating. *Psychological Review, 100,* 204–232. doi:10.1037/0033-295X.100.2.204

Buss, D. M., & Schmitt, D. P. (2011). Evolutionary psychology and feminism. *Sex Roles, 64,* 768–787. doi:10.1007/s11199-011-9987-3

Buss, D. M., & Shackelford, T. K. (2008). Attractive women want it all: Good genes, economic investment, parenting proclivities, and emotional commitment. *Evolutionary Psychology, 6,* 134–146.

Buunk, B. P., Angleitner, A., Oubaid, V., & Buss, D. M. (1996). Sex differences in jealousy in evolutionary and cultural perspective: Tests from the Netherlands, Germany, and the United States. *Psychological Science, 7,* 359–363. doi:10.1111/j.1467-9280.1996.tb00389.x

Cashdan, E. (2008). Waist-to-hip ratio across cultures: Trade-offs between androgen- and estrogen-dependent traits. *Current Anthropology, 49,* 1099–1107. doi:10.1086/593036

Cavalli-Sforza, L. L., & Feldman, M. W. (1981). *Cultural transmission and evolution: A quantitative approach.* Princeton, NJ: Princeton University Press.

Chisholm, J. S. (1993). Death, hope, and sex: Life-history theory and the development of reproductive strategies. *Current Anthropology, 34,* 1–24. doi:10.1086/204131

Clutton-Brock, T. H. (1991). *The evolution of parental care.* Princeton, NJ: Princeton University Press.

Clutton-Brock, T. H., & Parker, G. A. (1992). Potential reproductive rates and the operation of sexual selection. *Quarterly Review of Biology, 67,* 437–456. doi:10.1086/417793

Costa, P. T., Terracciano, A., & McCrae, R. R. (2001). Gender differences in personality traits across cultures: Robust and surprising findings. *Journal of Personality and Social Psychology, 81*, 322–331. doi:10.1037/0022-3514.81.2.322

Cronk, L. (1999). *That complex whole: Culture and the evolution of human behavior.* Boulder, CO: Westview Press.

Cross, S. E., & Madson, L. (1997). Models of the self: Self-construals and gender. *Psychological Bulletin, 122*, 5–37. doi:10.1037/0033-2909.122.1.5

Cunningham, S. J., & Russell, P. A. (2004). The influence of gender roles on evolved partner preferences. *Sexualities, Evolution & Gender, 6*, 131–150. doi:10.1080/14616660412331332909

Daly, M., & Wilson, M. (1988). *Homicide.* New York, NY: Aldine de Gruyter.

Davies, A. P. C., & Shackelford, T. K. (2008). Two human natures: How men and women evolved different psychologies. In C. Crawford & D. Krebs (Eds.), *Foundations of evolutionary psychology* (pp. 261–280). New York, NY: Taylor & Francis Group.

Del Giudice, M. (2009a). Author's response: Human reproductive strategies: An emerging synthesis? *Behavioral and Brain Sciences, 32*, 45–67. doi:10.1017/S0140525X09000272

Del Giudice, M. (2009b). Sex, attachment, and the development of reproductive strategies. *Behavioral and Brain Sciences, 32*, 1–21. doi:10.1017/S0140525X09000016

Del Giudice, M. (2011). Sex differences in romantic attachment: A meta-analysis. *Personality and Social Psychology Bulletin, 37*, 193–214. doi:10.1177/0146167210392789

DeSteno, D., Bartlett, M. Y., Braverman, J., & Salovey, P. (2002). Sex differences in jealousy: Evolutionary mechanism or artifact of measurement? *Journal of Personality and Social Psychology, 83*, 1103–1116. doi:10.1037/0022-3514.83.5.1103

Durkheim, E. (1962). *The rules of sociological method.* New York, NY: Free Press. (Original work published 1895)

Eagly, A. H. (1987). *Sex differences in social behavior: A social-role interpretation.* Hillsdale, NJ: Erlbaum.

Eagly, A. H., & Steffen, V. J. (1986). Gender and aggressive behavior: A meta-analytic review of the social psychological literature. *Psychological Bulletin, 100*, 309–330. doi:10.1037/0033-2909.100.3.309

Eagly, A. H., & Wood, W. (1999). The origins of sex differences in human behavior. *American Psychologist, 54*, 408–423. doi:10.1037/0003-066X.54.6.408

Eastwick, P. W., Eagly, A. H., Glick, P., Johannesen-Schmidt, M. C., Fiske, S. T., Blum, A. M. B., . . . Volpato, C. (2006). Is traditional gender ideology associated with sex-typed mate preferences? A test in nine nations. *Sex Roles, 54*, 603–614. doi:10.1007/s11199-006-9027-x

Ellis, L. (2011). Identifying and explaining apparent universal sex differences in cognition and behavior. *Personality and Individual Differences, 51*, 552–561. doi:10.1016/j.paid.2011.04.004

Feingold, A. (1992). Gender differences in mate selection preferences: A test of the parental investment model. *Psychological Bulletin, 112,* 125–139. doi:10.1037/0033-2909.112.1.125

Frayser, S. (1985). *Varieties of sexual experience: An anthropological perspective.* New Haven, CT: HRAF Press.

Frederick, D. A., & Haselton, M. G. (2007). Why is muscularity sexy? Tests of the fitness indicator hypothesis. *Personality and Social Psychology Bulletin, 33,* 1167–1183. doi:10.1177/0146167207303022

Gabriel, S., & Gardner, W. L. (1999). Are there "his" and "hers" types of interdependence? The implications of gender differences in collective versus relational interdependence for affect, behavior, and cognition. *Journal of Personality and Social Psychology, 77,* 642–655. doi:10.1037/0022-3514.77.3.642

Gaeddert, W. P. (1985). Sex and sex role effects on achievement strivings: Dimensions of similarity and difference. *Journal of Personality, 53,* 286–305. doi:10.1111/j.1467-6494.1985.tb00367.x

Gangestad, S. W. (2011). Human adaptations for mating: Frameworks for understanding modern family formation and fertility? In A. Booth, S. M. McHale, & N. S. Landale (Eds.), *Biosocial foundations of family processes* (pp. 117–148). New York, NY: Springer Science + Business Media.

Gangestad, S. W., & Buss, D. M. (1993). Pathogen prevalence and human mate preferences. *Ethology & Sociobiology, 14,* 89–96.

Gangestad, S. W., Haselton, M. G., & Buss, D. M. (2006). Evolutionary foundations of cultural variation: Evoked culture and mate preferences. *Psychological Inquiry, 17,* 75–95. doi:10.1207/s15327965pli1702_1

Gangestad, S. W., & Simpson, J. A. (2000). The evolution of human mating: Trade-offs and strategic pluralism. *Behavioral and Brain Sciences, 23,* 573–587. doi:10.1017/S0140525X0000337X

Gaulin, S. J. C. (1997). Cross-cultural patterns and the search for evolved psychological mechanisms. In G. R. Bock & G. Cardew (Eds.), *Characterizing human psychological adaptations* (pp. 195–207). Chichester, England: Wiley.

Geary, D. C. (2010). *Male, female: The evolution of human sex differences* (2nd ed.). Washington, DC: American Psychological Association. doi:10.1037/12072-000

Geertz, C. (1973). *The interpretation of cultures.* New York, NY: Basic Books.

Guimond, S., Chatard, A., Marinot, D., Crisp, R. J., & Redersdorff, S. (2006). Social comparison, self-stereotyping, and gender differences in self-construals. *Journal of Personality and Social Psychology, 90,* 221–242. doi:10.1037/0022-3514.90.2.221

Gwynne, D. T. (1984). Sexual selection and sexual differences in Mormon crickets. *Evolution, 38,* 1011–1022. doi:10.2307/2408435

Hamilton, W. D., & Zuk, M. (1982). Heritable true fitness and bright birds: A role for parasites? *Science, 218,* 384–387. doi:10.1126/science.7123238

Harris, C. R. (2003). A review of sex differences in sexual jealousy, including self-report data, psychophysiological responses, interpersonal violence, and morbid jealousy. *Personality and Social Psychology Review, 7,* 102–128. doi:10.1207/S15327957PSPR0702_102-128

Harvey, P. H., & Reynolds, J. D. (1994). Sexual selection and the evolution of sex differences. In R. V. Short & E. Balaban (Eds.), *The difference between the sexes* (pp. 51–66). Cambridge, England: Cambridge University Press.

Hassett, J. M., Siebert, E. R., & Wallen, K. (2008). Sex differences in rhesus monkey toy preferences parallel those of children. *Hormones and Behavior, 54,* 359–364. doi:10.1016/j.yhbeh.2008.03.008

Henrich, J., Heine, S. J., & Norenzayan, A. (2010). The weirdest people in the world? *Behavioral and Brain Sciences, 33,* 61–83. doi:10.1017/S0140525X0999152X

Hoffman, L. W. (1977). Changes in family roles, socialization, and sex differences. *American Psychologist, 32,* 644–657. doi:10.1037/0003-066X.32.8.644

Hundhammer, T., & Mussweiler, T. (2012). How sex puts you in gendered shoes: Sexuality-priming leads to gender-based self-perception and behavior. *Journal of Personality and Social Psychology, 103,* 176–193. doi:10.1037/a0028121

Hupka, R. B., & Bank, A. L. (1996). Sex differences in jealousy: Evolution or social construction? *Cross-Cultural Research: The Journal of Comparative Social Science, 30,* 24–59. doi:10.1177/106939719603000102

Hyde, J. S. (1986). Gender differences in aggression. In J. S. Hyde & M. C. Linn (Eds.), *The psychology of gender: Advances through meta-analysis* (pp. 51–66). Baltimore, MD: Johns Hopkins University Press.

Imada, T., & Yussen, S. R. (2012). Reproduction of cultural values. *Personality and Social Psychology Bulletin, 38,* 114–128. doi:10.1177/0146167211421938

Jackson, J. J., & Kirkpatrick, L. A. (2007). The structure and measurement of human mating strategies: Toward a multidimensional model of sociosexuality. *Evolution and Human Behavior, 28,* 382–391. doi:10.1016/j.evolhumbehav.2007.04.005

Kaplan, H., & Lancaster, J. B. (2003). An evolutionary and ecological analysis of human fertility, mating patterns, and parental investment. In K. W. Wachter & R. A. Bulatao (Eds.), *Offspring: Human fertility behavior in biodemographic perspective* (pp. 170–223). Washington, DC: National Academy Press.

Kavanagh, P. S., Robins, S., & Ellis, B. J. (2010). The mating sociometer: A regulatory mechanism for mating aspirations. *Journal of Personality and Social Psychology, 99,* 120–132. doi:10.1037/a0018188

Keller, H. (1990). Evolutionary approaches. In J. W. Berry, Y. H. Poortinga, & J. Pandey (Eds.), *Handbook of cross-cultural psychology* (2nd ed., Vol. 1, pp. 215–255). Boston, MA: Allyn & Bacon.

Kelly, R. L. (1995). *The foraging spectrum: Diversity in hunter-gatherer lifeways.* Washington, DC: Smithsonian Institution Press.

Kenrick, D. T. (1987). Gender, genes, and the social environment: A biosocial interactionist perspective. In P. Shaver & C. Hendrick (Eds.), *Review of personality and social psychology* (Vol. 7, pp. 14–43). Newbury Park, CA: Sage.

Kenrick, D. T., Nieuweboer, S., & Buunk, A. P. (2010). Universal mechanisms and cultural diversity: Replacing the blank slate with a coloring book. In M. Schaller, A. Norenzayan, S. J. Heine, T. Yamagishi, & T. Kameda (Eds.), *Evolution, culture, and the human mind* (pp. 257–272). New York, NY: Psychology Press.

Khaleque, A., & Rohner, R. P. (2012). Transnational relations between perceived parental acceptance and personality dispositions of children and adults: A meta-analytic review. *Personality and Social Psychology Review, 16,* 103–115. doi:10.1177/1088868311418986

Kirkpatrick, L. A. (1998). Evolution, pair-bonding, and reproductive strategies: A reconceptualization of adult attachment. In J. A. Simpson & W. S. Rholes (Eds.), *Attachment theory and close relationships* (pp. 353–393). New York, NY: Guilford Press.

Laland, K. N., Odling-Smee, F. J., & Myles, S. (2010). How nature has shaped the human genome: Bringing genetics and the human sciences together. *Nature Reviews Genetics, 11,* 137–148. doi:10.1038/nrg2734

Lancaster, J. B. (1994). Human sexuality, life histories, and evolutionary ecology. In A. S. Rossi (Ed.), *Sexuality across the life course* (pp. 39–62). Chicago, IL: University of Chicago Press.

Li, N. P., Bailey, J. M., Kenrick, D. T., & Linsenmeier, J. A. W. (2002). The necessities and luxuries of mate preferences: Testing the tradeoffs. *Journal of Personality and Social Psychology, 82,* 947–955. doi:10.1037/0022-3514.82.6.947

Lippa, R. A. (2009). Sex differences in sex drive, sociosexuality, and height across 53 nations: Testing evolutionary and social structural theories. *Archives of Sexual Behavior, 38,* 631–651. doi:10.1007/s10508-007-9242-8

Little, A. C., Jones, B. C., DeBruine, L. M., & Caldwell, C. A. (2011). Social learning and human mate preferences: A potential mechanism for generating and maintaining between-population diversity in attraction. *Philosophical Transactions of the Royal Society B: Biological Sciences, 366,* 366–375. doi:10.1098/rstb.2010.0192

Low, B. S. (1989). Cross-cultural patterns in the training of children: An evolutionary perspective. *Journal of Comparative Psychology, 103,* 311–319. doi:10.1037/0735-7036.103.4.311

Low, B. S. (1990). Marriage systems and pathogen stress in human societies. *American Zoologist, 30,* 325–340.

Low, B. S. (2000). *Why sex matters.* Princeton, NJ: Princeton University Press.

Lytton, H., & Romney, D. M. (1991). Parents' differential socialization of boys and girls: A meta-analysis. *Psychological Bulletin, 109,* 267–296. doi:10.1037/0033-2909.109.2.267

Maccoby, E. E. (1998). *The two sexes: Growing up apart, coming together.* Cambridge, MA: Harvard University Press.

Mace, R., & Holden, C. J. (2005). A phylogenetic approach to cultural evolution. *Trends in Ecology & Evolution, 20,* 116–121. doi:10.1016/j.tree.2004.12.002

Marlowe, F. M. (2003). The mating system of foragers in the standard cross-cultural sample. *Cross-Cultural Research: The Journal of Comparative Social Science, 37,* 282–306. doi:10.1177/1069397103254008

McCarthy, M. M., & Arnold, A. P. (2011). Reframing sexual differentiation of the brain. *Nature Neuroscience, 14,* 677–683. doi:10.1038/nn.2834

Mealey, L. (2000). *Sex differences: Developmental and evolutionary strategies.* San Diego, CA: Academic Press.

Mesoudi, A. (2009). How cultural evolutionary theory can inform social psychology and vice versa. *Psychological Review, 116,* 929–952. doi:10.1037/a0017062

Mesoudi, A., Whiten, A., & Laland, K. N. (2006). Towards a unified science of cultural evolution. *Behavioral and Brain Sciences, 29,* 329–347. doi:10.1017/S0140525X06009083

Nettle, D. (2007). Empathizing and systemizing: What are they, and what do they contribute to our understanding of psychological sex differences? *British Journal of Psychology, 98,* 237–255. doi:10.1348/000712606X117612

Nettle, D. (2009). Ecological influences on human behavioural diversity: A review of recent findings. *Trends in Ecology & Evolution, 24,* 618–624. doi:10.1016/j.tree.2009.05.013

Nettle, D. (2010). Dying young and living fast: Variation in life history across English neighborhoods. *Behavioral Ecology, 21,* 387–395. doi:10.1093/beheco/arp202

Nettle, D. (2011). Flexibility in reproductive timing in human females: Integrating ultimate and proximate explanations. *Philosophical Transactions of the Royal Society B: Biological Sciences, 366,* 357–365. doi:10.1098/rstb.2010.0073

Ngun, T. C., Ghahramani, N., Sánchez, F. J., Bocklandt, S., & Vilain, E. (2011). The genetics of sex differences in brain and behavior. *Frontiers in Neuroendocrinology, 32,* 227–246.

Oliver, M. B., & Hyde, J. S. (1993). Gender differences in sexuality: A meta-analysis. *Psychological Bulletin, 114,* 29–51. doi: 0033-2909/93/S3.00

Olson, L. R. (2011). The essentiality of "culture" in the study of religion and politics. *Journal for the Scientific Study of Religion, 50,* 639–653. doi:10.1111/j.1468-5906.2011.01608.x

Pasternak, B., Ember, C., & Ember, M. (1997). *Sex, gender, and kinship: A cross-cultural perspective.* Upper Saddle, NJ: Prentice Hall.

Pedersen, F. A. (1991). Secular trends in human sex ratios: Their influence on individual and family behavior. *Human Nature, 2,* 271–291. doi:10.1007/BF02692189

Penke, L., Todd, P. M., Lenton, A. P., & Fasolo, B. (2007). How self-assessments can guide human mating decisions. In G. Geher & G. F. Miller (Eds.), *Mating intelligence: Sex, relationships, and the mind's reproductive system* (pp. 37–75). Mahwah, NJ: Erlbaum.

Pinker, S. (1994). *The language instinct: How the mind creates language.* New York, NY: HarperCollins.

Plotkin, H. (2004). *Evolutionary thought in psychology: A brief history*. London, England: Blackwell. doi:10.1002/9780470773840

Pratto, F., Sidanius, J., & Levin, S. (2006). Social dominance theory and the dynamics of intergroup relations: Taking stock and looking forward. *European Review of Social Psychology, 17*, 271–320. doi:10.1080/10463280601055772

Quinn, N. (1977). Anthropological studies on women's status. *Annual Review of Anthropology, 6*, 181–225. doi:10.1146/annurev.an.06.100177.001145

Ridley, M. (2003). *Nature via nurture*. New York, NY: HarperCollins.

Roese, N. J., Pennington, G. L., Coleman, J., Janicki, M., Li, N. P., & Kenrick, D. T. (2006). Sex differences in regret: All for love or some for lust? *Personality and Social Psychology Bulletin, 32*, 770–780. doi:10.1177/0146167206286709

Rogers, A. R. (1988). Does biology constrain culture? *American Anthropologist, 90*, 819–831. doi:10.1525/aa.1988.90.4.02a00030

Rose, A. J., & Rudolph, K. D. (2006). A review of sex differences in peer relationship processes: Potential of trade-offs for the emotional and behavioral development of girls and boys. *Psychological Bulletin, 132*, 98–131. doi:10.1037/0033-2909.132.1.98

Ross, N. (2004). *Culture and cognition: Implications for theory and method*. Thousand Oaks, CA: Sage.

Schaller, M., & Murray, D. R. (2008). Pathogens, personality and culture: Disease prevalence predicts worldwide variability in sociosexuality, extraversion, and openness to experience. *Journal of Personality and Social Psychology, 95*, 212–221.

Schmitt, D. P. (2005). Sociosexuality from Argentina to Zimbabwe: A 48-nation study of sex, culture, and strategies of human mating. *Behavioral and Brain Sciences, 28*, 247–275. doi:10.1017/S0140525X05000051

Schmitt, D. P. (2008). Evolutionary perspectives on romantic attachment and culture: How ecological stressors influence dismissing orientations across genders and geographies. *Cross-Cultural Research: The Journal of Comparative Social Science, 42*, 220–247. doi:10.1177/1069397108317485

Schmitt, D. P. (2011). Psychological adaptation and human fertility patterns: Some evidence of human mating strategies as evoked sexual culture. In A. Booth, S. M. McHale, & N. S Landale (Eds.), *Biosocial foundations of family processes* (pp. 161–170). Mahwah, NJ: Erlbaum. doi:10.1007/978-1-4419-7361-0_11

Schmitt, D. P., Alcalay, L., Allensworth, M., Allik, J., Ault, L., Austers, I., . . . Scrimali, T. (2003). Are men universally more dismissing than women? Gender differences in romantic attachment across 62 cultural regions. *Personal Relationships, 10*, 307–331. doi:10.1111/1475-6811.00052

Schmitt, D. P., & Buss, D. M. (1996). Strategic self-promotion and competitor derogation: Sex and context effects on the perceived effectiveness of mate attraction tactics. *Journal of Personality and Social Psychology, 20*, 1185–1204. doi: 0022-3514/96/S3.00

Schmitt, D. P., Jonason, P. K., Byerley, G. J., Flores, S. D., Illbeck, B. E., O'Leary, K. N., & Qudrat, A. (2012). A reexamination of sex differences in sexuality: New studies reveal old truths. *Current Directions in Psychological Science, 21*, 135–139. doi:10.1177/0963721412436808

Schmitt, D. P., Realo, A., Voracek, M., & Allik, J. (2008). Why can't a man be more like a woman? Sex differences in Big Five personality traits across 55 cultures. *Journal of Personality and Social Psychology, 94*, 168–182. doi:10.1037/0022-3514.94.1.168

Silverman, I., Choi, J., & Peters, M. (2007). On the universality of sex-related spatial competencies. *Archives of Human Sexuality, 36*, 261–268. doi:10.1007/s10508-006-9168-6

Smith, E. A. (2011). Endless forms: Human behavioural diversity and evolved universals. *Philosophical Transactions of the Royal Society B: Biological Sciences, 366*, 325–332. doi:10.1098/rstb.2010.0233

Smuts, B. (1995). The evolutionary origins of patriarchy. *Human Nature, 6*, 1–32. doi:10.1007/BF02734133

Sprecher, S., Sullivan, Q., & Hatfield, E. (1994). Mate selection preferences: Gender differences examined in a national sample. *Journal of Personality and Social Psychology, 66*, 1074–1080. doi:10.1037/0022-3514.66.6.1074

Surbey, M. K., & Brice, G. R. (2007). Enhancement of self-perceived mate value precedes a shift in men's preferred mating strategy. *Acta Psychologica Sinica, 39*, 513–522.

Tinbergen, N. (1963). On aims and methods of ethology. *Zeitschrift für Tierpsychologie, 20*, 410–433. doi:10.1111/j.1439-0310.1963.tb01161.x

Tooby, J., & Cosmides, L. (1992). Psychological foundations of culture. In J. Barkow, L. Cosmides, & J. Tooby (Eds.), *The adapted mind* (pp. 19–136). New York, NY: Oxford University Press.

Tooby, J., & Cosmides, L. (2005). Conceptual foundations of evolutionary psychology. In D. M. Buss (Ed.), *The handbook of evolutionary psychology* (pp. 5–67). Hoboken, NJ: Wiley.

Triandis, H. C. (1994). *Culture and social behavior.* New York, NY: McGraw-Hill.

Trivers, R. (1972). Parental investment and sexual selection. In B. Campbell (Ed.), *Sexual selection and the descent of man: 1871-1971* (pp. 136–179). Chicago, IL: Aldine.

Tybur, J. M., & Gangestad, S. W. (2011). Mate preferences and infectious disease: Theoretical considerations and evidence in humans. *Philosophical Transactions of the Royal Society B: Biological Sciences, 366*, 3375–3388.

Vandermassen, G. (2005). *Who's afraid of Charles Darwin? Debating feminism and evolutionary theory.* Lanham, MD: Rowman & Littlefield.

Way, B. M., & Lieberman, M. D. (2010). Is there a genetic contribution to cultural differences? Collectivism, individualism, and genetic markers of social sensitivity. *Social Cognitive and Affective Neuroscience, 5*, 203–211. doi:10.1093/scan/nsq059

Whiting, B. B., & Edwards, C. P. (1988). *Children of different worlds*. Cambridge, MA: Harvard University Press.

Whiting, J. W. M., & Whiting, B. B. (1975). Aloofness and intimacy of husbands and wives: A cross-cultural study. *Ethos, 3,* 183–207. doi:10.1525/eth.1975.3.2.02a00080

Williams, J. E., & Best, D. L. (1990). *Sex and psyche: Gender and self viewed cross-culturally*. Newbury Park, CA: Sage.

Wood, W., & Eagly, A. H. (2002). A cross-cultural analysis of the behavior of men and women: Implications for the origins of sex differences. *Psychological Bulletin, 128,* 699–727. doi:10.1037/0033-2909.128.5.699

Wood, W., & Eagly, A. H. (2010). Gender. In S. Fiske, D. Gilbert, & G. Lindzey (Eds.), *Handbook of social psychology* (5th ed., Vol. 1, pp. 629–667). New York, NY: Wiley.

Wood, W., & Eagly, A. H. (2012). *Biosocial construction of sex differences and similarities in behavior*. In M. P. Zanna & J. M. Olson (Eds.), *Advances in experimental social psychology* (pp. 55–123). San Diego, CA: Academic Press. doi:10.1016/B978-0-12-394281-4.00002-7

9

RELIGIONS AS CULTURAL SOLUTIONS TO SOCIAL LIVING

AZIM F. SHARIFF, BENJAMIN GRANT PURZYCKI, AND RICHARD SOSIS

Scholars of religion have long assumed that religions offer benefits and fulfill the needs of individuals and that these benefits can explain why religions exist. Religion's ascribed functions include pacifying existential angst (e.g., Darwin, 2004; Durkheim, 1915/2001; Geertz, 1973), creating meaning in a natural world inherently devoid of meaning (Bering, 2011; Inzlicht, Tullet, & Good, 2011; Rappaport 1979), and coping with death anxiety (e.g., Becker, 1973; Spiro, 1987). Religions are, however, more than answers and cures for the psychological concerns of individuals. Religions also solve social and ecological problems faced by groups of people, and it is likely that religions have responsively adapted to serve these roles from their beginnings. In this chapter, we explore evolutionary analyses of religion that aim to explain how

We thank the following institutions for generous support: the Social Sciences and Humanities Research Council of Canada–funded Cultural Evolution of Religion Research Consortium at the University of British Columbia; Oxford University's Cognition, Religion and Theology Project; the University of Connecticut's Anthropology Department; the Economic and Social Research Council (REF RES-060-25-0085); and the Center of Theological Inquiry at Princeton University.

http://dx.doi.org/10.1037/14274-008
Culture Reexamined: Broadening Our Understanding of Social and Evolutionary Influences,
A. B. Cohen (Editor)

religions solve many of the social and ecological challenges faced by communities of individuals trying to live together.

First, we discuss the major distinctions between cultural functionalist theory and evolutionary functionalism. Evolution-minded social scientists are often faced with charges of endorsing functionalism, which continues to be a "dirty word in the social sciences" (Sharrock, Hughes, & Martin, 2003, p. 15). Here, we focus on a number of commonly expressed problems associated with cultural functionalism and on how in both theory and practice, evolutionary functionalism overcomes such limitations. We then review some of the evidence that demonstrates the conditions under which religions provide solutions to social and ecological problems faced by particular communities. Finally, we discuss avenues for further research and stress the importance of maintaining the theoretical and methodological pluralism that currently flourishes within the evolutionary study of religion.

CULTURAL FUNCTIONALISM VERSUS EVOLUTIONARY FUNCTIONALISM

In anthropology, functionalism has come in many forms over the years, ranging from the more sociologically oriented structural–functionalist schools of Lévi-Strauss (1983) and Durkheim (2001) to the cultural materialist and ecological schools of Harris (1966) and Rappaport (1979, 2000). Malinowski (1964), the titular founder of functionalism, defined *function* as the "satisfaction of a need" (p. 159). He offered five components that make up his vision of culture, three of which are key to understanding his thought:

- Culture is essentially an instrumental apparatus by which man is put in a position the better to cope with the concrete specific problems that face him in his environment in the course of the satisfaction he needs.
- It is a system of objects, activities, and attitudes in which every part exists as a means to an end.
- Such activities, attitudes, and objects are organized around important and vital tasks into institutions such as the family, the clan, the local community, the tribe, and the organized teams of economic cooperation, political, legal, and educational activity. (Malinowski, 1964, p. 150)

Malinowski considered the essential core of cultural domains to be functional; they contain within them the means by which to overcome environmental problems to satisfy needs and "every part exists as a means to an end" (p. 150). Therefore, any successful functional analysis of a cultural system, such as religion, entails understanding the constituent parts' relationships and what their particular end is, even if that end is merely to fulfill the other components' functions. However, a number of problems have been identified with such functionalist accounts of human social systems.

For example, many have taken issue with some cultural functionalists' heavy reliance on interpretation and their lack of a systematic method for data collection (e.g., Sperber, 1996). Harris's (1966) classic explanation of the sacralization of cattle in India, for example, is a regular target for such critiques. Harris argued that Indians taboo the killing of cattle because the utility of keeping them alive for things such as fuel and milk outweighs the benefits reaped by eating them. Bloch (1983) critically pointed out the ad hoc nature of the explanation: "Harris notes that cows are holy in India and then looks around for anything that will show the belief to be reasonable in terms of the economy" (p. 133). Indeed, strong correlative interpretivism and weak methodology characterize much functionalist and other anthropological research throughout the middle of the 20th century. Evolutionary functionalists, however, have made use of a vast array of research methods to avoid the trappings and limitations of interpretive ethnographic inquiry, as is evinced by the studies we review next (which are themselves just a small sampling).

The apparent lack of agency in functionalist accounts has been another target for criticism (for further discussion, see Elster, 1979). In other words, functionalist accounts often lack consideration or minimize the significance of individual motivations and decision making in the formation of institutions and social systems. As a response to this, rational choice theorists have emphasized individuals' beliefs and desires in the process of decision making. However, the classic (but often confused) distinction between *teleology*—an intentional function—and *teleonomy*—functional by design of evolutionary processes—has to be taken into consideration here (Pittendrigh, 1958). Individuals' intentions and decisions may indeed have something to do with their well-being (see Spiro, 1987), and their internal states can, at times, accurately represent the fitness value of a particular strategy. That is, proximate intentions can align with ultimate explanations. Alternatively, however, the proximate, consciously obvious goal can be quite removed from the ultimate, teleonomic purpose for a given behavior, ritual, or teaching. That is to say that group members engaging in a particular ritual might understand the teleonomic group benefit offered by the ritual, or they may conceive of it as beneficial for a radically different reason. People's conscious intentions can consist of a wide range of things, but what matters for evolutionary functionalism is how the behavior affects fitness (see Hames, 1991, 2007; Smith & Wishnie, 2000, for excellent discussions of this distinction with respect to the evolution of conservation practices).

Another common problem identified with functionalism stems from an alleged essentialization of culture. For instance, Collier et al. (1997) noted that

> the flaw in Malinowski's argument is the flaw common to all functionalist arguments: Because a social institution is observed to perform a necessary function does not mean either that the function would not be performed if the institution did not exist or that the function is responsible for the existence of the institution. (p. 73)

In other words, Collier et al. took issue with the idea that an institution is inextricably linked with its function or that a function plays some causal role in the formation of an institution. Moreover, they suggested that functionalist analyses essentialize the social context with the institution. Of course, an institution can exist longer than its constituent participants and its function can change, and humans are particularly adept at finding ways to solve problems by formalizing behaviors that work around them. Analytically, however, all one needs to see are an institution's effects to claim it has a function, regardless of whether it is true. This problem with functionalist institutional analysis is that institutions are thought of as essential to a society. Evolutionary analyses (*pace* Gould, 2002) tend to essentialize functions for traits because traits often serve different purposes in different contexts. Likewise, anyone with a modicum of understanding of the ethnographic record cannot deny the diversity in content of religion, and careful arguments must address the possibility that different religions overcome or address problems posed by local environments.

In fact, in some situations, ignorance of the individual over the ultimate teleonomic purpose of a behavior is critical to convincing the individual to partake. Although individuals may be content to engage in an activity because they are aligned with its proximate purpose (say, pleasing the gods), the hidden ultimate purpose may be something that runs counter to their interests. For example, compelling people to avoid cheating, resource hogging, or promiscuity may, as we describe, be instrumental to group success but can often come at a cost to a rationally acting individual. The powerful proximate reasons that religions provide to compel individuals to engage in ultimately self-sacrificing (but group-beneficial) behaviors is, from the perspective of evolutionary functionalism, one of the great strengths of religious systems.

A third criticism of many functionalist accounts is the apparent lack of a feedback mechanism to sustain the movement of elements within the system. In other words, to be convincing and complete, functionalist accounts require a force external to the system to reconstitute, maintain, and reproduce elements within the system (Elster, 1979, 1982; Sperber, 1996). The combination of natural selection and genetic transmission is one obvious feedback mechanism, but as Stinchcombe (1968) pointed out, other forms of selection and transmission—for example, cultural evolution—can serve as feedback mechanisms as well. What functionalist accounts often lack is attention to the ecological pressures that led to the emergence of an institution and the fitness effects that could explain its persistence.

Again, methodologically, cultural functionalism has largely been interpretative; one studies an institution and discovers the problem it solves, and this analysis is carried through to other domains of a population's experience. However, researchers must empirically demonstrate that the institution or trait under examination produces benefits that are not available to those who lack the institution or trait. The problem for those who study religion, however, is finding a sufficient control sample (cf. Sosis & Bressler, 2003) and, as such, researchers are often limited to evidence that allows them to abductively conclude that particular traditions benefit individuals and communities in particular contexts.

HOW EVOLUTIONARY FUNCTIONALISM CAN EXPLAIN RELIGION

Currently, a complete evolutionary functionalist analysis of any religious system is lacking; however, plenty of evidence has nonetheless suggested that religion is adaptive in specific ecological contexts. Although this evidence relies primarily on cultural evolutionary processes by which cultural information—in the form of beliefs, rituals, and teaching—are selected and transmitted, the approach mimics that which naturalists use to understand why organisms have the particular features they do.

Here, we review the arguments and evidence for six of the most prominent hypotheses regarding religion's cultural adaptations for enabling, sustaining, and facilitating social interaction in human groups. We also note open questions that remain and avenues of future research that may address them.

Hypothesis 1: Monitoring and Punishing Selfish Behavior

Although many nonstate traditions have traces of moralistic deities (Boehm, 2008), anthropologists have understood for at least half a century that these types of morally involved "big" gods are found predominantly in state-level social organizations (Swanson, 1960; Wallace, 1966). In the absence of effective top-down secular institutions, such as policing and court systems, to regulate ethical behavior, groups of this size face considerable challenges in preventing the destabilizing forces of free riding and defection. Genetically evolved mechanisms, such as kin-based altruism and reciprocity with nonkin, are only able, on their own, to sustain very small groups—much smaller even than the towns that sprang up 9,000 to 11,000 years ago in the Levant (Dunbar, 2003; Henrich, 2004). At this size, anonymous encounters become increasingly frequent and, with them, so too do the opportunities to engage in selfish, other-damaging, unethical behavior without sacrificing one's reputation.

A number of researchers have argued that commitment to omniscient and morally judging supernatural agents facilitated cooperation by discouraging believers from cheating in these otherwise anonymous situations (Lahti, 2009; Rappaport, 1979; Sanderson, 2008; Schloss & Murray, 2011; Shariff & Norenzayan, 2007; Stark, 2001). Furthermore, knowing that a potential interaction partner fears supernatural reprisal for violating social norms builds faith in the moral constraints on this partner's behavior and thus heightens trust among people. These hypotheses have received ample empirical support from several different fields. First, psychological studies have shown that people primed to think about God and other supernatural agents are more cooperative, more honest, and more generous to strangers in anonymous situations (Ahmed & Salas, 2011; Piazza, Bering, & Ingram, 2011; Randolph-Seng & Nielsen, 2007; Shariff & Norenzayan, 2007). Second, cross-cultural research has shown that these types of effects are significantly more likely to occur when individuals believe in powerful, omniscient, and moralizing big gods than in localized gods (Henrich et al., 2010; Johnson, 2005). Third, people do indeed use other people's religiosity as a powerful cue of trust (Gervais, Shariff & Norenzayan, 2011; Tan & Vogel, 2008)

The threat of supernatural punishment, in particular, seems to have a much stronger effect than the promise of supernatural reward. Controlling for relevant variables, people who more strongly believe in a punishing God than a loving and comforting God are less likely to cheat in academic settings (Shariff & Norenzayan, 2011), and those countries that have higher rates of belief in hell and lower rates of belief in heaven also tend to have lower crime rates (Shariff & Rhemtulla, 2012). In fact, indications are that when individuals emphasize God's forgiveness over God's vindictiveness, it actually encourages norm violations (DeBono, Shariff, & Muraven, 2012).

Anthropological work has shown that those societies in which cooperation was especially important and especially difficult to sustain using basic processes of kin selection and close reciprocity—such as larger societies or societies that faced acute resource shortages—were more likely to develop widespread beliefs in big gods (Roes & Raymond, 2003; Snarey, 1996). These findings suggest that supernatural punishment may have emerged to facilitate the management of limited resources. Considered together, the results emerging from this line of research suggest that of the multitudes of forms supernatural deities have taken and could have taken, those now endorsed by the greatest number of people—specifically, powerful, omniscient, and morally involved gods—evolved because of the moral cohesion that they offered large groups of people. These types of gods thrived because the societies they were attached to managed to succeed where less cohesive groups could not.

Hypothesis 2: Resource Regulation and Management

One of the avenues by which regulated behavior among individuals fosters greater success among groups is the wise management of shared resources—preventing "commons" from becoming tragedies (Hardin, 1968). Durkheim (1915/2001) noted that this type of resource regulation was an example of religion's secular utility. In a well-known example—mentioned earlier—Harris (1966) argued that cattle are sacralized in India because the benefits from the prohibition of slaughter outweigh the benefits of eating cattle. According to Harris, this institutionalized prohibition makes ecological sense for Indians engaging in the practice; if cattle are sacred and not to be slaughtered, then Indians maintain the secular utility of keeping cattle alive for plowing, milk, and dung for fuel. However Harris's analysis failed to demonstrate that those living under similar conditions who did not sacramentally conserve cattle had lower caloric returns or fertility or wealth or any other indicator of fitness.

In Rappaport's (1968/2000) classic study, *Pigs for the Ancestors*, he argued that ritual among the Tsembaga Maring of New Guinea serves a variety of functions. First, ritualized mass pig slaughters are timed at points when pig population sizes become too cumbersome and parasitic on resources used by humans. The slaughter, according to Rappaport,

> helps to maintain an undegraded environment, limits fighting to frequencies that do not endanger the existence of the regional population, adjusts man-land ratios, facilitates trade, distributes local surpluses of pig in the form of pork throughout the regional population, and assures people of high-quality protein when they most need it. (p. 224)

Subsequent theoretical models have been mixed in their support for Rappaport's (1968/2000) suggestion about the social utility of the rituals (e.g., Anderies, 1998; Foin & Davis, 1984; Samuels, 1982; Shantzis & Behrens, 1973), but such models still await quantitative empirical testing.

Nevertheless, some studies have produced reliable evidence of higher returns for religiously sanctioned resource management. In a landmark study, Lansing (1987, 1991; Lansing & Kremer, 1993) argued that the religious system among the Balinese teleonomically and strategically mediates water distribution to complex networks of artificially constructed terraced rice paddies operated by cooperative units of people (*subak*). The rice paddies depend on supernaturally sanctioned irrigation practices that affect the nutrient content of the water, regulate pests, and maximize sunlight exposure to plants. Lansing and Kremer (1993) demonstrated that each *subak*'s yield is better on average than it would be otherwise by virtue of the religiously facilitated wide-scale coordination of competing *subak*.

Unfortunately, studies as detailed and comprehensive as that of Lansing and Kremer (1993) are rare. This scarcity of research is particularly unfortunate because as markets increasingly engulf local economies, the need is greater than ever to understand the hard-won and time-tested cultural solutions for resource acquisition and management that have stabilized and ultimately sustained their communities.

Hypothesis 3: Signaling Rituals

Many have referred to religion as a social glue that binds people together (see, e.g., Graham & Haidt, 2010). Indeed, the likely Latin derivative of the word *religion, religare*, means "to bind." But how is this binding accomplished? The currency of social bonds is prosocial behavior, but one question that haunts evolutionary analyses of human cooperation is the problem of how to determine whom to trust in times of need. In the context of religious prosociality, ritual behavior is a strong candidate. Specifically, because of their public visibility and associated costs, rituals can serve as proxies for reputation and reliably indicate trustworthiness (Sosis, 2005). Across the animal kingdom, costly signals often reliably convey fitness, fertility, and mate quality (see Searcy & Nowicki, 2005; Zahavi & Zahavi, 1997). Religious groups often provide social and resource benefits to adherents, benefits that are susceptible to exploitation. Ritual systems that entail somatic, economic, social, time, or opportunity costs can, however, protect these benefits. Ritual performance not only conveys commitment to the supernatural agents accepting or receiving the sacrifice, but it also conveys commitment to the community that proclaims the agent. Such rites can also serve as an effective cultural bulwark against various forms of exploitation if costs are high enough to prevent likely defectors from performing rituals without concomitant beliefs and commitment.[1] A number of studies have bolstered the explanatory power of the signaling theory of religion.

Sosis and Bressler (2003) found that religious communes outlast secular ones by a significant margin; at the end of each year, religious communes were 4 times as likely to still exist than secular ones. Notably, the strongest predictor of which religious communes survived the longest was the number of costly displays of commitment to the group. Those communities that offered their

---

[1] In Henrich's (2009) model of credibility-enhancing displays, the signals of commitment need not be costly to the honest signaler, only too costly for a dishonest signaler to fake.

individual members more opportunities to display their commitment to the group saw the lowest rates of dissolution from internal or external strife. Sosis, Kress, and Boster (2007) found that those societies that needed the high levels of coordination required for warfare also engaged in riskier and more taxing rituals. Soler (2012) found a significant relationship between increased cooperation and commitment to ritual participation among Candomblé cult members in Brazil. Similarly, Sosis and Ruffle (2003, 2004; Ruffle & Sosis, 2007) found that religious kibbutzim engaging in expensive religious commitments are more cooperative and generous with each other than with their secular equivalents. Berman (2009) argued that even actions such as sending one's children to religious schools (which he showed provides demonstrably lower future returns on investment per year of education) serve as a form of sacrificial display of commitment to one's religious group. These studies suggested that, indeed, costly religious rituals reliably convey commitment to other people. As such, it overcomes problems inherent in human relationships regarding who is trustworthy; reliable partners in cooperative ventures are those willing to demonstrate commitment at a cost to themselves. This commitment therefore translates to increased cooperation and establishes social bonds that promote individual well-being, which is ritual's adaptive function. Among other things, what religious concepts do is provide an unverifiable, powerful, and agentive impetus for engaging in and maintaining costly ritualistic traditions as well as provide a means by which people can communicate shared mental states (Purzycki & Sosis, 2010).

However, although these studies may explain why rituals build trusting and cohesive societies, researchers have little understanding of the proximate psychological mechanisms responsible for equating costly, ritualized displays of commitment with trustworthiness. Can other factors mediate perceptions of trustworthiness in a religious context? What are the factors involved in changing the perceived cost of ritual acts? These questions likely revolve around the nature of human institutions in which people have shared expectations and meanings for things. The operative word here is *shared*. However, as discussed next and in Exhibit 9.1, various traditions appear to measure sharedness and conformity in different ways.

Hypothesis 4: Cohesion Rituals—The Case of Synchrony

What are the proximate mechanisms involved in behavioral conformity? One answer may lie in the recent research on synchrony, wherein multiple people engage in identically coordinated behaviors such as singing or dancing. In a seminal article, Wiltermuth and Heath (2009) showed that individuals instructed to move in time with other research participants (as opposed to engaging in the same behaviors but doing so out of sync)

EXHIBIT 9.1
Religious Conformities: Doxa and Praxis

One popularly entertained idea is that religions function to maximize ideological conformity. Perhaps surprisingly, though, with the notable exception of a few imperialistic traditions, having faith or belief in the same religious concepts as others in the community is not considered vital to most of the religious traditions that have existed through the ages. These traditions often emphasize behavioral consistency and participation, that is, practice, as the mark of religiosity rather than consensus in belief (see Fernandez, 1965). It tends to be only the universalizing and often imperialistic religious traditions—which seek to include a wide variety of diverse groups—in which faith is indicative of religiosity (Purzycki & Sosis, 2011). In other words, different contexts appear to influence the factors that indicate what it means to be religious. A. B. Cohen, Siegel, and Rozin (2003) predicted that an emphasis on practice—and not on faith—is likely associated with ethnicity-bound traditions. Indeed, if a religious group considers itself to be different by virtue of some internal essence (see Gil-White, 2001), then likely less need exists to demonstrate ideological conformity than in those traditions—such as Christianity, Islam, and Buddhism—in which anyone can be a member. In support of this thesis, A. B. Cohen et al. (2003) showed that that Protestants are significantly more likely than Jews to emphasize faith as an indicator of religiosity. The distinction between an emphasis on belief versus one on practice presents a compelling and illustrative example of different adaptive solutions that culturally evolved from different social needs and pressures.

reported higher levels of similarity, connection, and trust with their group members and also showed higher levels of coordination and self-sacrifice for their group. Paladino, Mazzurega, Pavani, and Schubert (2010) found that watching others receive identical sensory stimulation (in this case having their cheek brushed) in synchrony rather than out of synchrony not only felt more resemblance to and attraction for their sensation partner, but actually tended to, at some level, confuse themselves with the other subject, perceiving more agency over the other person and experiencing "body illusions" of feeling one's own sensations in the location of the other person. Notably, the synchronous participants also showed more conformity in their responses than the asynchronous ones.

Similarly, synchronic behavior has been shown to increase both pain tolerance and, perhaps as a consequence, work output (E. E. A. Cohen, Ejsmond-Frey, Knight, & Dunbar, 2010). Moreover, neuroimaging research has revealed that the intense audiovisual sensory experiences that often accompany religious rituals actually inhibit self-related processing (Goldberg, Harel, & Malach, 2006). The effectiveness of synchrony at promoting the importance of the group at the expense of the individual likely explains its persistence across a vast variety of religious rituals—from the Sufi whirling dervishes to the coordinated movements (*Raka'ah*) performed during Muslim prayers to the collective hymn singing that is found throughout religions. Of course, religions are not the only institutions to have leveraged the socially cohesive effects of synchronic behaviors. As Wiltermuth and Heath (2009) pointed out, modern militaries maintain frequent marching drills even though marching has all but been abandoned as an actual strategy in military engagement. Various forms of dancing, such as the coordinated step dances of primarily African American fraternities and sororities, likely achieve the same type of social binding.

Future research would do well to investigate whether other aspects common to religious rituals—for example, subordination postures—produce similar effects for submitting individual interests to those of the group.

Hypothesis 5: Management of Competitors, Defectors, and Other Threats to Influence

As religious systems bind ingroup members, religions also often endorse mechanisms that manage potential outgroup disruptions to social order. For example, Steadman and Palmer (2008) argued that the various witch hunts around the world have been directly tied to perceptions of threats to the social order. They predicted that "witch-killings occur only when there is a significant threat to the social hierarchy of the killers and those supporting them," noting that the rash of witch hunts in Europe "began and ended with the Reformation and Counter-Reformation" (p. 168). Such killings appear to have little to do with fear that witchcraft has efficacy but more with the social consequences of killing witches. This explains why suspected witches are typically vulnerable individuals; they are a less risky group of people to publicly decry to demonstrate the authority of leaders.

In the Abrahamic traditions, antiatheist teachings are explicit and pervasive in scriptures and sermons. For example, the Shemoneh Esrei, which is recited thrice daily by observant Jews, includes a paragraph against nonbelievers who can threaten the continuity of the community. The Qur'an, meanwhile, instructs that bodily harm should be done to unbelievers in this life (e.g., 8:59–60) and promises even more grievous punishment in the next (22:19–20). The worst fate is reserved not for pagans or Jews but for apostates who were formerly Muslim but have left the faith (3:90)—thereby doubling as a powerful disincentive for doubt among current believers. (Apostasy in Islam can include a rejection of either the existence of God [religious belief] or of obligatory rituals [practice]. The distinction between these two forms of religious conformities is discussed more in Exhibit 9.1.) Certain hadiths imply that the appropriate punishment for apostasy should be death for men and life imprisonment for women, and although the meaning and application of these hadiths are topics of active debate among modern Islamic scholars (e.g., Saeed & Saeed, 2004), apostasy remains illegal in a number of Muslim-majority countries and a capital crime in Saudi Arabia and Iran.

The codified disparagement of atheism can be understood as a self-protective device on the part of religions aiming to discourage defection from their cultural system. From the perspective of religious prosociality, however, antiatheist prejudice can also be understood as a reaction against a moral threat. If cooperation and trust rely on the shared religious beliefs of those surrounding one, then members of one's society who explicitly reject these beliefs are immediately morally suspect. This theory fits recent empirical findings. Examining the virulent antiatheist prejudice in North America—polls have consistently shown atheists at the top of lists of most disliked groups (Edgell, Gerteis, & Hartmann, 2006)—Gervais et al. (2011) found that these intense negative attitudes are driven by a profound moral distrust. Antiatheist prejudice appears most prominently in high-trust situations. Participants were not overwhelmingly concerned about being served food by an atheist (a low-trust situation) but were highly unwilling to hire one for babysitting (a high-trust situation). When given a scenario briefly describing a man of dubious moral character, participants were as likely to implicitly attribute the description to an atheist as they were to a rapist.

Research has also found that antiatheist prejudice does not exhibit the typical signature of standard social identity–driven ingroup–outgroup psychology. As Gervais et al. (2011) discussed, these standard models fail to account for the domain specificity of the antipathy (confined to trust-based situations) or the lack of a corresponding ingroup preference on behalf of nonbelievers. Instead, the distrust of non- and other-believers can be seen as the direct—and selected-for—outcome of the emphasis religions put on a trusted community of common believers. In a sense, these are flip sides of the same cultural adaptation.

Open questions remain. How does the distrust people feel toward nonbelievers compare with the distrust they feel toward believers of other religions? Consistent with theoretical predictions that the fear of any God is preferable to the fear of none, preliminary research has indicated that people are more inclined to trust a believer from another religion than someone from their own religion who thereby shares a social identity but who nonetheless claims nonbelief (Shariff & Clark, 2012).

The bulk of the research on attitudes about atheists has, however, been conducted primarily with Christian participants. Another open question is how differently members of religions that rely more on religious practice than belief as a cue of religiosity (see Exhibit 9.1) feel toward atheism. Might the level or kind of prejudice differ in, say, Judaism? Finally, what role will the vastly increasing number of atheists have on antiatheist prejudice and on religion in general? Gervais (2011) showed that people led to believe that atheists were more, rather than less, prevalent in their community showed higher levels of trust. As the "otherness" of atheists decreases, so too might the prejudice directed against them. That said, it remains possible that the rise of a more coalitional form of atheism, which could unify nonbelievers into a coherent ingroup, may provoke more aggressive responses.

Hypothesis 6: Marriage and Other Regulations on Sexuality and Reproduction

Religion may also be credited with the salutary effects that monogamous marriage norms have had on societies. Polygyny is common among other primates and has been a demonstrable feature of human mating patterns throughout history—the vast majority of societies in the anthropological record permitted men to take multiple wives (White et al., 1988). The historical transition from nomadic hunter–gatherer lifestyles to permanent settlements, however, amplified the destabilizing effect that such polygyny norms had on human groups. As the wealth inequality between men grew, so did the inequality in the number of wives that men could acquire. The ability of a handful of wealthy, high-status men to monopolize a disproportionate share of mating opportunities led to a large and particularly socially disruptive underclass of unpaired men. Facing restricted sexual opportunities, unpaired men of reproductive age are liable to engage in increasingly desperate, risky, and often violent behavior (Wilson & Daly, 1985). Consistently, the historical anthropological record has shown that polygynous societies had higher rates of crime and engaged in higher levels of warfare than did predominantly monogamous ones (Bacon, Child, & Barry, 1963; White & Burton, 1988). Even today, societies with higher rates of polygyny show higher levels of murder, rape, and robbery (after controlling for relevant variables such as gross domestic product per capita and economic inequality; Kanazawa & Still, 2000).

Modern monogamous marriage norms, which originated in ancient Greece 2,500 years ago and spread via the vehicles of Christian expansion and European colonialism, are thus likely to be adaptive cultural innovations that offer increased stability to large, unequal groups (Henrich, Boyd, & Richerson, 2012). Had those societies that adopted monogamous marriage norms been more able to restrict the antisocial consequences that accompany polygyny (while at the same time increasing paternal investment in offspring and generally redirecting the energy men devoted to finding ever-increasing numbers of wives), then the increased stability of these societies would make them more competitive in the cultural evolutionary market (Henrich et al., 2012).[2]

---

[2]As Buss and Schmitt (1993) argued, the high rates of singledom, divorce, and adultery in modern Western societies make it difficult to argue that they are purely monogamous societies. However, monogamous marriage norms limit the number of women that can be explicitly tied to one man, leaving unmarried women at least theoretically available to other men.

Although they are likely to have strengthened groups, these norms ran counter to the evolved sexual strategies of individual men—and were particularly unappealing for high-status men who had the greatest opportunities for polygynous pursuits, thus making marriage a hard sell, especially for those with power. As with other group-beneficial but personally costly phenomena, tying these norms to religion would have been a particularly efficacious way of ensuring they had the strength to restrict behavior. Research has shown that norms are more likely to be adopted when they are backed by religious edict (Bushman, Ridge, Das, Key, & Busath, 2007).[3] Moreover, in societies with weak legal enforcement, religion served not only as the primary moral authority but also as the only one whose sanctions could be mostly trusted to apply equally to those at the top of the hierarchy (whose behavior, in this case, needed the most regulating).

Today, ample evidence exists for the relationship between religion and monogamous sexual behavior. In the United States, religious adherents have significantly fewer lifetime sexual partners than those who are not religious (Billy, Tanfer, Grady, & Klepinger, 1993). They also have lower rates of premarital sex (Beck, Cole, & Hammond, 1991; Herold & Goodwin, 1981; Zelnik & Shah, 1983), are more likely to get married (Thornton, Axinn, & Hill, 1992), have higher marital satisfaction (Call & Heaton, 1997; Wilson & Filsinger, 1986), and have fewer extramarital affairs (Atkins, Baucom, & Jacobson, 2001; Reiss, Anderson, & Sponaugle, 1980). Although these findings are supportive, future research would do well to explore historical trends to see whether the spread of religions with monogamous norms indeed increased levels of monogamy and social stability.

Aside from providing social stability via marriage norms, religions may also have contributed to the success of culture groups by maximizing fertility. Today, fertility rates have declined all across the world but have done so at a slower rate among those who are religious—and particularly those of the more conservative and orthodox religious sects (Berman, 2000). At both the individual and the national level, religiosity is one of the strongest predictors of family size, even after controlling for important related variables (Blume, 2009; Frejka & Westhoff, 2008; Kaufmann, 2010; Lehrer, 1996). One provocative suggestion as to why religious people have lagged behind the general trend of reduced fertility is that religiously backed norms maintain entrenched gender roles while simultaneously promoting a "cult of motherhood and fertility" (Beit-Hallahmi, 1997, p. 167). Restrictions preventing women in highly religious cultures from accessing education and economic

---

[3]Aside from just monogamy norms, the enveloping of other important group-beneficial norms in the power of supernatural sanction has likely been a highly effective and frequently used cultural strategy for ensuring compliance. Violating sacred values, after all, is a much weightier offense than breaking secular norms.

autonomy have prevented these women both from exercising as much control over their reproductive decisions and seeing alternative opportunities to motherhood as women in other cultures. This suggestion has received some support, especially among rural populations (Amin & Alam, 2008); however, it is an important topic that is ripe for more research. Although historically these high rates of fertility likely allowed religious groups to grow into very populous cultural groups that could outcompete less fertile ones, these norms may today be a double-edged sword. High birth rates in modern times are tied to cycles of poverty and economic stagnation—drawing into question just how culturally adaptive these norms should still be considered.

CONCLUSION

The preceding sections are not meant to be an exhaustive list of cultural adaptations that religions offer groups. We have scarcely mentioned many other likely important group functions that religious rituals and proscriptions may serve—mostly because of a lack of available research. For example, researchers have begun to discuss the idea of a cultural immune system consisting of cultural practices that are devoted to avoiding and managing the spread of virulent pathogenic diseases. The preferential culinary use of spices with antibacterial properties in areas of high pathogenic load is one oft-cited example (Sherman & Billing, 1999; see Henrich & Henrich, 2010, for another example). It is very likely that many religiously sanctioned dietary and cleansing rituals serve similar disease-avoidance purposes. Although much anthropological research has been devoted to the great variety of these types of rituals, little of it has adopted the functionalist perspective featured here. Doing so in the future, however, may provide a critical tool for understanding the culturally adaptive reasons why these and other rituals and edicts exist.

Investigating the culturally evolved group utility that religions serve must, however, resist the pull of naïve pan-adaptationism. Not every aspect of religions evolved to serve the group. For one thing, as briefly discussed in the introduction, many aspects may have developed to directly serve the individual. In addition, though, many aspects of religions can be destructive to both groups and individuals. Cases such as the Jonestown and Heaven's Gate mass suicides illustrate the disastrous results for constituents when the costs of commitment so drastically outweigh the benefits of devotion. Indeed, aspects of religions that convey no adaptive advantages to the group or to the individual can persist for generations without being extinguished simply because they effectively sustain belief in that religion (see Shariff, 2008, for a discussion).

Finally, as changes occur to the sociocultural environment in which religions exist—including the growth of competition from other religions, ideologies, and social institutions, hitherto adaptive elements can become inert and even negative to the welfare and survival of the group and group members. As typically conservative and tradition-rich institutions, religions may be slow to adapt to these changes, leading them to lose market share, or they may maintain the devotion of their adherents but condemn them to diminishing returns in comparison with other contemporary social institutions. The future, ultimately, will belong to those religions that combine the best group- and individual-level cultural adaptations for the current environment and provide the best solutions to both the persistent and the novel challenges of modern life.

REFERENCES

Ahmed, A. M., & Salas, O. (2011). Implicit influences of Christian religious representations on dictator and prisoner's dilemma game decisions. *Journal of Socio-Economics, 40*, 242–246. doi:10.1016/j.socec.2010.12.013

Amin, S., & Alam, I. (2008). Women's employment decisions in Malaysia: Does religion matter? *Journal of Socio-Economics, 37*, 2368–2379. doi:10.1016/j.socec.2008.04.012

Anderies, J. M. (1998). Culture and human agro-ecosystem dynamics: The Tsembaga of New Guinea. *Journal of Theoretical Biology, 192*, 515–530. doi:10.1006/jtbi.1998.0681

Atkins, D. C., Baucom, D. H., & Jacobson, N. S. (2001). Understanding infidelity: Correlates in a national random sample. *Journal of Family Psychology, 15*, 735–749. doi:10.1037/0893-3200.15.4.735

Bacon, M. K., Child, I. L., & Barry, H. (1963). A cross-cultural study of correlates of crime. *Journal of Abnormal and Social Psychology, 66*, 291–300. doi:10.1037/h0042395

Beck, S. H., Cole, B. S., & Hammond, J. A. (1991). Religious heritage and premarital sex: Evidence from a national sample of young adults. *Journal for the Scientific Study of Religion, 30*, 173–180. doi:10.2307/1387211

Becker, E. (1973). *The denial of death*. New York, NY: Simon & Schuster.

Beit-Hallahmi, B. (1997). Biology, density and change: Women's religiosity and economic development. *Journal of Institutional and Theoretical Economics, 153*, 166–178.

Bering, J. (2011). *The God instinct*. London, England: Nicolas Brealy.

Berman, E. (2000). Sect, subsidy and sacrifice: An economist's view of ultra-orthodox Jews. *Quarterly Journal of Economics, 115*, 905–953. doi:10.1162/003355300554944

Berman, E. (2009). *Radical, religious, and violent: The new economics of terrorism.* Cambridge, MA: MIT Press.

Billy, J. O. G., Tanfer, K., Grady, W. R., & Klepinger, D. H. (1993). The sexual behavior of men in the United States. *Family Planning Perspectives, 25,* 52–60. doi:10.2307/2136206

Bloch, M. (1983). *Marxism and anthropology.* New York, NY: Oxford University Press.

Blume, M. (2009). The reproductive benefits of religious affiliation. In E. Voland & W. Schiefenhoevel (Eds.), *The biological evolution of religious mind and behavior* (pp. 117–126). Berlin, Germany: Springer. doi:10.1007/978-3-642-00128-4_8

Boehm, C. (2008). A biocultural evolutionary exploration of supernatural sanctioning. In J. Bulbulia, R. Sosis, E. Harris, R. Genet, C. Genet, & K. Wyman (Eds.), *Evolution of religion: Studies, theories, and critiques* (pp. 143–152). Santa Margarita, CA: Collins Foundation Press.

Bushman, B. J., Ridge, R. D., Das, E., Key, C. W., & Busath, G. M. (2007). When God sanctions killing: Effect of scriptural violence on aggression. *Psychological Science, 18,* 204–207. doi:10.1111/j.1467-9280.2007.01873.x

Buss, D. M., & Schmitt, D. P. (1993). Sexual strategies theory: A contextual evolutionary analysis of human mating. *Psychological Review, 100,* 204–232. doi:10.1037/0033-295X.100.2.204

Call, V. R. A., & Heaton, T. B. (1997). Religious influence on marital stability. *Journal for the Scientific Study of Religion, 36,* 382–392. doi:10.2307/1387856

Cohen, A. B., Siegel, J. I., & Rozin, P. (2003). Faith versus practice: Different bases for religiosity judgments by Jews and Protestants. *European Journal of Social Psychology, 33,* 287–295. doi:10.1002/ejsp.148

Cohen, E. E. A., Ejsmond-Frey, R., Knight, N., & Dunbar, R. I. M. (2010). Rowers' high: Behavioural synchrony is correlated with elevated pain thresholds. *Biology Letters, 6,* 106–108. doi:10.1098/rsbl.2009.0670

Collier, J. F., Rosaldo, M. Z., & Yanagisako. S. (1997). Is there a family? New anthropological views. In R. N. Lancaster & M. di Leonardo (Eds.), *The gender/ sexuality reader: Culture, history, political economy* (pp. 71–81). New York, NY: Routledge Chapman & Hall.

Darwin, C. (2004). *The descent of man.* New York, NY: Penguin Classics. (Original work published 1872)

DeBono, A., Shariff, A. F., & Muraven, M. (2012). *Forgive us our trespasses: Priming a forgiving (but not a punishing) god increases theft.* Unpublished manuscript.

Dunbar, R. I. M. (2003). The social brain: Mind, language, and society in evolutionary perspective. *Annual Review of Anthropology, 32,* 163–181. doi:10.1146/annurev.anthro.32.061002.093158

Durkheim, É. (2001). *The elementary forms of religious life.* New York, NY: Oxford University Press. (Original work published 1915)

Edgell, P., Gerteis, J., & Hartmann, D. (2006). Atheists as "other": Moral boundaries and cultural membership in American society. *American Sociological Review, 71,* 211–234. doi:10.1177/000312240607100203

Elster, J. (1979). *Ulysses and the sirens*. Cambridge, England: Cambridge University Press.

Elster, J. (1982). The case for methodological individualism. *Theory and Society, 11*, 453–482.

Fernandez, J. (1965). Symbolic consensus in a Fang reformative cult. *American Anthropologist, 67*, 902–929. doi:10.1525/aa.1965.67.4.02a00030

Foin, T. C., & Davis, W. G. (1984). Ritual and self-regulation of the Tsembaga Maring ecosystem in the New Guinea highlands. *Human Ecology, 12*, 385–412. doi:10.1007/BF01531125

Frejka, T., & Westhoff, C. F. (2008). Religion, religiousness and fertility in the US and Europe. *European Journal of Population, 24*, 5–31. doi:10.1007/s10680-007-9121-y

Geertz, C. (1973). *The interpretation of cultures*. New York, NY: Basic Books.

Gervais, W. M. (2011). Finding the faithless: Perceived atheist prevalence reduces anti-atheist prejudice. *Personality and Social Psychology Bulletin, 37*, 543–556. doi:10.1177/0146167211399583

Gervais, W. M., Shariff, A. F., & Norenzayan, A. (2011). Do you believe in atheists? Trust and anti-atheist prejudice. *Journal of Personality and Social Psychology, 101*, 1189–1206. doi:10.1037/a0025882

Gil-White, F. J. (2001). Are ethnic groups biological "species" to the human brain? Essentialism in our cognition of some social categories. *Current Anthropology, 42*, 515–554. doi:10.1086/321802

Goldberg, I. I., Harel, M., & Malach, R. (2006). When the brain loses its self: Prefrontal inactivation during sensorimotor processing. *Neuron, 50*, 329–339. doi:10.1016/j.neuron.2006.03.015

Gould, S. J. (2002). *The structure of evolutionary theory*. Cambridge, MA: Harvard University Press.

Graham, J., & Haidt, J. (2010). Beyond beliefs: Religion binds individuals into moral communities. *Personality and Social Psychology Review, 14*, 140–150. doi:10.1177/1088868309353415

Hames, R. (1991). Wildlife conservation in tribal societies. In M. Oldfield & J. Alcorn (Eds.), *Biodiversity: Culture, conservation, and ecodevelopment* (pp. 172–199). Denver, CO: Westview Press.

Hames, R. (2007). The ecologically noble savage debate. *Annual Review of Anthropology, 36*, 177–190. doi:10.1146/annurev.anthro.35.081705.123321

Hardin, G. (1968). The tragedy of the commons. *Science, 162*, 1243–1248. doi:10.1126/science.162.3859.1243

Harris, M. (1966). The cultural ecology of India's sacred cattle. *Current Anthropology, 7*, 51–66. doi:10.1086/200662

Henrich, J. (2004). Cultural group selection, coevolutionary processes and large-scale cooperation. *Journal of Economic Behavior & Organization, 53*, 3–35. doi:10.1016/S0167-2681(03)00094-5

Henrich, J. (2009). The evolution of costly displays, cooperation, and religion: Credibility enhancing displays and their implications for cultural evolution. *Evolution and Human Behavior, 30*, 244–260. doi:10.1016/j.evolhumbehav.2009.03.005

Henrich, J., Boyd, R., & Richerson, P. J. (2012). The puzzle of monogamous marriage. *Philosophical Transactions of the Royal Society of London B: Biological Sciences, 367*, 657–669. doi:10.1098/rstb.2011.0290

Henrich, J., Ensimger, J., McElreath, R., Barr, A., Barrett, C., Bolyanatz, A., . . . Ziker, J. (2010). Markets, religion, community size, and the evolution of fairness and punishment. *Science, 327*, 1480–1484. doi:10.1126/science.1182238

Henrich, J., & Henrich, N. (2010). The evolution of cultural adaptations: Fijian food taboos protect against dangerous marine toxins. *Proceedings of the Royal Society B: Biological Sciences, 277*, 3715–3724. doi:10.1098/rspb.2010.1191

Herold, E. S., & Goodwin, M. S. (1981). Adamant virgins, potential virgins and non-virgins. *Journal of Sex Research, 17*, 97–113. doi:10.1080/00224498109551105

Inzlicht, M., Tullet, A. M., & Good, M. (2011). The need to believe: A neuroscience account of religion as a motivated process. *Religion, Brain & Behavior, 1*, 192–251.

Johnson, D. D. P. (2005). God's punishment and public goods: A test of the supernatural punishment hypothesis in 186 world cultures. *Human Nature, 16*, 410–446. doi:10.1007/s12110-005-1017-0

Kanazawa, S., & Still, M. C. (2000). Why men commit crimes (and why they desist). *Sociological Theory, 18*, 434–447. doi:10.1111/0735-2751.00110

Kaufmann, E. (2010). *Shall the religious inherit the earth?* London, England: Profile Books.

Lahti, D. C. (2009). The correlated history of social organization, morality, and religion. In E. Voland & W. Schiefenhövel (Eds.), *The evolution of religious mind and behavior* (pp. 67–88). New York, NY: Springer. doi:10.1007/978-3-642-00128-4_5

Lansing, J. S. (1987). Balinese "water temples" and the management of irrigation. *American Anthropologist, 89*, 326–341. doi:10.1525/aa.1987.89.2.02a00030

Lansing, J. S. (1991). *Priests and programmers: Technologies of power in the engineered landscape of Bali.* Princeton, NJ: Princeton University Press.

Lansing, J. S., & Kremer, J. N. (1993). Emergent properties of Balinese water temple networks: Coadaptation on a rugged fitness landscape. *American Anthropologist, 95*, 97–114.

Lehrer, E. L. (1996). Religion as a determinant of marital fertility. *Journal of Population Economics, 9*, 173–196. doi:10.1007/s001480050013

Lévi-Strauss, C. (1983). *Structural anthropology* (Vol. 2). Chicago, IL: University of Chicago Press.

Malinowski, B. (1964). *A scientific theory of culture and other essays.* Chapel Hill: University of North Carolina.

Paladino, M.-P., Mazzurega, M., Pavani, F., & Schubert, T. W. (2010). Synchronous multisensory stimulation blurs self-other boundaries. *Psychological Science, 21*, 1202–1207. doi:10.1177/0956797610379234

Piazza, J., Bering, J. M., & Ingram, G. (2011). "Princess Alice is watching you": Children's belief in an invisible person inhibits cheating. *Journal of Experimental Child Psychology, 109*, 311–320. doi:10.1016/j.jecp.2011.02.003

Pittendrigh, C. S. (1958). Adaptation, natural selection, and behavior. In A. Roe & G. G. Simpson (Eds.), *Behavior and evolution* (pp. 390–416). New Haven, CT: Yale University Press.

Purzycki, B. G., & Sosis, R. (2010). Religious concepts as necessary components of the adaptive religious system. In U. Frey (Ed.), *The nature of God: Evolution and religion* (pp. 37–59). Marburg, Germany: Tectum Verlag.

Purzycki, B. G., & Sosis, R. (2011). Our gods: Variation in supernatural minds. In U. J. Frey, C. Störmer, & K. P. Willführ (Eds.), *Essential building blocks of human nature* (pp. 77–93). New York, NY: Springer-Verlag. doi:10.1007/978-3-642-13968-0_5

Randolph-Seng, B., & Nielsen, M. E. (2007). Honesty: One effect of primed religious representations. *International Journal for the Psychology of Religion, 17*, 303–315. doi:10.1080/10508610701572812

Rappaport, R. A. (1979). *Ecology, meaning, and religion.* Berkeley, CA: North Atlantic Books.

Rappaport, R. A. (2000). *Pigs for the ancestors: Ritual in the ecology of a New Guinea people.* New Haven, CT: Yale University Press.

Reiss, I. L., Anderson, R. E., & Sponaugle, G. C. (1980). A multivariate model of the determinants of extramarital sexual permissiveness. *Journal of Marriage and the Family, 42*, 395–411. doi:10.2307/351237

Roes, F. L., & Raymond, M. (2003). Belief in moralizing gods. *Evolution and Human Behavior, 24*, 126–135. doi:10.1016/S1090-5138(02)00134-4

Ruffle, B. J., & Sosis, R. H. (2007). Does it pay to pray? Costly ritual and cooperation. *B.E. Journal of Economic Analysis & Policy, 7*, 1–35. doi:10.2202/1935-1682.1629

Saeed, A., & Saeed, H. (2004). *Freedom of religion, apostasy and Islam.* Burlington, VT: Ashgate.

Samuels, M. L. (1982). POPREG I: A simulation of population regulation among the Maring of New Guinea. *Human Ecology, 10*, 1–45. doi:10.1007/BF01531103

Sanderson, S. K. (2008). Religious attachment theory and the biosocial evolution of the major world religions. In J. Bulbulia, R. Sosis, E. Harris, R. Genet, C. Genet, & K. Wyman (Eds.), *The evolution of religion: Studies, theories, and critiques* (pp. 67–72). Santa Margarita, CA: Collins Foundation Press.

Schloss, J. P., & Murray, M. J. (2011). Evolutionary accounts of belief in supernatural punishment: A critical review. *Religion, Brain and Behavior, 1*, 46–99.

Searcy, W. A., & Nowicki, S. (2005). *The evolution of animal communication: Reliability and deception in signaling systems.* Princeton, NJ: Princeton University Press.

Shantzis, S. B., & Behrens, W. W. (1973). Population control mechanisms in a primitive agricultural society. In D. L. Meadows & D. H. Meadows (Eds.), *Towards global equilibrium* (pp. 257–288). Cambridge, MA: Wright-Allen Press.

Shariff, A. F. (2008). One species under God? Sorting through the pieces of religion and cooperation. In J. Bulbulia, R. Sosis, C. Genet, R. Genet, E. Harris, & K. Wyman (Eds.), *The evolution of religion: Studies, theories, and critiques* (pp. 119–125). Santa Margarita, CA: Collins Foundation Press.

Shariff, A. F., & Clark, B. (2012). [Atheists versus Muslims: Comparing religious prejudices]. Unpublished raw data.

Shariff, A. F., & Norenzayan, A. (2007). God is watching you: Supernatural agent concepts increase prosocial behavior in an anonymous economic game. *Psychological Science, 18*, 803–809. doi:10.1111/j.1467-9280.2007.01983.x

Shariff, A. F., & Norenzayan, A. (2011). Mean gods make good people. *International Journal for the Psychology of Religion, 21*, 85–96. doi:10.1080/10508619.2011.556990

Shariff, A. F., & Rhemtulla, M. (2012). *Divergent effects of heaven and hell beliefs on national crime*. Unpublished manuscript.

Sharrock, W. W., Hughes, J. A., & Martin, P. J. (2003). *Understanding modern sociology*. Thousand Oaks, CA: Sage.

Sherman, P. W., & Billing, J. (1999). Darwinian gastronomy: Why we use spices. *Bioscience, 49*, 453–463. doi:10.2307/1313553

Smith, E. A., & Wishnie, M. (2000). Conservation and subsistence in small-scale societies. *Annual Review of Anthropology, 29*, 493–524. doi:10.1146/annurev.anthro.29.1.493

Snarey, J. (1996). The natural environment's impact upon religious ethics: A cross-cultural study. *Journal for the Scientific Study of Religion, 35*, 85–96. doi:10.2307/1387077

Soler, M. (2012). Costly signaling, ritual and cooperation: Evidence from Candomblé, an Afro-Brazilian religion. *Evolution and Human Behavior, 33*, 346–356. doi:10.1016/j.evolhumbehav.2011.11.004

Sosis, R. (2005). Does religion promote trust? The role of signaling, reputation, and punishment. *Interdisciplinary Journal of Research on Religion, 1*, Article 7. Retrieved from http://www.religjournal.com

Sosis, R., & Bressler, E. R. (2003). Cooperation and commune longevity: A test of the costly signaling theory of religion. *Cross-Cultural Research: The Journal of Comparative Social Science, 37*, 211–239. doi:10.1177/1069397103037002003

Sosis, R., Kress, H. C., & Boster, J. S. (2007). Scars for war: Evaluating alternative signaling explanations for cross cultural variance in ritual costs. *Evolution and Human Behavior, 28*, 234–247. doi:10.1016/j.evolhumbehav.2007.02.007

Sosis, R., & Ruffle, B. (2003). Religious ritual and cooperation: Testing for a relationship on Israeli religious and secular kibbutzim. *Current Anthropology, 44*, 713–722. doi:10.1086/379260

Sosis, R., & Ruffle, B. (2004). Ideology, religion, and the evolution of cooperation: Field tests on Israeli kibbutzim. *Research in Economic Anthropology, 23*, 89–117. doi:10.1016/S0190-1281(04)23004-9

Sperber, D. (1996). *Explaining culture: A naturalistic approach*. Malden, MA: Blackwell.

Spiro, M. E. (1987). *Culture and human nature: Theoretical papers of Melford E. Spiro* (B. Kilborne & L. L. Langness, Eds.). Chicago, IL: University of Chicago Press.

Stark, R. (2001). Gods, rituals, and the moral order. *Journal for the Scientific Study of Religion, 40*, 619–636. doi:10.1111/0021-8294.00081

Steadman, L. B., & Palmer, C. T. (2008). *The supernatural and natural selection: Religion and evolutionary success*. Boulder, CO: Paradigm.

Stinchcombe, A. L. (1968). *Constructing social theories*. New York, NY: Harcourt, Brace & World.

Swanson, G. E. (1960). *The birth of the gods: The origin of primitive beliefs*. Ann Arbor: University of Michigan Press.

Tan, J. H. W., & Vogel, C. (2008). Religion and trust: An experimental study. *Journal of Economic Psychology, 29*, 832–848. doi:10.1016/j.joep.2008.03.002

Thornton, A., Axinn, W. G., & Hill, D. H. (1992). Reciprocal effects of religiosity, cohabitation, and marriage. *American Journal of Sociology, 98*, 628–651. doi:10.1086/230051

Wallace, A. F. C. (1966). *Religion: An anthropological view*. New York, NY: McGraw-Hill.

White, D. R., Betzig, L., Borgerhoff Mulder, M., Chick, G., Hartung, J., Irons, W., . . . Otterbein, K. F. (1988). Rethinking polygyny: Co-wives, codes, and cultural systems. *Current Anthropology, 29*, 529–572. doi:10.1086/203674

White, D. R., & Burton, M. L. (1988). Causes of polygyny—Ecology, economy, kinship, and warfare. *American Anthropologist, 90*, 871–887. doi:10.1525/aa.1988.90.4.02a00060

Wilson, M., & Daly, M. (1985). Competitiveness, risk-taking, and violence: The young male syndrome. *Ethology & Sociobiology, 6*, 59–73. doi:10.1016/0162-3095(85)90041-X

Wilson, M. R., & Filsinger, E. E. (1986). Religiosity and marital adjustment: Multidimensional interrelationships. *Journal of Marriage and the Family, 48*, 147–151. doi:10.2307/352238

Wiltermuth, S. S., & Heath, C. (2009). Synchrony and cooperation. *Psychological Science, 20*, 1–5. doi:10.1111/j.1467-9280.2008.02253.x

Zahavi, A., & Zahavi, A. (1997). *The handicap principle: A missing piece of Darwin's puzzle*. New York, NY: Oxford University Press.

Zelnik, M., & Shah, F. H. (1983). First intercourse among young Americans. *Family Planning Perspectives, 15*, 64–70. doi:10.2307/2134848

INDEX

Independence
  ethos of, 94
  explicit, 96–100, 106, 111
  in frontier settlement, 96–105,
      119–120
  implicit, 100–105, 109, 111–113
  interdependence vs., 98–100
  and preference among city types,
      117–118
  regional variation in, 106, 109
  and residential mobility, 115–116
  schemas of self based on, x, xi
  in urban vs. rural areas, 116–117
India
  caste system in, 60–61
  food taboos in, 162
  sacralization of cattle in, 219, 223
Individual development
  in cross-temporal research, 37–39
  in generational change model, 34
  in mutual constitution model, 33
Individualism
  in cross-temporal research, 40–43
  defined, 40
  as fundamental to U.S. society, 96
  in regional culture, 79–81
  and social class, 58–59
Individualist culture, United States as, 79
Individual level
  aggregations of adaptations at, 67
  culture at, 13
Industrialized countries, 69
Inertia, continuance of regional cultures
    and, 87
Influence, threats to, 227–229
Information, in cultural transmission
    process, 25
Informational influence, in disciplinary
    and professional cultures, 14
Information processing, in disciplinary
    and professional cultures, 15–16
Inglehart, R., 96–98, 134–136
Innovations, 93–94
Institutional actors (in food cultures),
    166, 167, 175–184
  and broader social trends, 182–184
  corporations and media, 179–182
  government agencies, 177–179
Institutionalization, in disciplinary and
    professional cultures, 12, 13

Integrity, elite, 135
Intellectual traditions. *See* Professional
    and disciplinary cultures
Interdependence
  explicit, 98–100
  implicit, 100–105
  schemas of self based on, x
Interdisciplinary collaboration, 16–18
Internalization stage (cultural evolution
    and perpetuation), 84–85
Interpretation, in cultural functional-
    ism, 219
Intersubjective perceptions of culture, 13
Inventions, 93–94
Iran, 227
Ishii, K., 111–113
Islam, 138
  antiatheist teachings in, 227
  apostasy in, 227
  and ideological conformity, 226
  Sufi whirling dervishes, 226
Italy
  civic culture in, 132
  food culture of, 172
  regional cultures in, 78
  rice as gift in, 164
  workplace and values in, 54

Jack-in-the-Box, 181
Jambor, E., 80
Japan
  cultural stability in, 33
  food culture in, 161, 165
  Hokkaido as frontier in, 111–113
  independence in, 111
  independence in the U.S. vs., 103
  modes of being in North America
      vs., x
  regional cultures in, 78
  workplace and values in, 54
Jokela, M., 114
Journal of Counseling Psychology, 24
*Journal of Experimental Psychology:
    Animal Behavior Processes,* 24
*Journal of Experimental Psychology:
    General,* 24
*Journal of Experimental Psychology: Learn-
    ing, Memory, and Cognition,* 24
*Journal of Personality and Social Psychol-
    ogy,* 21–23, 26

ABOUT THE EDITOR

Adam B. Cohen, PhD, is an associate professor of psychology at Arizona State University. Dr. Cohen's research fuses cultural and evolutionary approaches to religion. He is the author of more than 40 peer-reviewed articles (including "Many Forms of Culture," published in *American Psychologist* in 2009). He is associate editor of the *Journal of Personality and Social Psychology: Personality Processes and Individual Differences* and is a former associate editor of *Personality and Social Psychology Bulletin*.